The Politics of Interpretation

The Politics
of Interpretation

*Ideology, Professionalism,
and the Study of
Literature*

PATRICK COLM HOGAN

New York   Oxford
OXFORD UNIVERSITY PRESS
1990

Oxford University Press

Oxford   New York   Toronto
Delhi   Bombay   Calcutta   Madras   Karachi
Petaling Jaya   Singapore   Hong Kong   Tokyo
Nairobi   Dar es Salaam   Cape Town
Melbourne   Auckland

and associated companies in
Berlin   Ibaden

Library of Congress Cataloging-in-Publication Data
Hogan, Patrick Colm.
The politics of interpretation : ideology, professionalism,
and the study of literature / Patrick Colm Hogan.
p. cm.   Includes bibliographical references.
ISBN 0-19-506272-8
1. Criticism—Political aspects.   2. Ideology and literature.
I. Title.
PN98.P64H64   1990   89-26589
801'.95—dc20

9 8 7 6 5 4 3 2 1

Printed in the United States of America
on acid-free paper

*For the courageous men and women
who made the Nicaraguan revolution—
in the military, in politics, and in art.*

PREFACE

This book, and the concerns which animate it, grew out of three sets of related experiences. The first was my own involvement—however limited—in Central America solidarity work. I had developed since high school a serious, if ambivalent, intellectual interest in radical political theory, principally in the Marxist tradition. But politics became something real and practical for me, something more than an intellectual curiosity, only through the work of a handful of non-Marxist or even anti-Marxist writers—such as Noam Chomsky and Bertrand Russell—who, through ordinary methods of rational enquiry, unencumbered by dialectical causality or dubious economics, sought to discover the facts of U.S. foreign and domestic policy and to evaluate these by reference to universal moral principles.

At roughly the same time that I began reading authors such as Chomsky and engaging in some practical political activity, I also began reading politically oriented literary criticism and theory—Marxist, post-structural, and so on. I found myself shocked by what I frequently perceived to be a lack of intellectual rigor and a cavalier attitude to real political issues. I was even more shocked by the elitism of faculty and graduate students who adopted fashionable political approaches to criticism and viewed all who did not as retrogressive and naive.

The third, and most personal experience which underlies and motivates this book derives from my first academic job. After passing through a fairly open and congenial graduate program, I was unprepared to enter a department which was rigidly hierarchical and which operated to a great extent through fear and general distrust, a department where one had to be very careful about what one said, with whom one was seen, what causes one championed, and how one championed them.

In writing this book, I have sought to deal with the general problems which arise in experiences such as these. I have tried to analyze the weaknesses of some prominent contemporary theories of criticism and offer in their place some positive critical principles which I believe to be simpler, more logically rigorous, more empirically adequate, and closer to the political concerns of real human life. Moreover, I have tried to do this with attention to the serious intellectual and political constraints imposed by the university and the various professions, for it is as important to understand and criticize the political circumstances *in* which critics typically write as it is to understand those *about* which they typically write.

Specifically, in the first chapter, I seek to define, in practical and empirical terms, the nature and domain of political interpretation. In the second and third chapters, after introducing ideological critique as a particularly important form of political interpretation, I criticize some prominent, post-structural alternatives to the position I am advocating. In the fourth chapter, I develop a psychological analysis of ideology and the critique of ideology. And, finally, in Chapter 5, I turn to the structure of the university, examining some of the ways in which it now contributes to the dissemination of oppressive ideologies, as well as how it might be restructured so as to inhibit such dissemination, and even to foster the sort of critical thinking which is (along the lines indicated in chapter four) antithetical to such ideologies.

In contrast to many contemporary theorists and critics, I believe that the principles of political interpretation and critique are relatively simple. However, I do not believe that the moral and practical problems to which such principles may be applied are in any way simple. Nor do I believe that there is anything at all simple about establishing a truly free intellectual community in which human beings can be treated decently and can pursue their work and study rationally and with critical cooperation. Yet it is precisely the practical political and moral difficulties we face which make clarity and rigor about principles—as well as goals, possibilities, and so on—all the more crucial. My hope, then, is that the following arguments and analyses may begin to shed some light on political and moral issues which are of more than merely intellectual concern, and that the views which they express will help to encourage the sort of rational dialectic which it is the function of ideology to foreclose.

As I emphasize in the following pages, any political study of literature must ultimately be tied to real issues of concrete political concern, if it is to be political in anything but name or rhetoric alone. For this reason, I make repeated reference to extra-literary sexism, racism, imperialism, and so on. Of these various references, the most controversial are no doubt to imperialism—especially regarding U.S. actions in Southeast Asia, the Middle East, and Central America. Needless to say, I cannot defend my views on, for example, Nicaragua in the present context. For this reason, I include the following brief and introductory bibliography, for readers wishing to pursue these important issues.

Armstrong, Robert, and Shenk, Janet. 1982. *El Salvador: The Face of Revolution*. Boston: South End Press.

Berman, Karl. 1986. *Under the Big Stick: Nicaragua and the United States Since 1848*. Boston: South End Press.

Brody, Reed. 1985. *Contra Terror in Nicaragua/ Report of a Fact-Finding Mission: September 1984–January 1985*. Boston: South End Press.

Burns, E. 1988. *At War in Nicaragua: The Reagan Doctrine and the Politics of Nostalgia*. New York: Harper & Row.

Chomsky, Noam. 1983. *The Fateful Triangle: The United States, Israel, and the Palestinians*. Boston: South End Press.

———. 1985. *Turning the Tide: U.S. Intervention in Central America and the Struggle for Peace*. Boston: South End Press.

———, and Herman, Edward. 1979. *The Political Economy of Human Rights, Volume I: The Washington Connection and Third World Fascism, Volume II: After the Cataclysm: Postwar Indochina and the Reconstruction of Imperial Ideology*. Boston: South End Press.

Collins, Joseph. 1986. *Nicaragua: What Difference Could a Revolution Make?* 3rd ed. (With Frances Moore Lappe, Nick Allen, and Paul Rice.) New York: Grove Press.

Herman, Edward. 1982. *The Real Terror Network: Terrorism in Fact and Propaganda*. Boston: South End Press.

———, and Brodhead, Frank. 1984. *Demonstration Elections: U.S.-Staged Elections in the Dominican Republic, Vietnam, and El Salvador*. Boston: South End Press.

Kornbluh, Peter. 1987. *The Price of Intervention: Reagan's Wars Against the Sandinistas*. Washington: Institute for Policy Studies.

Manz, Beatriz. 1988. *Refugees of a Hidden War: The Aftermath of Counterinsurgency in Guatemala*. Albany: State University of New York Press.

Morley, Morris, and Petras, James. 1987. *The Reagan Administration and Nicaragua: How Washington Constructs Its Case for Counter-revolution in Central America*. New York: Institute for Media Analysis.

Poelchau, Warner, ed. 1981. *White Paper Whitewash: Interviews with Philip Agee on the CIA and El Salvador*. New York: Deep Cover Books.

Robinson, William, and Norsworthy, Kent. 1987. *David and Goliath: The U. S. War Against Nicaragua*. New York: Monthly Review Press.

Rosset, Peter, and Vandermeer, John. 1983. *The Nicaragua Reader: Documents of a Revolution Under Fire*. New York: Grove Press.

Sklar, Holly. 1988. *Washington's War on Nicaragua*. Boston: South End Press.

Vickery, Michael. 1984. *Cambodia: 1975–1982*. Boston: South End Press.

This is only a small fraction of the relevant bibliography. However, each of these works includes further bibliographical references which, in conjunction, should constitute a fairly extensive, if still very incomplete list of studies now available. Interested readers might wish to keep an eye on the South End Press Collective in Boston and their journal, *Zeta Magazine*, as well as the various authors mentioned above, for relevant work in the future. Several specialized periodicals are extremely valuable on these issues—for example, *NACLA Report on the Americas*, *MERIP Reports*, and the *Bulletin of Concerned Asian Scholars*. The reports of Amnesty International and Americas Watch are very important in this connection also. Finally, a number of associations are good sources of information as well—for example, Clergy and Laity Concerned (New York), Witness for Peace (Washington), the American Friends Service Committee (Philadelphia), CISPES (the Committee in Solidarity with the People of El Salvador) (New York), and Oxfam America (Boston).

A note on punctuation: In the following pages, double inverted commas are used for direct quotation only; scare-quotation, metalinguistic citation, etc., are marked by single inverted commas.

Storrs, Conn.   P.C.H.
December 1989

ACKNOWLEDGMENTS

There are many people to whom I am grateful for intellectual and other considerations during the composition of this book. Of these I should particularly like to mention Gerald Graff, who suggested the project in the first place and provided useful comments on several chapters; Walter Benn Michaels, who was inconceivably supportive with regard to my argument against his position in Chapter 1; Norman Holland who made very helpful comments on an earlier version of sections from Chapter 1; Dr. Merton Gill, who gave incisive criticisms of an oral version of the treatment of the transference in Chapter 4; Joe Bryant, who made sensitive stylistic suggestions on an earlier draft; Lance Olsen and Greg Stump, who read the entire manuscript and made helpful suggestions throughout; Armando Prats, who gave concrete administrative support to the project at a difficult time; Ruth Marcus who provided encouragement and solid practical advice; and a reader for Oxford University Press who made extremely useful suggestions for revision.

I would like to give particular and warm thanks to Noam Chomsky who helped turn me away from total nonsense and obscurantism in ideological analysis, who read the bulk of this manuscript, providing helpful comments and encouragement, and who has been a constant source of intellectual stimulation, moral support, and, indeed, personal inspiration.

My greatest debt of gratitude goes to Lalita Pandit. Before the book was written, and while it was being written, she was subjected to regular diatribes on its various concerns. After the second draft was completed, she read the entire manuscript. To a great extent, insofar as the book is free from offensive or embarrassing stupidities, she is to be credited. Self-evidently, I am to be credited with any offensive, embarrassing, or other stupidities which might remain.

I am grateful to the University of Kentucky for reducing my teaching load during the writing of this book and for awarding me a summer fellowship as it neared completion. I am grateful also to the Research Foundation of the University of Connecticut for awarding me a summer fellowship while I was preparing the final manuscript.

Finally, I should like to recall my friend and fellow-'dissident,' Mike Newman, whose early death was a great tragedy, a great evil which one cannot help but blame on the vast human indecency and intolerance fostered by our society.

A draft of a portion of Chapter 2 was delivered at the conference on "Post-Structuralism" (Ottawa, 1984). An early version of the section appeared in the Belgian periodical, *Restant: Tijdschrift voor Recente Semiotische Teorievorming en de Analyse van Teksten/ Review for Semiotic Theories and the Analysis of Texts*. A version of the discussion of Lacan and the transference was presented at the seminar on Jacques Lacan sponsored by the Center for Psychoanalytic Study (Chicago, 1986).

CONTENTS

The Politics of Interpretation

1

Political Interpretation:
Can a Construal be Ethical?

In recent years, the politics of interpretation has been one of the most widely and passionately discussed topics of literary study. Disparate theories, generating incompatible conclusions through antithetical methods, have been presented by their respective theorists as the most politically liberating choices amongst a bewildering array of alternatives. We hear that reader response, deconstruction, intentionalism, historicism, feminism, Marxism, and other approaches are the most likely to inhibit domination, limit ideological constraint, and so on. Indeed, in a recent book on *The Ethics of Criticism*, Tobin Siebers maintains that this intensive focus on ethical/political issues, and on the ethical/political status of one's own theoretical work, is one of the defining characteristics of contemporary criticism.

Throughout the various debates surrounding the politics (or ethics) of interpretation, it has been widely—and, it would seem, reasonably—assumed that there is such a thing as the politics of interpretation, that one can examine it, discuss it, invoke it, make claims about it, evaluate criticism in light of it, and so on. However, in a recent, influential, and rigorously argued article on the topic, Walter Benn Michaels has denied that criticism, and by implication the theory of literature, has any possible political status. He has, in other words, sought to controvert the notion that there is any such thing as the politics of interpretation in the sense crucial to the various debates just mentioned—and thus, it would seem, in the sense crucial to the present undertaking. If Michaels is right, it would appear that there is no scope for the present study or any like it. Thus, I should like to begin by examining and disputing Michaels' arguments. In doing this, I hope to be able not only to defend the notion of political interpretation, but also to outline some general criteria for its definition, criteria which will serve to guide the rest of our study.

Disputing the Possibility of Political Interpretation

Having at one time worn the fashionable cap of Maoism, and still maintaining sympathy for cultural revolution theory—most crucially, its valorization of art *and the interpretation of art* as media for mobilization, or ideologization—I was dumbfounded to find critics such as Walter Benn Michaels and Terry Eagleton debating whether or not literary interpretation could or could not be political (see Michaels 1983 and Eagleton 1983). As I had always conceived criticism to be often *actually* political, a debate on the *possibility* of such seemed to me redundant. For example, the Cultural Revolution could arguably be dated from the publication of Yao Wenyuan's "On the New Historical Play *The Dismissal of Hai Jui*"—as Mao himself put it, "Our great Proletarian cultural revolution should begin with Yao Wenyuan's criticism of *The Dismissal of Hai Jui* in the winter of 1965" (Mao 1974, p. 261, altered)—and much of the Cultural Revolution could be understood as a direct result of the work of 'radical' literary critics such as Yao and Chi Benyu, as well as journalists such as Zhang Chunqiao (see Christensen and Delman 1981; and Milton and Milton 1976, pp. 105–6, 123, and elsewhere). Clearly, if there is any such thing as ideology, if it has any of the effects it is thought and claimed to have, and if it is true that art is, along with education and religion, the major 'ideological apparatus' by which the populace may be presented with either a pacifying fantasy of its own conditions or a mobilizing criticism thereof, then the act of literary interpretation is not only *possibly a* political act, but, in the proper circumstances, *necessarily the* political act *par excellence*.

But Michaels' argument against the possibility of political criticism is far more compelling than might seem. It is really quite immune to the preceding argument that criticism is actually political and, thereby, *a fortiori* possibly so. Presumably, Michaels would begin his response to the example of the cultural revolution by asking the evidently innocuous question, 'Well, now, don't you think that when Yao interpreted *The Dismissal of Hai Jui* as a play about a peasantry passive in the face of beneficent officialdom, or when Mao identified Hai Jui with P'eng Teh-huai, that they either believed their interpretations to be accurate or they did not?' It seems, of course, indisputable that they either believed their interpretations to be accurate or they did not believe them to be accurate. 'So,' Michaels would presumably continue, 'let us assume they did *not* believe their interpretations to be accurate. In this case, you must admit that they offered their 'interpretations' for the effect that they believed such 'interpretations' would produce, but they did not do anything in their *actual interpretation*, which is to say in their construal of the play as they actually understood it, which contributed to this. In other words, they acted politically, most certainly, but whatever their actual interpretation of *The Dismissal of Hai Jui*, it itself was not political, or at least we cannot conclude it to have been such on the basis of a political act which duplicitously invokes the title of 'interpretation.'' It seems once again clear that we cannot infer to politicality of interpretation from duplicitous invocation thereof. In this case it is not interpretation which is political, but at best the use of the word 'interpretation.'

'Good—then let us go on to the more difficult case, that in which Yao and Mao accept, believe, are convinced of the accuracy of their interpretations. Evidently, they could offer their interpretations of the play either because they believe them to be accurate—as they do believe, *ex hypothesi*—or they could offer their interpretations because they believe that the statement of such interpretations, whatever their accuracy, would produce desirable results. We make the simplifying assumption that they do not offer their interpretations for each reason in part, for clearly such a complex, if common, situation would not affect the present argument.' It seems, once more, that Michaels would be completely correct in this. 'So let us assume that the interpretations are offered for political effect, independent of accuracy. This case is, then, indistinguishable from that in which Yao and Mao do not believe their interpretations to be true. It is mere coincidence that what they say and what they believe coincide. They act politically, but their political acts are entirely independent of their interpretive acts. Therefore we have no warrant to infer to a politicality of their interpretations.' Right again, I think.

'Thus all that remains is the case in which Mao and Yao offer their interpretations entirely because they believe them to be true. But it seems quite obvious that much the same holds here. Mao and Yao are acting politically, but their political acts concern *announcing* their interpretations of *The Dismissal of Hai Jui*, choosing *Hai Jui* as the object of their interpretive scrutinies, etc., but *not* in interpreting *Hai Jui per se*. In other words, when Yao looks at *Hai Jui*, he begins to see certain patterns, allusions, similarities to present political situations, etc. In the course of his perusal, he eliminates various interpretations of the play as inaccurate, eventually arriving at a set of interpretations to each of which he would, with greater or lesser confidence, attribute accuracy. If he is judging the play on the basis of an interpretation he deems accurate (our present assumption), then it must be only at this point that he forms his most nearly final evaluation of the work. Contrast, once again, the situation in which Yao is concerned to support a certain evaluation which he believes to be politically expeditious, and scrutinizes the work with an eye toward rhetorically effective 'evidence' therefor, independent of concern for interpretive accuracy. In this latter case, the scrutinizing is political, but not, in any usual sense, interpretive. But in the former case, is it not clear that the situation is, in the usual sense, interpretive but not political?

'In other words, is it not clear that when Yao actually interprets, he concerns himself with accuracy in interpretation (what this is needs some spelling out, of course, but we need not concern ourselves with that for the moment—we can take it to be simply what Yao takes it to be [full stop])? Now, when Yao concerns himself with accuracy in interpretation, he is concerning himself with what he takes to be certain *facts*, rather than with political options, even if he goes on to claim that these facts are 'multiple,' 'contradictory,' 'plurivalent,' etc. In announcing his interpretation in certain circumstances, Yao is acting politically, which is to say, choosing one or another political option, one or another possibility with supposed political ramifications. However, in taking one set of interpretations to be probably accurate, Yao is not acting politically, that is, choosing one or another political option. Yao's deciding which interpretations are likely to be accurate is no more a political act than my deciding who are the gubernatorial candidates for Kentucky or who are the presidential candidates for the United States. No matter how much I would like Ronald Dellums to be the Democratic presidential candidate, he is not, and my deciding he is not is in no way a political position. It is only what I do on the basis of these decisions that is political. Thus interpretation itself can never be political.'

This is a very rigorous and compelling argument, I think—and, unfortunately, Eagleton offers little solace. At the beginning of his essay, Eagleton adopts a sort of Kantian position with regard to belief—it is in fact free, insofar as it is rational, and it is precisely this rational freedom which makes belief belief and not, for example, ideological prejudice. As Eagleton puts it, "I can still hold my beliefs freely even when I find them magnificently convincing. Indeed, the more convincing I find them, the more freely I hold them. I hold them because I have been convinced by the arguments and the evidence. . . . Because I find my beliefs reasonable I would abandon them if they came to seem unreasonable, which is not so easily done with a spontaneous ideological prejudice. To be rationally convinced is thus a 'freer' matter than being ideologically controlled. Michaels ignores the relation between freedom and reason" (p. 376). Here Eagleton presents half of his argument against Michaels. The other half of his argument consists in maintaining that, not only is interpretation a less constrained matter than Michaels ever suspected, political action is a more constrained matter than he ever imagined. As Eagleton puts it, "it is surely the case that you cannot choose the political if you live on Belfast's Falls Road: it has already chosen you in the shape of those British soldiers" (p. 378).

At one level, I completely agree with Eagleton on both points, and feel that it is important they be made. Specifically, I agree that rational belief may be changed more readily than ideological prejudice. We all know this from everyday experience. Thus I agree that an effort to be rational is a political decision *par excellence*. It is a decision to do one's best to ascertain the facts, to judge on the basis of evidence, logic, and the Principle of Minimal Interpretation, rather than blind trust in a person, a dogma, or whatever. (We will discuss this in more detail in the following chapters.) However, a decision to be rational is, presumably, not part of interpretation *per se*, at least in the sense in which the term is used in the question as to whether or not interpretation can be political. In other words, I take it that the gist of the question at issue is: Are there interpretations of which we can say, 'That interpretation is politically bad,' where we do not mean 'The utterance of that interpretation would produce unfortunate political results,' 'That interpretation is simply wrong,' and so on? The politicality of a decision to be rational in interpretation does not extend to a subsequent decision about what interpretation actually is accurate. The former alone is open to free choice in the politically relevant sense. Indeed, Michaels makes a similar point when he argues that "You can, for example, choose to interpret a text as opposed to putting it aside. . . . Going one step further, you can choose to do a Marxist (or deconstructive or . . .) interpretation of the text. . . . But can you choose to believe your Marxist interpretation?" (p. 336). Eagleton's contrast of rational belief with ideological prejudice indicates very clearly the degree to which any decision as to whether or not one will aim for a thorough gathering of evidence, consider alternative accounts for such evidence, etc., is rife with political import, the degree to which it is a political act. However, it says nothing about any politicality of interpretation *per se*.

In other words, Eagleton demonstrates only that one's decision as to how one will gather data, evaluate them, and so on, has political consequences, and that, leaving aside problems of chance, the most rational method of inquiry is the most politically beneficial. This is true because political action concerns itself with the facts. If we seek to house the Salvadoran peasant rather than the bourgeois, it is because the fact of the matter is that the bourgeois has a mansion with a swimming pool, while the peasant has a corrugated tin affair smaller than the bourgeois' tool-shed. If the fact of the matter were different, our political aims would be different as well. Thus it is politically well-advised to seek the facts. Consequently, a decision to seek the facts, rather than doing something else, is a political, and politically admirable, decision. However, given our decision to determine the facts, rather than fanta-size, lie, or just not think about it, we are simply not free to then use political criteria to determine what those facts are. It is only once our political decision to ascertain the facts has been made that interpretation begins. But this interpretation cannot be political, precisely because the prior, political decision to seek the facts precludes considerations other than likely truth. On the other hand, were we to make the political decision *not* to seek the facts, but just to make the most expeditious claims, then there would be no question of interpretation at all—political or not. Interpretation would not even enter into the picture.

As to Eagleton's second point, that political action is not quite as free as Michaels seems to imagine, this seems to me an important observation as well, and one which I, once again, fully endorse. In a sense, the Muslim Palestinian living in the occupied West Bank, with friends tortured, family imprisoned or bussed to work on three hours of sleep (in keeping with the sinister laws of Israeli apar-theid), relatives massacred in refugee camps, has little choice but to be political. Or to use Eagleton's example, the fellow living on the Falls Road has no choice but to be political when the British soldier breaks down his door and beats his son—everything, from shooting the soldier to sitting passively by to joining in as proof of loyalty, is political. In a case such as this there simply is no option which is not political. This is important, for in giving an extreme example Eagleton indicates the extent to which 'non-political' action in less extreme cases may be political also.

However, the argument about the politicality of interpretation does not concern the degree to which we can or cannot choose to act politically in interpreting (or not interpreting). Certainly there are or could be interpretive situations parallel to those just cited. For example, in a theocracy where sacred texts are ordained by law to have particular meanings, one's relation to those texts would necessarily be political—whether one chose to interpret those texts or not to interpret them, one's choice would be political. Once again, however, this is irrelevant to the topic at issue. The point here is that, once someone has chosen to interpret, that person cannot choose what he or she will accept as a correct interpretation; once a citizen of the theocracy has chosen to interpret the sacred texts, that citizen cannot choose whether he or she will come to believe that the standard interpretations are true or false, whether he or she will come to accept some different or contradictory interpretation, and so on. This is the point Michaels is arguing and Eagleton has not addressed it. Thus, in his discussion of the limits of political choice, just as in his discussion of the freedoms of reason, Eagleton's arguments simply do not bear upon the act of interpretation *per se*, but rather upon decisions made prior to that act.

Before going on to dispute Michaels' conclusions myself, I should like to address one further objection of Eagleton. Eagleton argues that, insofar as it is true that we have no choice about our beliefs, it is trivially true, for it comes down to saying that I cannot believe *p* and not believe *p* at the same time. In other words, it is true only in the sense in which it is true that if I am in Lexington, Ky., I cannot be in Paris, Ky. Now, I might go to Paris, if I choose and am able—and, likewise, Eagleton maintains, I might alter my beliefs, if I choose and am able. But this is clearly ludicrous. No matter how much I wish to do so, I simply cannot change my beliefs, or retain them, on will. For example, no matter how unpleasant it may be for me to believe that a book manuscript of mine will not be published, I simply cannot 'up and believe' it will be published. No matter how pleasant it would be for me to believe that George Bush is not President of the United States, I cannot decide to believe he is not. Moreover, this is true independent of my wealth, position, physical strength, etc.

On the other hand, should I decide to go to Paris, given some minimal physical requirements, I can. I may, of course, decide that it would be best not to skip teaching for a long, unpleasant hike, but that is irrelevant. I do not decide not to alter my belief about who is President because it would be best not to—I just cannot do so. Of course, the Salvadoran peasant has fewer real possibilities than I do. The peasant cannot go to Paris, Ky., no matter how much he or she tries, for the peasant will probably be shot by U.S.-trained soldiers, with U.S. weapons, when he or she tries to cross the border into Honduras. However, the point is not that one can do whatever one wishes, as long as it is not changing one's beliefs, but rather that, given the physical means, one can choose to do lots of things—but one cannot choose to alter one's beliefs no matter what one is given. Thus the landlord can choose to do many more things than the peasant, but when it comes to changing individual beliefs, the landlord and the peasant are in the same boat—neither has any say in the matter. Of course, either may choose to investigate the sources of individual beliefs, and may come to believe different things as a result of these investigations, as Eagleton indicated, but this is clearly an entirely different matter, as we have already discussed.

It seems that Eagleton can maintain the position that beliefs are open to choice in the way that being in Lexington is open to choice because he frequently elides belief and the expression of belief. For example, speaking of a medieval bishop, Eagleton asserts, "The bishop's belief is ideologically determined, but it is still free in the sense that a belief one adopts at gunpoint is not" (p. 377). I can make little sense of the notion of adopting a belief at gunpoint. The very idea is ludicrous to me. However, I can make sense of the notion of *asserting* a belief at gunpoint, just as I can make sense of leaving or entering Lexington at gunpoint, and I suspect that this is what Eagleton had in mind. If so, this makes at least some sense of Eagleton's otherwise incomprehensible insistence upon the assimilation of belief to eating, travelling, etc. *Asserting* a belief is so assimilable—and we have already indicated that such assertion can quite clearly constitute a political act. *Believing*, however, is not so assimilable. Again, Eagleton has crucially failed to address the point at issue.

The Nature and Limits of Political Interpretation

Fortunately, however, none of this indicates that there just cannot be any political interpretation. Michaels' argument implies only that there cannot be any political interpretation *in the sense of interpretation whose truth-decisions are governed by political criteria.* Michaels' argument limits the possibilities of political interpretation. It limits these possibilities in an absolutely crucial way and through an important argument which indicates that concerns of truth or validity, in interpretation or elsewhere, cannot be understood as, let alone *made* contingent upon, political concerns. But Michaels' argument by no means eliminates the possibilities of political interpretation. Indeed, Michaels' sense of 'political interpretation' is not at all our ordinary sense of the term; it is, rather, an unusual sense tacitly employed by various post-structuralists and others (often in arguments from political authority and in implicit telic emplotments, such as we will discuss in the following chapter). Our ordinary sense of 'political' in such contexts is quite different. For example, when we judge, say, Noam Chomsky to be a 'political' writer, we do not thereby assert that the descriptions he believes true of the world are *chosen* by him *as true* for political reasons. In other words, when we say that Chomsky is political in a way that, say, Hartman is not, we are not saying that Chomsky opts to term certain things 'facts' for political reasons whereas Hartman opts to call the same or other things 'facts' for other reasons. Rather, what we are saying in terming someone a 'political' writer is that the person is concerned with those descriptions of the world which are of direct political importance. We are saying that he or she chooses to examine certain of the infinite number of truths which may be uttered concerning the world, and those truths which the person chooses to examine are, precisely, the political ones, or amongst the political ones. In other words, if Chomsky argues that the U.S. press has systematically distorted the condition, history, and policies of the Palestinians and the Palestine Liberation Organization, he does so in much the way that Yao argues for a certain political reading of *The Dismissal of Hai Jui*—he either believes it or does not. (Of course, he does believe it, and with excellent reason, but that does not really matter here.) However, no matter whether he believes it or not, makes his case because he believes it true or because he believes it expeditious, he is doing something political simply because he is focussing his attention on political facts. In this sense, Chomsky's and Yao's acts are *political* no matter what they believe; however, they are *interpretations* also only if they are not duplicitous.

Thus, if our *ordinary* criteria for politicality of interpretation—or construal, explanation, etc.—in general do not demand that decisions about what the facts are to be made by reference to political principles, but rather demand only that attentions be directed to certain questions, the answers to which may be classed as political truths, then why should we adopt the more rigorous standards for politicality when it comes to literature in particular? There are, presumably, infinitely many true things that one can say about a literary work. Of this infinity some truths would concern class relations, racial or sexual characterizations, and other topics we should normally term political, while others would concern astrological theories, general psychological principles, non-generalizable peculiarities of individual characterization, etc. Now, when someone speaks of astronomy, we usually consider that speech not to be, in and of itself, political. In contrast when someone speaks of class relations or sexual stereotyping we usually do consider that speech to be, in and of itself, political. It seems to me clear that much the same loose criteria should be applied to literary studies— and, indeed, it seems clear that much the same loose criteria *are* applied to literary studies. In other words, we generally consider critics who examine the function of astrological theories in literary works contemporary therewith to be non-political and critics who examine the characterization of minorities or women to be at least somewhat political, and I see no reason to change this.

However, merely to say that political interpretation is interpretation attending to political considerations is clearly inadequate. By this definition, a discussion of which character in a novel holds which governmental position and an elaboration of what responsibilities, etc., such positions would have involved at the time of the story, might be termed a 'political interpretation.' But obviously this sort of 'political interpretation' is quite different from, say, that attending to the representation of minorities. In a similar way, we might term 'political' an encyclopedia article on the structure of the Israeli government, an article detailing, for example, the powers of the Knesset, but we would not consider this article political in the way Chomsky's discussions of Israeli policy in the occupied territories are such.

What, then, distinguishes Chomsky's writings from those of the encyclopedist? There are two widely held views on this issue. The first is that writing such as Chomsky's advocates a position, policy, or whatever. The second is that writing such as Chomsky's involves moral judgments. Certainly the two can go together. In fact, in my view—which is pretty much in accord with commonsense views on this issue—moral judgments should lead to advocacy and advocacy should be guided by moral judgment. In this way, the two are not opposed, but interrelated. On the other hand, however necessary advocacy might be, however much moral judgment and advocacy might go together, moral judgment is, in this view, clearly primary, for it is precisely through moral judgment that we initially determine what we should advocate. For those who accept this view, the distinguishing characteristic of, say, Chomskyan political interpretation is, first of all, that it is *normative*, that it involves *ethical evaluation*.

However, not all contemporary writers would agree with this commonsense view. For many, it is advocacy or, even more narrowly, the taking of sides which is crucial. Indeed, for writers such as these, ethical evaluation is at best secondary and at worst inhibiting or retrograde. One clear case of a theorist who separates the taking of sides from moral judgment is Fredric Jameson. In *The Political Unconscious*, Jameson speaks disparagingly of "ethical politics" and asserts that "ideological commitment is not first and foremost a matter of moral choice but of the taking of sides in a struggle between embattled groups." Moreover, he ties this taking of sides to a "dawning sense of solidarity with other members of a particular group or class" in a form of "class consciousness" which is "found not in . . . 'contents' or ideological motifs" but precisely in a feeling of group unity (Jameson 1981, p. 290). Jameson, I should emphasize, is not alone in voicing such views. Many of the most prominent theorists writing in recent years—for example, Michel Foucault—have affirmed or at least implied affirmation of similar principles.

But the position of Jameson, Foucault, and others seems open to quite obvious objections. Primarily, those advocating this view cannot possibly believe that any act of solidarity is as good as any other. However, they have no principled way of drawing relevant distinctions. For example, they have no way of defending their preference for, say, Martin Luther King over George Wallace. Sometimes marginality is invoked as an appropriate non-moral criterion in these cases. In this view, our guiding principle in political judgment should be to valorize the marginal. But this clearly will not do. Fascist survivalists of the Aryan Brotherhood are, if anything, more marginalized than members of the NAACP, but clearly Jameson, Foucault, and others in this school of thought, would never even consider supporting the former group, despite that marginalization. (John Ellis has made a similar point; see Ellis 1989, p. 96.)

Possibly more important, the 'us vs. them' construal of politics implied by this position is grossly oversimple. In some cases, analysis into opposing groups is just not relevant. For example, in certain sorts of environmental work we might seek to alter the actions of particular people without supporting or opposing anyone, conceiving of the situation in terms of opposition, etc. If someone convinces his or her neighbors to save and recycle glass and paper products, that person has done something political but has not in any obvious way taken sides in an opposition between embattled groups. In other cases, there are indeed opposed and embattled groups, but none of these groups deserves our support. No doubt the best political response to, for example, the war in Afghanistan is to seek to end the war, not to take the side of the government or that of the rebels. Finally, even when there are opposed groups and one group clearly deserves our support, our relation to that group should not be guided by an uncritical feeling of solidarity. Our solidarity with the members of an oppressed group—for example the Palestinian people and their representatives in the Palestine Liberation Organization—should not allow us to condone or look with indifference upon a heinous crime committed in the name of their liberation.

Clearly, writers who propose a conception of politics based upon solidarity removed from ethical evaluation cannot justify preferences between groups or preferences within groups. Moreover, they cannot even allow for preferences which are indifferent to groups, preferences which do not involve taking sides. It would appear, then, that principled political action must be action which, far from eschewing ethical evaluation, is based firmly upon it.

Thus, returning to the topic at hand, political interpretation in the appropriate sense might best be construed as interpretation toward the end of political critique, which is to say, interpretation toward the end of ethical evaluation attending to specifically political considerations. Hence we might construct a further reformulation of our preceding definition: Political interpretation is interpretation which attends to considerations of justice, that is to say, political considerations (in the ordinary sense) which lie in the realm of the ethical.

In and of itself, this seems roughly adequate, but it leads to another problem—the delimitation of the ethical. To speak of the realm of the ethical without giving criteria for its circumscription is virtually meaningless. It leaves us with the same set of problems regarding justification which, as we saw, arose for writers such as Jameson when they dismissed or downgraded ethical evaluation. Ethics without criteria is tantamount to no ethics at all. Unfortunately it is by no means self-evident how we might determine ethical criteria. Indeed, before we even undertake any specification of the ethical, the prior question arises as to whether or not there is an 'objective' or non-arbitrary notion of 'the ethical,' a notion which we might *discover*—by intuition, for example, as advocated by Thomas Nagel (in Nagel 1986, pp. 138–48, and elsewhere)—rather than merely *stipulate*.

In fact, I believe that there is and can be no such notion independent of arbitrary stipulation. It is widely believed among philosophers and literary theorists that questions such as 'What is justice?,' 'What is beauty?,' etc., are open to rational debate. However, they are not, for they are not empirical or logical questions, but definitional questions—and definitional questions can be answered only by stipulation. More exactly, any given referential term has both an extension, a set of objects to which it refers or may be used to refer, and a definition. Rational debate about definitions is possible only relative to an extension. We can dispute a definition of, say, 'dog' by saying that it fails to include poodles, or fails to exclude wolves. Alternative definitions can be adjudicated only by reference to their conformity with a pre-established extension. But rational debate on extensions is possible only relative to a definition. We can decide whether or not Spot is a dog only by ascertaining whether or not Spot has the characteristics specified in the definition of 'dog.' Alternative extensions may be adjudicated only by reference to their conformity with a pre-established definition. Clearly, the extension and definition of a given term are not simultaneously open to rational debate. One of the two must be arbitrarily stipulated. Of course, we may, indeed will, rely on intuition to help us sort out our own preferences for stipulation. However, to rely on intuition for anything more—as, for example, Nagel advocates—is merely to rely on implicit, but still arbitrary stipulations, and now to mystify those arbitrary stipulations by presenting them as discoveries.

Thus we have no choice but arbitrarily to stipulate a definition or an extension for goodness or justice. However, before going on to this, I wish to emphasize that this does not involve us in moral relativism (and thus subject us to the criticisms of, for example, Dworkin 1983 and others). Indeed, it is the only way to *remove* such relativism. Debates over moral relativism concern whether or not there is one thing which is really 'the good.' As no rational debate can be had on this matter, absolutists cannot establish their point and thus relativism seems the only alternative. The point here is not that the relativists are correct, but that the entire debate rests upon an essentialist mistake to the effect that such questions as 'What is The Good?' make sense and might, at least in principle, be answered. There can be no question of goodness or justice being universal or non-universal prior to the stipulation of a definition or an extension. In other words, the question, 'Is justice the same for all societies and at all times?' just makes no sense. It is not that justice is *not* the same. Rather, prior to stipulation, 'justice' is meaningless and thus there can be no question of sameness or difference in its regard. Subsequent to stipulation, the problem disappears. Thus, for example, the notion of 'decreasing human misery' does not change across time or place, and neither does the notion of 'treating others as ends in themselves,' and so on. Certainly the degree of observation of these principles or the general esteem in which they are held varies drastically, but this is quite a different matter. There is, then, no question of relativism here. The entire debate about ethical relativism rests upon an illusion, the illusion that the idea of a nature of goodness *per se* is a coherent idea. It is not and we might well be better off if we were entirely to stop speaking in terms of goodness and speak only in terms of our stipulations, saying 'That involves the treatment of others as mere means' or 'That increases human misery,' and so on, rather than 'That is evil' or 'That is unjust.' In the following, however, I will retain the latter terms, once their definitions have been stipulated, to more clearly convey the evaluative nature of the relevant judgments.

Turning to the problem of stipulation, Immanuel Kant's influential criteria seem particularly well suited to our purposes, for they attend not only to the 'private' morality of 'treating others as ends in themselves and never as mere means,' but equally to the 'public' morality of 'establishing a kingdom of ends,' which is to say a society in which *all* are *systematically* treated as ends in themselves and not as mere means. They accord with, systematize, and develop, our, or at least my, notion of the appropriate extension of terms such as 'justice' and 'injustice,' provide a relatively clear delimitation of the ethical, and so intimately connect personal morality and justice as to make redundant any further account of access from one to the other.

Specifically, Kant argues that there are three criteria by which one might adjudicate ethical obligations (see Kant 1964). The first criterion defines as ethical that which I might universalize, which is to say, that which I might will of *all* other subjects. Put simply, the first criterion tells me to act in a particular fashion if and only if I could will all others to act likewise. As Kant rigorously puts it, "Maxims [to which we conform our actions] must be chosen as if they had to hold as universal laws of nature" (Kant 1964, p. 104). Or, equivalently, "So act that the maxim of your will could always hold at the same time as a principle establishing universal law" (Kant 1956, p. 30). The second criterion defines as ethical the treatment of others as ends in themselves and never as mere means. As Kant has it, "A rational being, as by his[/her] very nature an end and consequently an end in him[/her]self, must serve for every maxim as a condition limiting all merely relative and arbitrary ends," or, in another formulation, "Act in such a way that you always treat humanity, whether in your own person or in the person of any other, never simply as a means, but always at the same time as an end" (Kant 1964, pp. 104, 96). The third and final criterion defines the ethical as that which conduces toward, or rather, if universalized, would conduce toward, the establishment of a kingdom of ends, which is to say, as we have already remarked, a society in which everyone is systematically treated as an end and never as a mere means. Emphasizing the social and political nature of morality, if in a typically overlegalistic form, Kant urges "All maxims as proceeding from our own making of law ought to harmonize with a possible kingdom of ends as a kingdom of nature," which is to say an ideal or model of a kingdom or society "used to bring into existence what does not exist but can be made actual by our conduct" (Kant 1964, p. 104).

As is well known, much subsequent socially or politically oriented ethics—for example, the "existentialist ethics" proposed
by Sartre and subsequently developed by Simone de Beauvoir in
a specifically feminist direction—has its roots in Kantianism,
reformulating these principles in various ways and sometimes providing more detailed criteria both for the ideal itself and for the
transition thereto. Moreover, Kantian ethics, reformulated in relation to practical and utopian socialisms and conjoined with unhappily Hegelian analyses of history and economy, to a great extent
forms the normative foundation of both Marxism and Anarchism.
Following Kant and his many progeny, I will take something to be
of ethical concern insofar as and to the degree that it involves
considerations of the treatment of men and women as ends in
themselves or as mere means and to be of political concern insofar
as and to the degree that a decision in its regard would, if practiced
universally, conduce toward or from the establishment of a kingdom of ends.

It should be clear that our Kantian criteria (or now, criterion)
indicate that an interpretation attending to mere questions of what
governmental positions carried what responsibilities when would
not necessarily be any more political in our sense than an interpretation attending to questions of astrology. On the other hand, an
interpretation attending to questions of the characterizations of
women or minorities would be thus political—or, rather, could be
thus political *given a certain situation in the world which makes
questions appertaining to the characterization of women and minorities questions appertaining to the treatment of individuals as
ends in themselves and the establishment of a kingdom of ends.* The
characterization of women or blacks is an ethical question, while
the characterization of, say, people from Connecticut, or that of
men and women with curled little toes, is not an ethical question.
This is because women and blacks are not in fact universally and
systematically treated as ends in themselves *in the actual world*,
which is to say, *our society does not constitute or approximate or
conduce toward a kingdom of ends in their regard*, whereas this is
not the case for people from Connecticut or people with curled little
toes. Were this situation to change, the realm of the ethical would
change, and thus what would count as political interpretation
would alter, in precisely the same manner.

Thus we see that even our third definition of political interpretation is not quite fully adequate and hence we might, finally, reformulate it in the following manner: political interpretation is interpretation which attends to that subset of political considerations (in the usual sense) which are at once ethical considerations in the sense that they involve concerns of the establishment of a kingdom of ends *specifically in the manner in which and degree to which that kingdom has not been established*, which is to say, the manner in which and the degree to which *the society in question does not itself conform to the ideal of such a kingdom*. Thus a political interpretation always and necessarily recurs to *both* textual and mundane facts. Our evaluation of the fictional must always be grounded in our evaluation of the actual.

From the Determination of Intent to the Determination of Effect

Until now, we have drawn our examples from what is probably the most common form of political interpretation—the analysis and critique of single works, an analysis most often aimed at authorial intent or at 'the text itself.' For reasons that will become clear in subsequent chapters, I do not believe that the interpretation or ethical evaluation of 'the text itself' is a coherent project. In contrast, the parallel study of authorial intent—a study which seeks to uncover and evaluate the politically relevant aims and beliefs of a given writer as expressed in a particular work—is reasonable, and even at times quite valuable. Yet not all politically important forms of interpretation and critique focus on single works in isolation, however these are understood. Some, for example, involve broader, 'morphological' concerns. A single work with a single woman who is hysterical is not morally reprehensible insofar as it involves no claim about women in general. On the other hand, an entire set of works in which women are presented as hysterical quite generally is, indeed, as a set, morally reprehensible, not in the sense that anyone is necessarily to be *blamed* for the situation—after all, it might turn out that none of the authors intended generalization, etc.—but in the sense that the literary situation created by these works is, or is likely to be, in some sense unjust. But unjust to whom? Surely, we are not concerned about the fictional characters. Rather, our concern is with those actual women who might be affected by a misogynistic ideology fostered by the patterned repetition of a stereotypical characterization of women. Our concerns are principally with the facts, not with the fictions. The fictional treatment of women or minorities is ultimately a matter of indifference, ethically speaking, if the real treatment of women and minorities is in accord with the Kantian dicta and is not threatened by that fictional treatment.

This brings us to what is no doubt the most important sort of ethical interpretation: that which concerns the real effects of various works upon our beliefs and actions, whether these works are perfidious in intent or beneficent in intent, isolated or collocated. In the last two decades, the attention of literary critics has been drawn more and more toward a study of the *actual* responses of *actual* readers. Dissatisfied with vague and unsupported generalizations of the 'Here, readers feel that Hamlet's suffering is their own'-variety, a number of theorists have turned to an examination of exactly what readers do feel when they are supposed to be feeling that Hamlet's suffering is all their own, or whatever. Clearly, this sort of study is crucially relevant to political interpretation.

Unfortunately, the positive results of reader-response criticism are nil. The methods used to gather data concerning response are so faulty, on the one hand so biased and on the other hand so imprecise, that the so-called data themselves are entirely unreliable, and I do not even enter into the problem of their representativity. For example, a particularly significant methodological flaw in reader-response criticism is the widespread reliance of response researchers on the introspection and self-observation of experimental subjects. As Edith Klemenz-Belgardt points out, response "investigators usually content themselves with the exploration of the expressed response" and assume that "the relationship between the *inner response . . .* and the *overt response*" is "unproblematic" (Klemenz-Belgardt 1981, p. 359). The method of investigation in these cases basically involves asking people how they respond to given works and why (see, for example, Holland 1982 for an approach of this sort to humor). Now, to most people this seems, intuitively, quite reasonable. Unfortunately, the data of introspection and self-observation are often highly unreliable, as several studies have demonstrated (see, for example, Grunbaum 1984, pp. 29f. and citations, and Cameron 1985, p. 34; we will have occasion to return to this topic below). Thus research which is based upon introspection and self-observation does not tell us much of anything about response; in fact, it does not really advance beyond the unsupported intuitions which it sets out to criticize and replace.

Despite the problems with positive work in this area, however, the negative result of reader-response criticism is quite clear: Do not draw conclusions about response from inferences concerning, for example, authorial intent, but make response an independent object of study. Clearly, this advice applies no less to political interpretation than to any other variety. For example, a film which is politically pernicious by intentional criteria need not have politically pernicious effects. Conversely, a work which manifests the most virtuous of intents might prove morally degrading. Moreover, as we have already indicated, a series of works might conjunctively produce ideological effects entirely unrelated to the effects the works might have produced or even did produce in isolation. The point here is not, of course, that what a work means and what it does are unrelated, but simply that their relation is not as simple as might be thought, that it is not a matter for *a priori* reasoning, but for empirical investigation.

Again, the present tools of response critics are, it appears, useful mainly for 'proving' the particular theories of those who forge and use them. For this reason, it is likely that at the moment little of genuine interest can be uncovered with regard to ideological effect, by using specifically literary and response-oriented methods. However, for the present, the study of such effect can be pursued along other lines, and at least the more gross examples of speculation as to effect (e.g., 'the wide-angle shots in *Gandhi* make people view Indians as animals in wildlife documentaries, the genre in which such shots are most frequently employed'—really, people actually say things like this) can be kept to a minimum. More exactly, when studying ethical effect, we can follow the lead of researchers in other disciplines and begin to base our conclusions upon such data as may be derived from controlled psychological experimentation, the statistical study of social phenomena, and so on. Outside of literary study, the empirical investigation of effect is common (for an overview of some relevant empirical/psychological studies, see Klemenz-Belgardt 1981, pp. 365–68 and citations). For example, in a typical sort of experiment, a psychologist might take two groups of children, show them different sorts of television programs and then examine their subsequent behavior under controlled circumstances. Specifically, the psychologist might show one group 'violent' programs and another 'non-violent' programs and then count up the number of subsequent arguments, fights, and so on, in each group. Such a study can provide important data for the examination of the general effect of violent programming and thus, on the assumption that contentiousness and pugnacity are at least mildly unethical, it can provide important data for the examination of the *ethical* effect of such programming.

Along similar lines, a sociological, linguistic, or other researcher might undertake a statistical study of voting patterns and, for example, the phonetics of campaign slogans. In such a study, one might seek a statistically significant positive correlation between, say, the poetical quality of the slogan and the success of the candidate (as in Jakobson's well-known—but empirically weak—analysis of "I like Ike"). Again, any such correlation could contribute important data both to the examination of the general effect of campaign slogans, and more specifically to the examination of the *ethical* effect thereof, assuming voting to be an ethical act, which is to say, an act relevantly judged by the lights of our 'kingdom of ends' criterion.

It must be emphasized that, like any controlled experiments, statistical surveys, or other empirical enquiries, the studies we have just conjectured would not somehow put us in direct contact with the facts of ethical effect. Rather, they would yield data which we could assume to be unproblematic only at a much lower level (and even then only with a certain degree of tentativeness). In other words, any conclusions which we might draw from such studies concerning ethical effect are highly inferential, and not by any means directly manifest in the 'results' of the studies. Most important, many possible explanations for any correlations may be discovered. To take an obvious example, if it turns out that slogans with certain subtle phonetic patterns are positively correlated with electoral success, this may merely indicate that candidates who are careful about slogans will be careful about other things and thus will win because of those other things, the slogans actually having nothing to do with it. In like manner, suppose it turns out that children who view violent programs get into more fights right after the programs than those subjected to more serene and harmonious dramas. This seems to indicate that the violent programs foster pugnacity. However, it might eventuate that the children quite generally are prone to involve themselves in brawls at regular intervals and that the violence of the programming merely affects their timing, not their frequency.

The point here is certainly not that no inferences can be drawn from data to effect. In fact, empirical data provide the only possible basis for such inferences. The point is rather that these and other investigations do not yield facts about effect *per se*, but rather some sort of data for its construal. It is extremely important that we recognize this and practice circumspection in our inferences. When we are circumspect, we are not only more likely to avoid error, we are also more likely to recognize the possibilities for further, clarificatory investigations, to follow up different avenues of enquiry, and quite generally to deepen our understanding of the phenomena in question. For example, the alternative interpretations offered above for our hypothetical data immediately suggest specific investigations which could contribute to a disambiguation of those data.

In my view, literary critics interested in examining the ethical effects of literary works would do well to emulate the procedures of experimental psychologists and social scientists—while at the same time remaining even more fully aware of the hypothetical nature of their inferences and conclusions. Indeed, I believe that little systematic progress can be made in this field until it is widely recognized that systematic, rigorous, circumspect empirical investigation is the primary method for determining ethical or other effects and until such investigation is in fact undertaken by large numbers of students of literature. There are no doubt certain limited sorts of inference which we can make, with reasonable confidence, on the basis of general principles and which thus do not require specific experimental or statistical justification. For example, it seems reasonable, in the context of our broad understanding of human cognition and affection, and without specific experimental or statistical study, to conclude that the almost universal cinematic, literary, and other representation of Arabs as terrorists will encourage people to view Arabs as terrorists, at least tendentially. On the other hand, even here empirical study is necessary to determine the extent and precise nature of actual anti-Arab racism, the degree to which literature, or news coverage, or whatever, contributes to this, and so on.

Preliminary to any serious empirical research into literary effect, however, it is important to draw some distinctions and isolate the various objects of such research. First of all, although I have been using 'effect' and 'response' synonymously in the preceding, there are significant differences between response, in the sense or senses of Holland, Fish, Jauss, and other response critics, and effect, in the ethical sense, in the sense relevant to our 'kingdom of ends' criterion. Specifically, the notion of response encompasses the affective, interpretive, and associative reactions of readers. Response concerns the reader's feelings regarding the work; his or her beliefs about its meaning, theme, etc.; and the reader's associations with its scenes, imagery, or whatever. Effect, on the other hand, concerns the behaviors fostered in the individual by the experience of the work—the behaviors germane to considerations of conduciveness toward or from a kingdom of ends, in the case of ethical effect. It is important to emphasize that response and effect are never simple matters of unconditioned subjectivity encountering a univocally causal text. As we have already emphasized, one text will tend to foster sexist behavior principally or solely because other texts do so, many people already engage in sexist behavior, and so on. It is a *series* of factors acting *in concert* which encourages the behavior, not the text alone. Much the same holds for response. One's response to a given work is conditioned not only by the work in question, but by one's responses to other works, one's non-literary experiences, and so on.

Intermediate between response and effect is worldly belief. Texts encourage us to believe certain things—or, rather, we come to believe certain things in part as a consequence of our perusal of certain texts. Again, the mundane beliefs we derive from a given work are derived *in the context of* other works, social practices, and so on. Thus one text might foster—or reenforce—sexist beliefs only because *other* texts foster such beliefs, such beliefs are otherwise common in our society, etc. It should be clear that belief will most often derive from response. Literary works contain logical arguments, pathetic arguments, and arguments from authority (to advert to Aristotle's distinctions), just as easily, if not just as frequently, as non-literary works. All these involve interpretation (i.e., interpretive response), in the usual way; the latter two crucially involve the other components of response—emotional reaction and association—as well. There may also be more general elements related to response which enter here—like our tendency to treat fiction as reality and thus to include fictional events, characters, etc., in our inductions concerning actuality; for example, when people say that 'in their experience' women act like *a* and men like *b*, one might wonder how high a percentage of the women and men in their relevant experiences have been fictional (though, in fact, such impressionistic generalizations would not be reliable even if based solely on real people—for reasons discussed in Holland, et al., pp. 191–95).

Now, just as beliefs are fostered primarily by response, behavior is effected principally by way of the inculcation of beliefs. For the most part, a text fosters, say, sexist behavior by fostering sexist beliefs upon which agents subsequently act. It is no doubt possible for a text to effect a behavior independent of any relevant beliefs. Thus, reading that men treat women in certain prejudicial ways, seeing women treated thus in society, and so on, some man might 'automatically' come to treat women in these ways without concurrently holding the prejudicial beliefs which quite generally underlie the practices. However, more often than not the inculcation of belief would appear to be critical to the affecting of behavior.

Thus, as belief is most often the condition of effect, and response is most often the condition of belief, the study of response is a necessary part of the study of effect. While the study of response and the study of belief do not at all exhaust the study of effect, they are crucial to such a study. Moreover, they are, in general, closer to the interests and research capacities of the literary critic.

I should emphasize in this context, however, that any study of belief should seek carefully to distinguish what might be called 'motivational beliefs' from what might be called 'prompted assent beliefs.' By 'motivational beliefs,' I refer to beliefs that actually do or that might readily foster action. These beliefs may be conscious or unconscious, but they are related to aims of adequate importance to a subject such that the person might act on them. By 'prompted assent beliefs' I refer to beliefs which surface when the believer is queried, but have no general motivational force for him

or her. For example, if I believe that the U.S. funding of counterrev-
olutionaries invading Nicaragua from Honduras and Costa Rica is
in effect the funding of fascist thugs and terrorists *and* I have a
strong desire that the United States not fund fascist thugs and
terrorists, then it is at least possible that I will act on my belief.
Thus my belief in this case is motivational. If, however, I never
much think about Nicaragua but someone calls asking, 'Do you
think the United States should send $100 million to Nicaraguan
insurgents?,' I may say 'No,' in just the same way as I may say
'Yes' to the question, 'Do you feel that organic prunes should be
widely available to those who want them?' Assuming I have no
strong desires connected with either belief, there is virtually no
chance that I will act on either belief. Thus both beliefs are, in this
case, merely prompted assents with no motivational force. (A
striking case of this, along similar lines, is reported in Olson
1988.) Ideology functions not only to inculcate motivational beliefs
favorable to domination, it functions also to render innocuous
any beliefs unfavorable to domination by encouraging ignorance
or apathy in the populace, by eliminating subversive beliefs *or
reducing them to prompted assents only*. This is, in my view, a
point of crucial importance in the study of ideology in general and
of literary ideology—and literary effect—in particular. Note again
that here, as in all other cases, the politics of literary effect are not
themselves rarified and literary, but exist in the real world and
involve real issues of practical moral significance.

Political interpretation is, then, a two-fold undertaking; it attends
to intent and to effect, to meaning and to consequence. But to
undertake political interpretation is not to live in two worlds, one
fictional and one actual; it is, rather, to remain always among the
facts. As we have repeatedly emphasized, it is the facts that we
judge and work to change, it is the facts which, in their distance
from or proximity to the ideal of a kingdom of ends, define our
judgment and labor as political, define the work of fiction as an
object of political concern, both initially and subsequently. Though
it recurs constantly to both the mundane fiction of literature and
the celestial fiction of a kingdom of ends, political interpretation
lives only in the real, interpreting and critiquing the one fiction in
the hopes of realizing the other.

2

The Critique of Ideology and the Place of Deconstruction

Critique of ideology is the centerpiece of virtually all theories of political interpretation, and for very good reason. Within the general category of ethical interpretation, ideological critique is distinguished both by its objects and by its aims. First, its object—ideology—comprises common sets of (false) beliefs and/or aims (including interests, preferences, desires, etc.) which function to promote and secure privileges for certain individuals or groups over other individuals or groups. In this way, ideology functions to discourage behaviors conducive toward the establishment of a kingdom of ends. Moreover, ideological beliefs and aims are widespread, systematically efficacious, and, most crucially, adopted by those whose interests they do not serve, by those who are disprivileged through their enactment.[1]

In classical Marxist thinking, ideology is paired with repression and the two are taken to constitute the means of social control administered by the ruling classes to maintain and extend their power (see Althusser 1981). In this conception, which seems to me fundamentally correct, with qualifications to be marked below, the repressive 'apparatuses' of power constitute the state quite generally, including prominently the judiciary, the armed forces, and so on, as well as certain non-state paramilitary organizations, etc. Repression is constituted by all forms of external coercion. Ideological apparatuses, on the other hand, comprise schools, entertain-

ment industries, religious institutions, and so on. Ideology is constituted by all forms of 'internal coercion.'

It is important to point out here that ideological beliefs and aims
are tenacious. Frequently, they are not mere mistakes, corrigible by
simple indication of the facts or a simple discussion of interests or
ethical consequences. As Raymond Geuss has pointed out, they are
more often on the order of pathological illusions—or even delusions—in the psychoanalytic sense of these terms (see Geuss 1981,
pp. 39ff.). In Chapter 4, I will seek to isolate some of the reasons for
this. For now, I should merely like to emphasize this crucial difference between ideology and simple factual error or confusion as to
one's own interests or the ethical implications of one's acts. We
frequently come to believe true, statements which are in fact false.
Related to this, we are often confused about our own interests and
the ethical implications of our acts. However, in most cases we are
open to rational argument and a preponderance of evidence will
dissuade us from maintaining our erroneous views, at least with
complete certainty. Ideological beliefs and aims, however, are to a
far greater degree secured against argument and evidence and are
far less frequently tempered through circumspection.

The recalcitrance of ideological beliefs and aims is in large part
the reason for the development of a critique of ideology distinct
from ordinary ethical interpretation. To recur to our above analysis
of belief, effect, etc., the critique of ideology functions first of all to
isolate ideological beliefs and aims; ideologically motivated acts;
and writings, events, situations, etc., which foster such beliefs, aims,
and acts. From this, it evaluates the aims and the behaviors in light
of ethical criteria—in our case, the 'kingdom of ends' criterion—
and examines the logical coherence and empirical adequacy of the
beliefs. This it shares with all forms of ethical interpretation. Also
common to all forms of ethical interpretation is the examination of
response. This examination involves both the actual tabulation of
responses and the analysis of such rhetorical manipulations, etc., as
contribute to such response. Entirely absent from ordinary ethical
interpretation, however, is a *functional* account of the (ideological)
beliefs and aims in question. Such an account is, in contrast,
absolutely central to ideological critique. Specifically, such critique
continues beyond ethical and logico-empirical evaluation of ideological aims, beliefs, and behaviors and beyond examination of how

particular works, etc., serve to foster such aims, beliefs, and behaviors. Such critique proceeds to an isolation and examination of the *interests* which an inculcation of such aims, beliefs, and behaviors might serve. Ideological critique thus endeavors to *explain* the genesis of ideologies through the determination of those individuals or groups to whose concrete benefit these ideologies redound, the manner in which such ideologies contribute to such benefit, etc.

Thus the critique of ideology attends to the ethics of aims and behaviors, the veracity of beliefs, the nature of response, and the character of those power relations which underlie all these. In classical Marxist analysis, these power relations are always the relations of economic classes or some derivatives of the relations between such classes. While I certainly acknowledge that such relations are crucial, and while I believe that the possibilities of rigorous economic analysis should be exhausted before other sorts of analysis of power are undertaken, I myself would not follow classical Marxism in this regard. Rather, I take it that in virtually all cases non-economic factors enter into the definition of power relations and in some cases non-economic factors predominate, at least temporarily. We will return to this topic below.

As we have already indicated, the objects of concern in the ideological critique of literature are authors and readers. Indeed, such critique concerns *only* authors and readers—people. People are, after all, what have beliefs and aims, and what engage in behaviors. For the most part different varieties of ideological critique recognize this limitation at least tacitly. As to its means, methods, or criteria, ideological critique is, again, fundamentally concerned with logical and empirical adequacy, justice, and explanatory rigor. For the most part, different varieties of ideological critique maintain and seek to promulgate basic principles of logic, empirical enquiry, and ethical adjudication also.

However, in recent years the forms of ideological critique most prominent in literary circles in the United States—Derridaean deconstruction and related post-structural 'feminisms'—explicitly eschew such limits or principles. Specifically, deconstructive critique aims to undermine ideological 'hierarchies' which are to be located primarily in relation to the system of language itself. Similarly, post-structural feminisms, often following deconstructive principles, regularly focus their critical attentions on language *per se*. Moreover, these same theories frequently condemn logical inference and empirical investigation, claiming that the principles of rational enquiry are necessarily patriarchal and oppressive. For these reasons, I should like to examine and criticize these theories before continuing on to a more substantive consideration of ideology.

Prefatory to this, however, I should say a few things about the very idea of language *per se* and about reason and empirical investigation. I hope to devote a separate volume to meaning and method in the theory of literature; however, I should here indicate the general intent of that study insofar as it is germane to the critique of ideology and most particularly to the evaluation of deconstruction and post-structural feminism.

First, I take it that our above argument concerning definition and extension applies to the notion of *meaning* itself. As far as I am aware, all conceptions of referential meaning encompass a definitional part and an extensional part. Accepting this, but without fixing either for 'meaning,' literary theorists engage in necessarily futile debates on the 'nature' of meaning. In these circumstances there is a 'nature' of meaning as little as there is a 'nature' of justice. As with the latter concept, we must fix the extension of 'meaning' before there is any fact of the matter about the definition, and we must fix the definition before there is any fact of the matter about the extension. Before one or the other is fixed, debate is pointless, for there is no fact there about which one might debate. Thus, I would argue, there is no 'true nature' of meaning any more than there is a 'true nature' of anything else. Rather, there are various *sorts* of 'meaning,' various ways in which the notion may be stipulated—utterer's expressive intent, utterer's aesthetical intent, auditor's interpretive response, common interpretive response in a given community, etc.—none of which is 'more truly' meaning than any of the others. In other words, there is no question of the nature of meaning *per se*; rather, there is only a question of the *varieties* of meaning, of the ways in which our vague notion of meaning—involving extension and definition—may be fixed.

Now, it is, presumably, uncontroversial that there are intents—of utterers, auditors, other members of various 'speech communities,' etc.—and thus that various intents may be stipulated in various definitions of meaning. The question then remains as to whether or not there is any sort of meaning beyond these intents. For example, is there such a thing as 'autonomous' meaning, the meaning of language *per se*? Derrida, following the structuralist tradition, clearly assumes that there is. However, I would maintain that the notion of autonomous meaning makes little sense, ontologically or epistemologically. Ontologically, we simply have no reason to posit autonomous meaning. There just are no data which can be accounted for in autonomist, but not intentionalist terms (including those of Katz 1981, as I hope to demonstrate in the volume mentioned above). Epistemologically, I can see no way of our having any access to autonomous meaning or of its entering into our 'data of meaning' in any way. In other words, even if there were such a thing as autonomous meaning I do not see how it could have any bearing upon actual linguistic communication, reflection, etc.[2] As we will see, Derrida maintains that the systematic, autonomous "dissemination" and "differance" of meaning produce a split by which meaning and intent are never fully identical. For Derrida, there is always a "remainder" of meaning inaccessible to intent. But for Derrida this is only a remainder. Thus, for Derrida intent and autonomous meaning can be partially, but not fully reconciled. I would argue, in contrast, that they cannot be even partially reconciled. If there is any such thing as autonomous meaning, we simply have no way of getting at it. Finally, independent of ontological and epistemological considerations, ideological critique must always be governed by ethical concerns—and ethical concerns are always concerns about people or their acts, not about disembodied signifiers. Thus it seems that the very object of deconstructive and related critique simply does not exist; that, furthermore, even if it did exist, we could have no access to it; and finally, even if we had access to it, it would not be the proper target of ethical critique anyway.

As to reason and empirical investigation, I will merely restate what I have already indicated. Moral concerns are posterior to concerns of truth or falsity, not prior thereto. Most often, moral propositions imply and thus presuppose assertions of fact. For example, if we say that the United States is behaving shamefully with regard to Nicaragua, or if we say that we should work to put an end to U.S. Nicaraguan policy, we quite clearly assume there to be a certain fact of the matter. It is precisely the *factual* state of affairs which we assume ourselves to be criticizing. Similarly, when we claim that women should be allowed access to high-level governmental positions, we assume that there is a fact of the matter, specifically, their being denied such access at present. It is precisely because and insofar as our factual assumption is true that we ourselves take our moral assertion to have force. One cannot, so to speak, be more moral than the facts. If one attempts to be such, and thus maintains, against the evidence, that what ought to be the case by the lights of a given theory, is, in fact, the case, one thereby surrenders not only one's credibility, but one's effectiveness. I can no more effect moral amelioration if I take the facts to be other than what they are than I can exit the room if I take the door to be other than where it is—in which case I would be, quite literally, running my head up against the wall. We can and should work to end U.S. support for Samocista terrorists who burn crops and gun down civilians precisely and only because there is such U.S. support for a group of terrorists, former supporters of Anastasio Somoza, who burn crops and gun down civilians. Lacking empirical and logical criteria, as Bertrand Russell so nicely put it, "truth can be [and, we might add, *will* be] determined by the police" (Russell 1956, p. 148), or whoever has power in the relevant area.

It is important to emphasize here that Derrida's influential position on the notion of truth is that we need to deconstruct it. For example, in *Of Grammatology*, Derrida adjures us to "the deconstruction, of all the significations that have their source in that of the logos. Particularly the signification of truth" (p. 10). Elsewhere, Derrida develops this exortation, now connecting logic and truth with "phallocentric dialectic," as well (Derrida 1981, p. 49). Throughout *Spurs* he makes, or appears to make, similar assertions. And in "Structure, Sign, and Play in the Discourse of the Human Sciences," he urges "the Nietzschean *affirmation*—the joyous affirmation of the world and without truth" (Derrida 1972, p. 264).

It is not easy to ascertain precisely what Derrida intends in such assertions. Most often when Derrida deconstructs a given notion, such as that of truth, he does not dismiss it entirely. He does not seek to demonstrate an absolute incoherence and complete dissemination, but only a limited incoherence and a dissemination which leaves a trace.

On the other hand, Derrida does often appear to hold explicitly and self-consciously to the stronger view. Thus, on one occasion, I asked him how he reconciled his call to deconstruct the notion of truth with the aim, announced in *Of Grammatology* to "remove" deconstruction "from all relativism" (p. 14). Derrida explained, quite sensibly in the context of his work, that relativists accept the validity of the notion of truth, but just say, 'We can't get to it' or 'There is no such thing.' They still accept the system of oppositions in which 'truth' finds its place in Western metaphysics. (I suppose Fish is a good example of a relativist in this sense—though now, having made truth relative to interpretative community rather than individual response, he incomprehensibly claims not to be relativist.) He, on the other hand, denied the very notion of truth, and undertook to displace the entire system. Thus, he concluded, "In this way, I am more relativist than the relativists."

Of course, given the situation (a garden party), I would not wish to hold Derrida too rigorously to these claims. However, they seem to me one good explanation for his seemingly contradictory positions on truth and relativism. Moreover, Gayatri Spivak makes a very similar point in her introduction to *Of Grammatology*. Deconstruction, she tells us, "might seem an attractively truant world of relativism. But the fearful pleasure of a truant world is the sense of an authority being defied. That absolute ground of authority Derrida would deny" (p. lxxiii).

In any event, whether Derrida intends the stronger thesis or the weaker one, the relevant point here is that Derridaean deconstruction at the very least aims to displace and limit concerns of truth (and empirical enquiry—see Dews 1987, pp. 6ff.). There is no obvious way in which this is or may be politically liberatory; and there are obvious ways in which it could be politically quite unfortunate.

Moreover, many deconstructionists have not confined themselves to criticisms of the notion of truth. Rather, they have expressed a disaffection for the principles of logic and even dialectic, as we have already noted briefly. To take the most obvious case, many deconstructionists (and possibly Derrida himself) deny the Principle of Non-Contradiction. For example, Christopher Norris explicitly repudiates scientific method, including "non-contradiction" (Norris 1982, pp. 86–87). Similarly, Barbara Johnson claims that Derrida deconstructs the "logic of noncontradiction that underlies Western [logophonophallocentric] metaphysics" (Johnson 1981, p. xvii, though the passage she quotes from Derrida, insofar as it is at all clear, seems aimed at the quite different, and more limited, Principle of the Excluded Middle).[3]

Of course, these statements and others to the same effect necessarily presuppose the very principle they are claiming to deny. However, this presupposition is a logical one, resting on logical principles, including the Principle of Non-Contradiction and thus it too is no doubt deconstructively repudiated (in a further statement presupposing the principle by way of a—repudiated—logical relation, and so on). Perhaps more important, it should be clear that, not only in disputes such as this over logical presuppositions, but in all manner of disputes, those who deny the Principle of Non-Contradiction quite literally allow no contradiction. There simply is no way of disputing their claim in this case *or in any other*. To controvert their claims one would need, for example, to present evidence in contradiction with their generalizations, or isolate fallacious inferences in their reasonings, but the claims themselves disallow this. A denial of the Principle of Non-Contradiction makes all of one's claims into dogma, brooking no dispute. However, *acceptance* of the Principle of Non-Contradiction *allows dispute on all points*—coherently, and on all sides. Granting this principle, if I present a certain analysis, then you, employing evidence I have or seem to have overlooked, and employing a logical analysis of my inferences, may endeavor to controvert my conclusions. Equally, I might respond by in part revising my intitial analysis and in part disputing your arguments in like manner, etc. Again, if the principle is not granted, such dialogue—indeed, any dialogue involving dispute, any dialogue involving anything beyond shared doctrine—is impossible. The political ramifications of a deconstructive denial of the Principle of Non-Contradiction or of other logical principles, like those of a deconstruction of truth, do not appear salutary.

Some Prefatory Remarks on the Rhetoric of Deconstruction

There is, of course, much more to deconstruction than these admittedly isolated and ambiguous references to truth and logical inference. There is primarily a broad linguistic theory, which serves as the basis for a form of political interpretation quite different from, and indeed opposed to, that outlined above. This linguistic theory has been widely characterized, especially in literary circles, as politically liberatory. More important, its opponents have been castigated for various sorts of politically retrograde thinking—all of this *prior* to any consideration of the validity of the theory in question. Indeed, deconstructionists have, intentionally or unintentionally, promulgated a dichotmous and politicized view of linguistic theory, a view in which, as we will see, one's acceptance or rejection of deconstructive principles is taken to provide good evidence of one's political virtue or vice. In my experience, this has served to intimidate those who find deconstructive arguments unconvincing and might otherwise have sought to dispute them. It has therefore functioned to inhibit rational criticism and rational dialogue. Before turning to a discussion of the crucial linguistic and related arguments and conclusions of deconstruction, I should like to look at the initial plausibility of certain of its political claims and at the persuasive function and argumentative validity or invalidity of its political rhetoric, thereby seeking to 'clear the ground,' so to speak, for serious discussion of the relevant linguistic and related issues. (For a number of points in this section, I am indebted to Graff 1983, to which I refer the reader for a complementary discussion.)

1. Political Argumentation and Literary Theory

A few years ago, I attended a convention in which deconstruction was lauded for its revolutionary and liberatory 'gestures' in roughly the following words: 'Deconstruction is an ideology which valorizes the fragment, the discontinuous, the differe/ant and thus supports, on the theoretical plane, the struggles of women and minorities in the face of White, patriarchal power structures of homogeneity and organicity.' It is difficult to say precisely what this speaker intended to claim. For example, was he trying to say that those who analyze, in this case, *Ulysses* as a discontinuous and unsynthesizable play of differance were more likely to support bussing, preferential hiring for minorities and women, and the ERA, whereas those who sought to uncover synthetic unities in the work were more likely to be organizing anti-bussing protests, filing reverse discrimination suits, and enthusiastically promoting the "Family Protection Act"? Or was he trying to say that if the bulk of literary criticism were deconstructive, and, thus, fragment-valorizing, that most people in the United States would support gay liberation and institute non-prejudicial policies with regard to non-heterosexuals?

But both the claims concerning intent and those concerning effect seem arrantly false. Moreover, in line with a tendency in deconstruction which we have just discussed, this speaker went on to denounce the 'repressive ideology' of reason, logic, and truth. If he really intended this disclaimer, it would seem that he was not even in a position to say that women are oppressed, that the overwhelming majority of high-level governmental and industrial positions are held by men, that there is a gross discrepancy in the United States between the educational opportunities of most blacks and those of most whites, and so on. Thus the possibilities for adjudicating any particular claim which presupposes such facts seem bleak.

What is significant about these assertions is that this speaker is not alone. While his claims may be more fully explicit, they are of the same general sort as those put forth by some of the most respected and sensitive critics writing today. Like Jacques Derrida, Jonathan Culler, J. Hillis Miller, and other deconstructionists, as well as non-deconstructive post-structuralist or post-modern thinkers such as Julia Kristeva and Stanley Fish, he was claiming a particular theory superior due to its supposed beneficial political ramifications. Equally, he was claiming that other theories, and thereby, one is left to suppose, those who accept and promulgate such theories, are not only inferior, but somehow politically and ethically reprehensible as well. He was drawing a line: on the one side, *us*—liberationists, feminists, civil rights advocates; on the other side, *them*—naifs, racists, sexists, possibly fascists. A division of this sort is, I believe, implicit in Derrida's opposition of the deconstructive to the logo-, phono-, and, most crucially, *phallo-* centric. Though Derrida and other prominent post-structuralists are usually more subdued in their related characterizations, the divisions are still present.

Take, for example, Julia Kristeva's description of the "new" ethics. It is no longer "a coercive, customary manner of ensuring the cohesiveness of a particular group through the repetition of a code." Today, ethics has been reformulated through the synthesis of "Marx, Nietzsche, and Freud," which is to say through the writings of Kristeva, Sollers, Derrida, and other 'post-structuralists' associated with *Tel Quel*. Specifically, now "the issue of ethics crops up whenever a code . . . must be shattered in order to give way to the free play of negativity." Thus Kristevaean semiotics is an *ethical* activity and, moreover, it lays claim to the only ethics which is not a mere "coercive" subjugation and ideologization. As if this were not clear enough, Kristeva then goes on to assert that the old ethics, which is to say pretty much everything which is opposed to Kristevaean semiotics, comprises precisely "Fascism and Stalinism" (Kristeva 1980, p. 23).

While avoiding such straightforward claims of political totalitarianism, Hillis Miller opines that non- or anti-deconstructionists seek a "sovereign command" of the text (quoted in Culler 1982, p. 251). Miller thus implies that opponents of deconstruction suffer from a totalitarian personality and pursue totalitarian aims, at least in their professional activities. Similarly, Jonathan Culler accuses John Searle, and, by extension, all mainstream speech-act theorists—and, indeed, intentionalists—of undertaking to "control" language (Culler 1982, p. 120), while Derrida finds "the police . . . always waiting in the wings" in any rule-based theory of meaning such as that of Searle (1977, p. 250).

In other contexts, Derrida and others are quite explicit about the putative political benefits and even necessity of deconstruction. For example, Derrida asserts that the 'overturning' of *linguistic* 'hierarchies' which characterizes deconstructive method is at once a *political* and *social* overturning of hierarchies. It is at once a revolution of the signifier and of society. As Derrida puts it in "Signature, Event, Context," by overturning linguistic hierarchies one might "intervene in the field of [linguistic] oppositions . . . which is also a field of nondiscursive forces" (Derrida 1982, p. 329). In *Dissemination*, Derrida makes the same point inversely by chastizing non-deconstructionists for their "attitude of . . . indifference" in the face of oppression. To refuse to deconstruct, Derrida informs us, is to "give free rein to the existing forces that effectively and historically dominate . . . to confirm the established equilibrium" (p. 6). However, Derrida does not explain how a deconstructive analysis, for example, one maintaining that speech is always already writing, might produce or even encourage actual social change. I for one see no evidence that it does or reason that it might. As Peter Dews puts it, "Derrida has not been noticeably successful in articulating the relationship between 'deconstruction' in its initial discursive sense, as concerned with the analysis of 'logocentrism' and the 'metaphysics of presence,' and his more concrete political concerns. Throughout his work, Derrida hints at a complicity between the fundamental assumptions of Western thought and the violences and repressions which have characterized Western history, but the nature of this complicity is never truly clarified" (Dews 1987, p. 35).

Jonathan Culler undertakes to reexplain these claims, but, I think, without much success. Culler explains that due to their "radical potential," we must recognize that deconstructive "attempts to reverse, and thus displace major hierarchical oppositions of Western thought open possibilities of change that are incalculable" (Culler 1982, p. 158). But once again, *how* these possibilities are opened remains obscure. Without addressing this problem, Culler goes on to dismiss his opponents thus: "Affirmations of equality will not disrupt the hierarchy. Only if it includes an inversion or reversal does a deconstruction have a chance of dislocating the hierarchical structure" (p. 166). As far as I am aware, no one ever suggested that merely affirming 'Women and men are equally capable' will suddenly end, say, prejudicial hiring practices. It is self-evident that such affirmation must be combined with education, legislation, and other forms of 'praxis.' Culler's antagonist appears to be a straw man. On the other hand, the claims made by Culler and Derrida and other deconstructionists very nearly imply that if you engage in the sort of verbal analysis that characterizes deconstruction, then you will overcome women's oppression, including hiring discrimination, etc., at least in part. Once again, the "field of oppositions" upon which deconstruction focusses is claimed to *be* a "field of nondiscursive forces" also. Thus the position Culler attacks is more similar to his own than to that of his opponents.

I should emphasize that deconstructionists are not alone in employing this sort of argument and rhetoric. Another sort of theory obviously employing the type of rhetoric we have been discussing is reader-response criticism, most particularly that of Stanley Fish and his followers. Specifically, the shift from a belief that 'meaning is in the text' (actually an incomprehensible notion) to a belief that 'meaning is in the reader,' or, more exactly, that meaning and truth are creative and discursive acts, has been widely praised as democratic and anti-authoritarian. It involves, as Jane Tompkins puts it, a laudable "appeal to humility . . . [and] to the notion of self-development." It makes the reader "independent, free, and responsible"—a citizen in a democratic "interpretive community," not a "prisoner" in the totalitarian state of a criticism seeking "objectivity" (Tompkins 1980, p. xxiii). Interestingly, Tompkins concludes that "The net result of this epistemological revolution is to repoliticize literature and literary criticism. When discourse is responsible for reality and not merely a reflection of it, then whose discourse prevails makes all the difference" (p. xxv). However, it is in precisely such a scheme of things that whose discourse prevails makes *no difference whatsoever*, because there isn't a fact of the matter there to make a difference about. However, independent of this, the claim that a reduction of interpretation to response is politically beneficial—hence, the use of a political argument in support of the theory—is obvious.

It should be clear to those familiar with the texts in question that, if they are not indefensible, claims of political superiority are at least undefended. How asking students of Milton to stop analyzing and pretending to argue rationally and start responding affectively or temporally and affirming their persuasive strategies is supposed to 'make all the difference' politically—to, say, end or inhibit, for example, racism—is entirely unclear. Tompkins certainly couldn't be claiming that, for example, if a few German intellectuals had gotten together and formed an "interpretive community" in which they decided to interpret Hitler's genocidal ravings as, say, pleas to Germans to mow their lawns with greater frequency, then the genocide would have stopped and at once the suburbs would have been tidied. But what other sense can be made of the notion that a specifically interpreter-defined "discourse" is "responsible for reality"? Of course, Tompkins says that it is the discourse that "prevails" which makes "all the difference." But I cannot see that great benefit would have resulted if our hypothetical intellectuals had convinced most Germans that good gardening was all *der Führer* and his henchmen were up to. Similarly, it seems rather implausible that widespread use of Fishean (or deconstructive or other) methods in German literary periodicals of the Fascist period would have made any difference in the success of Nazi genocide.

Thus, it is very difficult to puzzle out the precise nature of either responsive or deconstructive claims to ethical/political superiority, or to isolate any clear defense of such claims. It is unclear whether the claims pertain to intents or effects or both, or what if any evidence deconstructive and other theorists might have in mind in proposing such claims—which are indeed *highly* implausible already in the context of a broad range of empirically ascertainable principles, as already indicated. (Moreover, what sense can be made of such claims is not only quite dubious, but involves claims of truth that seem disallowed by the theories themselves.) Thus the political claims of deconstruction and various other post-structural and post-modern theories of criticism appear to be baseless. However, through their effective derogation of virtually all possible opposition, they do serve a persuasive function which, once again, appears to hinder serious rational engagement with the issues raised in deconstructive and related theory. Thus it is important to take a more systematic look at the persuasive and argumentative 'strategies' of such writing before continuing on to the crucial semantic and philosophical issues.

2. Persuasion, Argumentation, and the Uses of Political Rhetoric

In the *Rhetoric*, Aristotle distinguishes three varieties of argument: those from logic and evidence, those from authority, and those from pathos. The first sort of argument is that which follows general principles of logical reasoning on the basis of data and in accord with a few other general scientific principles, such as the Principle of Minimal Interpretation. (Clearly, I am extending the Aristotelian notion here.) The second sort of argument is that which endeavors to establish the authority of the speaker, and thereby the truth of that person's doctrine, or the lack of authority of the opponent, and thereby the falsity of his or her doctrine. It is important to note that this authority need not be confined to *disciplinary* authority (i.e., expertise in the field of study in which the debate takes place), or even more general *intellectual* authority, but may include, for example, *moral* authority. The final sort of argument is that which seeks to effect sympathies in the audience, sympathies which will spur those in the audience to accept the speaker's position—'But isn't he just a good ol' boy, born and raised right here, always near his home, taking care of his sick mother, working in the corner store—you saw him there every time you went in, didn't you? Now are you, ladies and gentlemen of the jury, going to allow this good, home-town boy, to be locked up in the federal penetentiary with a lot of murderers and perverts?,' etc.

To my mind, Aristotle provides as adequate a division of varieties of argumentation as we are likely to find; hence, I shall take these as my starting point. First, I should like to follow Aristotle in placing arguments from logic and evidence under the broader category of arguments concerning theses *per se* and add argument from analogy thereto. Thus I should like to put forth a tri-partite analysis of arguments concerning theses *per se*. Specifically, I should like to maintain that such arguments may be deductive, and, hence, proceed from accepted premises and the laws of logic; inductive, and hence proceed from experience along with the Principle of Minimal Interpretation; or analogical. Clearly, most arguments are a combination of the three, but a combination is not a further category. Neither of the first two varieties of argument is relevant to our present considerations. However, I should like to distinguish among arguments by analogy those which are such by explicit modelling, such as Freud's "A Note Upon the 'Mystic Writing Pad,'" and those which are such implicitly, by metaphor or ambiguity. Deconstructionists often focus their attentions upon analogical arguments of the former variety. Dwelling upon what most critics would previously have considered irrelevant details of the analogy, deconstructionists undertake to demonstrate the uncontrollable dissemination of 'writing' (see, for example, Derrida's "Freud and the Scene of Writing" for a 'deconstruction' of the essay just mentioned). However, it seems to me that analogies are analogies precisely insofar as they are taken to be not literally true, but roughly identical with what is true in certain respects, and of necessity different in other respects. In employing an analogy *consciously*, one endeavors to draw conclusions only from that part of the analogy in which there is similarity, and thus one avoids 'uncontrollable dissemination' in any non-trivial sense. Though I shall not enter into the details, this seems to me clear in the case of Freud, for example. In his very brief essay, Freud compares the mind to a "mystic writing pad." Freud is well aware that he is working with an analogy (see p. 210) and is most judicious in his use thereof.

The *implicit* operation of analogy, on the other hand, its operation by metaphor and ambiguity of which the speaker is unaware, is another matter entirely. Here conclusions may be drawn from points of difference as well as from points of similarity. For example, a friend of mine was outlining for me an article on which he was at work. In this article, he argued that the principle difference between continental and Anglo-American philosophy was that Anglo-American philosophy was the result of a tradition which never took part in the romantic movement. As he put it, 'the two streams of Analytical and Continental philosophy flowed together as one stream only to bifurcate in the eighteenth century, the romantic philosophy of the continent flowing off in one direction, the 'classical' philosophy of the analytical tradition flowing off in the other.' 'But,' he added with conviction, 'I must, of course, maintain that both the classical and romantic currents were there from the beginning.' Well, clearly, one does need to maintain that, in some sense, there is one set of waters (and possibly of currents—I certainly do not know anything technical about rivers and I imagine that my friend did not either) flowing through the river before it bifurcates and after. However, one need not maintain that, just because Hegel incorporates romanticism into his philosophy, romanticism, in its technical sense, must have been present in, say, the work of the scholastics. My friend was taken in by his own implicit analogy—as I was also, in fact. Unlike Freud with respect to the mind and the mystic writing pad, my friend did not consciously and reflectively set out to compare the history of philosophy to a stream. Rather, the comparison emerged unconsciously and unreflectively. Thus, again unlike Freud, my friend was unable to limit the conclusions he drew from the analogy to those which were appropriate.

I take this sort of argument to be important for two reasons. First, it seems to me that argument by tacit analogy is far more common and far more likely to give rise to spurious conclusions than is commonly realized, at least outside of the analysis of advertising techniques. Second, I believe such tacit analogizing is an especially common feature of political argumentation, especially in its deconstructive forms, and one which contributes crucially to the rhetorical effectiveness of political claims. As to deconstruction, the most obvious and most pervasive cases may well be those involving tacit analogies of domination or lordship, briefly mentioned above, and those involving a daring quest, a conquest, in fact, of the "wilderness," to which we will turn below. In each case, conclusions are prejudiced and rhetorical effects enhanced. For example, might we not expect a judgment of intentionalism as totalitarianism when the merely semantic theory of intentionalism is presented as the assertion that there is "a hidden omnipotent author (in full mastery of his product)" (Derrida 1981, p. 7)? Moreover, might we not expect an otherwise unconvinced reader to opt for deconstruction given such a ridiculous and offensive position as the alternative, stated as it is in terms of an irrelevant divine analogy? Similarly, can we not expect deconstruction to be tied to political questions of gender and sexuality, even to a revolutionary, feminist 'graphics of the hymen,' when an innocuous semantic position—that one can in most cases accede to the primary literal meaning of an utterance in one's own language—is deemed 'phallocentric' and is alluded to in terms of voyeurism ("If a speech could be purely present, unveiled, naked, offered up in person in its truth . . ." [p. 71]) and when those who adopt such a position are spoken of as suffering from an uncontrollable "desire" (Derrida 1976, p. 49)? Examples of tacit political, religious, and sexual analogies in deconstructionist writings, analogies involving 'dominance,' 'control,' 'penetration,' 'seduction,' and so on, could be multiplied almost indefinitely. Such analogies of deconstruction are not explicitly part of the *argument*; they are, rather, part of its style (i.e., though deconstructionists tend to deny this distinction, I am sure Derrida would claim that his conclusions would still hold if the phrasing were changed). However, in this case, the style prejudices the political case which is made for deconstruction. Specifically, this style implies a sort of argument for the political and ethical superiority of deconstruction. But this argument is entirely tacit and, thus, closed to refutation or qualification.

This mention of deconstructive style leads directly to the so-called 'pathetic' argument, the argument which concentrates not on the thesis *per se*, but rather on the relation between the audience and the speaker. Pathetic argument functions to establish identifications and oppositions, in-groups and out-groups. In the brief fictional example cited above, the purpose of the argument was to establish an identification between the jurors and the man on trial, a feeling that he was just like them and they were just like him. This method of argumentation by identification might play off of any point of narcissism in the characters of the audience members. In the fictional courtroom, hometown sympathies, as well as narcissistic feelings about one's youth, tenderness for a sickly mother, etc., are all nurtured. In other contexts, moral or intellectual narcissism might prove more central; in their crudest forms these two would go something like 'If you agree with *that*, then you must be a ——— [reactionary, pervert, etc.]' and 'If you agree with *that*, then you must be an ——— [idiot, imbecile, New Critic, etc.].'

Virtually all theories claiming political superiority, it seems, use pathetic arguments to establish an in-group along moral and intellectual lines. Most often, they do this by beginning their work with a division of the entire intellectual world into two camps, the revolutionary and the bourgeois, the deconstructive and the logocentric, and so on. From the very start, that which is not, say, Marxist, deconstructive, or whatever, is named by an opprobative and characterized as oppressive or patriarchal, naive, and so on.

Thus, for example, deconstruction has defined its opposition in such a way as to make of anyone who joins that opposition a phallocentric naif. To be deconstructive is, then, to be 'in,' both morally and intellectually. Deconstructive rhetoric further encourages pathetic identification by fostering feelings of complicity in a covert and 'revolutionary' undertaking, as in Derrida's implications about a struggling deconstructive underground acting in disconnected, but somehow coordinated, solidarity. As Derrida explains, grammatology "shows signs of liberation all over the world, as a result of decisive efforts. These efforts are necessarily discreet, dispersed, almost imperceptible" (Derrida 1976, p. 4). Together, we can forge, we *are forging* the brave new grammatological world— and right underneath the noses of the patriarchs of speech. In some writers, this rebellion takes on a distinctly adolescent character. Thus, we can take pride in the fact that what we do as deconstructionists is, as Christopher Norris opines, "an affront to every normal and comfortable habit of thought" (p. xi).

Of course, this rebellion, adolescent or not, requires almost superhuman courage, for, as Derrida warns, such an undertaking involves a "perilous movement" (pp. 14, 74) which brings us face to face with "absolute danger" and the "monstrosity" of the future (p. 5, and Derrida 1970, p. 265). We, steely nerved deconstructors, encounter the "terrible" (Derrida 1981, p. 36) and do not flinch. But the timid logophallocrats only want a theory that is "domesticated" (p. 45) and, most of all, "reassuring" (pp. 4, 36, 43, and Derrida 1976, pp. 18, 33, 49, and elsewhere). Indeed, not only are they cowardly, the non-deconstructionists are diseased as well. They manifest the "symptom" of "the repression of writing," Spivak tells us (p. lxix) and, unable to control their passions, are buffeted about by an "exigent, powerful, systematic, and irrepressible desire for . . . a [transcendental] signified" (Derrida 1976, p. 49) or a "rage for unity" (Spivak, p. xvi). Brave, or cowardly; vital, or degenerate; wise, or naive; wild and free, or domesticated and enchained; liberator, or phallocrat; us, or them. You choose. As Geert Lernout put it at a recent International James Joyce Symposium, in a personal and honest moment sadly uncommon in such situations, "Whenever I hear deconstructionists talk, I feel like I'm in the old Marx Brothers' joke: *Man*: 'I didn't come here to be insulted.' *Groucho*: 'That's what you think.'"

Turning to our final variety of argument, it should be clear that argument from authority is closely related to pathetic argument in its moral and intellectual forms. In fact, most of the characterizations we have just presented involve both tacit pathetic argument and tacit argument from authority as well (not to mention tacit and explicit analogical argument). Similarly, both appear in Derrida's division of interpretation into the bad sort that "dreams" of the "reassuring" "origin" and the good sort that "affirms freeplay" (Derrida 1970, pp. 264–65), as well as related characterization. The major difference between these two varieties of argument is that in arguments from authority the focus is on the writer or theorist, not on the audience (or, of course, the thesis *per se*). Thus, in argument from authority, the orator endeavors to establish either his or her own intellectual or moral superiority, or the opponents' intellectual or moral inferiority, outside of a consideration of the point at issue. Clearly, this variety of argumentation is almost a necessary accompaniment to intellectual and moral pathetic argumentation. If the members of the audience are intellectual or moral only insofar as they are not, say, naive and patriarchal, and they are not naive and patriarchal only insofar as they are not logocentric, and they are not logocentric only insofar as they are deconstructive, then the very same must hold for those who are themselves involved in the debate, and, furthermore, it must be established in precisely the same fashion.

One particularly cogent rhetorical tactic, often critical in both argument from authority and pathetic argument, is what might be called 'implicit telic emplotment.' By 'implicit telic emplotment,' I intend a tacit narrative organization of the history of a discipline such that the particular theorist in question is cast as a hero struggling against the dark forces of evil in order to prevent disciplinary tragedy by achieving the comic telos—that is, establishing his or her theory. Due to its pervasive, yet unrecognized presence in literary theoretical argument, an understanding of implicit telic emplotment is of considerable importance to an understanding and criticism of literary theory. Therefore, I should like to conclude with a brief indication of the nature and function of such argumentation in deconstruction.

3. Telic Emplotment

A telic plot is, first of all, a plot, and therefore either tragic or comic. The *dramatis personae* are most often theorists, one of whom is the hero, and the dramatic situations are theories, one of which is deemed the telos. Thus the telic narrative is comic to the extent that the telic theory supercedes the precedent theories or insofar as the telic protagonist overcomes his or her (usually elder) antagonists. It is tragic insofar as the precedent theories are maintained or the (elder) antagonists triumph. In other words, the narrative of theoretical supercession, from the point of view of an actually supercessive theory, manifests a comic recognition which manages to reverse the direction of (naive) disciplinary thought, averting impending tragedy from the history of intellect and returning the latter to the true path which leads to the telos. Furthermore, it does so in the context of a polarization of opposed positions. Specifically the range of discrepant belief, desire, etc., is understood to be defined by precisely two polar opposites, with other positions either reduced to one of the two or construed as (often feeble) approximations to one or the other. This polarization most often entails the 'crystallization' of the opposed views in the persons of a protagonist and an antagonist, a hero and a villain, most often two theorists, as already mentioned, but sometimes, especially in social theories, the groups to whose benefits the theories or their acceptance might redound (e.g., the bourgeoisie and the proletariat, represented by the vanguard party, in certain versions of Marxism). These agonists engage in a narrative struggle which often bears a striking resemblance to that of the oedipal phase. Furthermore, this agon, defined in terms of the other oppositions of the emplotment—naive/learned, tragic/comic, and so on—encourages our identification with one or the other contestant or agonist and thereby fosters, once again, narcissistic/pathetic, rather than logical, evaluation.

Briefly, I see post-structuralism being posited as the telos of such an emplotment from its very name to the detail of its rhetoric. It is 'beyond' structuralism, supercessant of that powerful movement and, indeed, of the tradition which it 'culminates,' moving to a different plane entirely and crystallized in the heroic figure of Jacques Derrida.[4] All that precedes, in the bildungsroman of literary theory, is now-superceded naiveté. (On the naiveté of the relevant antagonists, see, for example, de Man 1979, pp. 68–69 and de Man 1983, p. 115; see also Fish 1980, p. 29). Deconstruction leads us on a pathbreaking adventure—perhaps even a spiritual quest—beyond the naive and, more relevantly, beyond the known, the safe, the familiar, into the "wilderness," as Hartman has it (Hartman 1979, p. 206); going "beyond the repetitive generation" which marks all other methods, it leads to "a strange borderland, a frontier region which seems to give the widest glimpse into the other land," in Miller's words (Miller 1979, pp. 230–31); it forges ahead, progresses toward the telos of the promised land, struggling always, Derrida explains, against "regressing" (Derrida 1981, pp. 5, 44). This telos announces the (unapproached and unapproachable) end of metaphysics and with it the end of sexism, of phallo-phono-logo-centrism, thus turning us in our tracks (i.e., effecting a peripeteia) and, through struggle with the patriarchy of interpretation (i.e., through—specifically odeipal—agon), returning us from the possible tragedy of seeming-comic presence to the comedy of seeming-tragic dissemination. Woman is writing, repressed and subdued by patriarchal speech, but freed from her bondage, like the damsel from the dragon, by grammatology on a white steed.

The use by deconstructionists of a tacit telic emplotment, as well as other forms of analogical, pathetic, or authoritarian argument, to the end of establishing deconstruction as both the most valid and most liberatory of theories should be clear. Once again, deconstruction is, by no means, alone in this category. Virtually all post-structural and post-modern theories of literature are to some degree guilty of employing such rhetoric as well. Of course, this is *not* to say they are necessarily wrong. However, it is to say that all such theories should be more carefully scrutinized, denuded of their teleology, tacit analogy, and so on; that we should always have an eye to their eschatological and other rhetorics; that we should accept or reject them for their arguments concerning literature, discourse, etc., and not for their unsupported and implausible, explicit or implicit claims of moral and political superiority.

Nothing is more debilitating to all forms of intellectual investigation and theorization than the substituting of intimidation for dialectic. This is almost certainly the effect—however unintentional—of the sort of rhetoric and the sorts of claims we have been examining. One can only hope that the use of such implicit and explicit political argumentation will swiftly decline, so that theorists will no longer be inhibited by the fear of defamation, and will be able rationally to address issues of literary study—both interpretive and evaluative—without having to defend their character or motives.[5]

Theory and Practice of Deconstruction

> And it seems plain that, even if differences did differ, they would still have to have something in common. But the most general way in which two terms can have something in common is by both having a given relation to a given term. Hence if no two pairs of terms can have the same relation, it follows that no two terms can have anything in common, and hence that different differences will not be in any definable sense *instances* of difference.
>
> BERTRAND RUSSELL (1938, P. 51)

Isolated from its tendentious rhetoric, deconstruction, as a philosophical position addressing important linguistic and social issues, is probably best understood as a method for and a doctrine concerning the analysis and critique of 'centrism'—specifically in its three forms of logocentrism, phonocentrism, and phallocentrism—as presented by Jacques Derrida in a series of highly influential works. Beginning with logocentrism in his examination of Husserl, *Speech and Phenomena*, Derrida moves on to phonocentrism in *Of Grammatology* (actually published at roughly the same time), and addresses the question of phallocentrism in *Dissemination* (in which he continues his critique of logocentrism in new ways as well) and *The Postcard from Socrates to Freud*. In the following pages, I will examine in sequence these three centrisms and their deconstructive critiques.

1. Logocentrism and Difference

Logocentrism is, according to Derrida, the principal malady of Western thinking, or, as he puts it, Western metaphysics. It involves a twofold belief in the primacy of "presence," first with regard to meaning and second with regard to perception.

Beginning with the former, the first question to ask is: What is meaning that it might be conceived of as present or not present? Like his precursors, the maligned 'metaphysicians of presence,' Derrida tacitly assumes that there is such a thing as autonomous meaning. In my view, it is *this* assumption, more than the notion of presence, which is central to the metaphysical tradition—and in this sense, Derrida falls squarely within that tradition. For the most part, autonomism has been a tacit but absolutely critical presupposition of Western and, for that matter, Eastern philosophy—indeed, of all philosophy in which the conception of language is modelled implicitly upon specifically *written* language. This phenomenon has been examined by many authors and need not be further examined here (see, for example, Havelock 1963 on Plato and Ong 1982 on various Medieval and Renaissance writers, for the standard historical analyses; see Hogan 1980 on Hegel for a cognitive-psychological approach). What is crucial here is that in each case linguistic autonomy is assumed and at the same time full accessibility of meaning to intent is assumed also. In Plato this is the result of a dialectal ascent into the realm of the $\epsilon'\iota\delta\eta$—metaphorically represented, in the famous myth of the cave, as the physical ascent into the realm of daylight. Hegel achieves semantic presence in *Absolutes Wissen*. Contemporary autonomists, such as Jerrold Katz, see presence as the result of the operation of a faculty of intuition (see Katz 1981, pp. 192–220). In all cases, it is assumed that full access to autonomous meaning is possible.

Before going on, I should remark that these are all coherent positions. That of Katz is particularly interesting, due to its linguistic rigor. While I reject all of these, they are respectable positions and should be treated with respect. Derrida wishes to argue that it is mistaken to contend that 'full semantic presence' is possible. He provides a general argument to this effect, which we will consider momentarily. However, he refrains from addressing directly the arguments of any of his antagonists. Rather, his method involves the careful scrutiny of their writings to find counter-intentional meanings. We shall look at one famous case of this below—Derrida's examination of Rousseau. Most often I am of the opinion that Derrida's analyses are just plain wrong, that the meanings he construes are controverted directly by the text. For example, I believe that this is in part the case with his reading of Rousseau, as we will discuss. However, what is more important is that Derrida's arguments are irrelevant. Derrida's claim is that if we can discover counter-intentional meaning, we can demonstrate that the meaning which was thought to be fully present, and hence fully manipulable, was not. We discover that meaning resisted the full control of intent and was thus not fully present. This is certainly an interesting argument, but I believe that someone like Katz would simply reply that our semantic intuitions, and hence semantic presence, are complex. Thus we sometimes fail successfully to intuit what it was possible for us to intuit all the time. For example, Katz is quite explicit about the place of sentential ambiguity in semantic intuition—part of our intutition is precisely recognizing such ambiguity. In some cases, a speaker might not intuit such ambiguity even though he or she *could* do so. However, Katz would presumably conclude, the very fact that Derrida spotted the counter-intentional meaning indicates that *Derrida* intuited it and thus that it is indeed fully accessible and that there is no problem.

In fact, one need not even claim inattentiveness on the part of the speaker. A speaker/writer might well intuit the meanings Derrida descries, but not seek to 'control' them as the person assumes that his or her auditor/reader will be following ordinary interpretive practices and not deconstructive ones. For the most part, we interpret an utterance for intent. For example, if someone says something to me in broken English, I try to figure out what the person wants, and that is all I try to do. This is ordinary procedure. Thus if intent is relatively clear, rigorous disambiguation may be unnecessary. But, as we have remarked, Derridaean interpretation is specifically counter-intentional. As Derrida explains in *Dissemination*, the deconstructive "reading must always aim at a certain relationship, unperceived by the writer, between what he commands and what he does not command of the patterns of language that he uses" (Derrida 1981, p. 158). Similarly, Paul de Man tells us that "In the act of anthropological intersubjective interpretation, a fundamental discrepancy always prevents the observer from coinciding fully with the consciousness he is observing. The same discrepancy exists in everyday language, in the impossibility of making the actual expression coincide with what has to be expressed" (de Man 1983, p. 11). Moreover, it is the function of a deconstructive analysis to uncover precisely this discrepancy. Thus a deconstructive analysis aims to do precisely what we all assume no one will do—interpret counter-intentionally. Having set out to do this it is not surprising that 'uncontrolled' counter-intentional meanings are discovered.

I will explain momentarily why I reject the entire debate over presence, why I believe that the premises are grossly mistaken. However, my point here is that one can be a metaphysician of presence, accepting autonomous meaning and the possibility of its full presence, and still accept counter-intentional meaning. In other words, Derrida's discoveries of counter-intentional meaning do not, in and of themselves, contribute to an argument against the metaphysics of (semantic) presence.

Derrida has a more general argument against this notion of presence, however. This argument derives from his conception of language, a conception principally taken over from the structuralists. Specifically, Derrida tacitly accepts the notion that meaning is defined along two axes—the syntagmatic axis and the paradigmatic axis. Take, for example, the phrase, 'in the first place.' In the structuralist model, the meaning of 'first' derives in part from its place in a 'syntagmatic' sequence in which it immediately follows 'the,' immediately precedes 'place,' and so on. It also derives in part from its contrast with other terms—'last,' 'second,' etc.—along the 'paradigmatic' axis. The meaning of 'first' may be visually represented as shown in Figure 2-1. Syntagmatically, then, the meaning of a 'sign' is produced by sequence or *deferral*. Each signifier 'defers' what precedes and what follows and its meaning is in part a result of that cumulative and ongoing deferral. Paradigmatically, on the other hand, the meaning of a 'sign' is produced by *difference*, difference from other 'signs' in an entire signifying system. Thus, for Derrida, meaning is a function of difference and deferral, or, as he puts it, *differance*. Differance is both difference and deferral (see Derrida 1973, pp. 129ff), combined to indicate the systematic "play" which defines (autonomous) meaning. As Derrida explains, "*Differance* is the systematic play of differences, of the traces of differences, of the *spacing* [along the syntagmatic axis in writing— thus the defferal] by means of which elements are related to each other" (Derrida 1981, p. 27).

Granted this notion of meaning, it should be clear how Derrida argues that intent cannot "govern the entire scene and system of utterance," that there is "*a priori* an essential dehiscence and cleft" between intent and utterance (Derrida 1982, p. 326). The meaning which is thought to be open to introspection or intuition and thus fully present, at least potentially, is in fact constituted by *absences*—

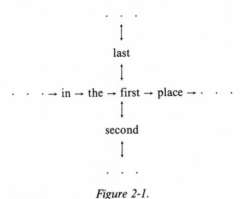

Figure 2-1.

the absent terms it defers and those from which it differs, the entire network of differance. Paul de Man nicely expresses the absencing function of deferral in this context when he speaks of "The repetitive erasures by which language performs the erasure of its own positions" (de Man 1979, p. 65). The syntagmatic aspect of meaning involves what Derrida would call a "sequence of supplements" which create "the mirage . . . of immediate presence" (Derrida 1976, p. 157) while endlessly deferring such presence. More generally, as Derrida puts it, "every sign . . . supposes a certain absence" (Derrida 1982, p. 314). Indeed, every sign is, at least in part, constituted by such an absence. And thus, as absence is part of the constitution of meaning, meaning cannot be fully present. As Maurice Merleau-Ponty argued in his 1951 "On the Phenomenology of Language," a text which almost certainly influenced Derrida, the "expressive value" of language "is not the sum of the expressive values which allegedly belong individually to each element of the 'verbal chain.' On the contrary, these elements form a system . . . in the sense that each of them signifies only its difference in respect to the others (as de Saussure says, signs are essentially 'diacritical'); and as this is true of them all, there are only differences of signification in a language. The reason why a language means and says something is not that each sign is a vehicle for a signification which allegedly belongs to it, but that all signs together *allude* to a signification which is always in abeyance" (Merleau-Ponty 1974, p. 85).

Thus, for Derrida, full semantic presence is impossible by the very nature of meaning. Meaning is differantial, and hence actually *defined by* absence. Because of this absence, Derrida tells us, it is important to recognize "the impossibility of reducing a text as such to its effects of meaning, content, thesis, or theme. Not the impossibility, perhaps, since *it is commonly done*, but the resistance—we shall call it the *restance*" (Derrida 1981, pp. 7–8). Each text resists intent and thus for each text there is a *remainder* ("*restance*"), something left over when intent is subtracted. Thus deconstructive interpretation or analysis comes to focus on this resisting remainder and its tense relation to and 'subversion of' intent. In its main outlines, deconstructive method follows directly.

This is certainly a fascinating argument, but one which, I think, ultimately fails. It fails, however, not for any internal reasons, but because of its presuppositions. Knowing the meaning of a term or a sentence just has nothing to do with presence or absence. Rather it has to do with being able to use the term or sentence and understand other people's uses thereof. Part of knowing the meaning of a term may be knowing to what sorts of things people use it to refer, or even how the term would be defined by other users. Incidentally, of course, this involves knowing that the term in question is different from other terms, but in this context, that is inconsequential. That is a phonological, not a semantic fact. Knowing how to use a term, form a sentence, etc., so as to be understood is, of course, a very complex sort of knowledge. What is important here, however, is that such knowledge is entirely intentional. The speaker who knows how to use and understand a term knows precisely and only how others in his/her speech community use and understand that term. Moreover, we have no reason to believe that there is anything to meaning beyond this. We have no reason to believe that there is an autonomous meaning which might be fully present, partially resistant, or whatever. To know the meaning of the noun 'orange' is simply to know what sort of thing to pick up when someone asks for an orange, the way to get what you want if you want an orange, and so on. It does not involve introspection or intuition of a sign in a differantial system. Moreover, if there were such a differantial system, it is extremely difficult to say how introspection or intuition would allow us even partial access thereto, or how it would enter into our speech, which would necessarily be intentional and aimed toward the intents of others anyway. As Peter Dews puts it, in a somewhat different context, Derrida "is unable to explain how the experience of meaning is able to occur at all" (Dews 1987, p. 98). Of course, our inferences to others' intents may be mistaken. It may always turn out that we are misusing or misunderstanding the term 'orange,' say. But this only means that our empirical inferences—including those upon which we base our speaking and understanding—are not infallible. It indicates nothing about the introspective or intuitive presence or absence of meaning.

Thus it would appear that there is not even a question of semantic presence or absence in Derrida's sense. The metaphysical tradition which Derrida both honors and disavows is a tradition in which autonomous meaning is presupposed. Thus it is a tradition in which the question of semantic presence or absence can be asked.

Derrida's forbears tended to opt for full presence. Derrida opts for a presence conditioned by absence. In my view, once one accepts autonomous language, the only option is full absence. However, there is no reason to accept the fundamental metaphysical presupposition of autonomy. To my mind, *this* is the presupposition most crucial to Western metaphysics. This presupposition ultimately underlies essentialism, the premier metaphysical doctrine. This presupposition allows the entire range of 'What is . . . ?' questions which span the history of Western metaphysics and against which we argued in the preceding chapter. In accepting this presupposition, Derrida has placed himself in the mainstream of the metaphysical tradition he claims to critique.

I should emphasize that none of this implies that interpretation must concern authorial intent. As we remarked in the preceding section, interpretation may concern authorial intent—aesthetical or expressive or whatever—but it may equally concern common lectorial interpretive response, individual interpretive response, and so on. Indeed, it may even concern the systematic discrepancy between, say, authorial aesthetical intent and common lectorial interpretive aesthetical response, if there is any such systematic discrepancy. What is important here is that no question of semantic presence does or even can enter.

As we remarked, Derrida's notion of logocentrism encompasses both the belief in semantic presence and the belief in perceptual presence. Full perceptual presence is a rather peculiar notion. On the one hand, it seems to involve the notion that an external object can be fully present to perception. But this is obviously wrong and no philosopher or anyone else has ever believed such a thing, as far as I am aware. As Derrida points out, following Husserl, perception is necessarily aspectual and constructive. For example, my perception of the paper-clip-filled "Folger's Crystals," "special trial offer" one-ounce jar before me, appears to me under a certain aspect. I judge the shape of the object, or its color, by projecting, with greater or lesser specificity, what I would see were I to turn to it. Thus the 'full presence' of this object is deferred until I have seen the other aspects of the jar, aspects which, in some sense, define this one. Now, of course, I can only get to these other aspects by turning the jar or the like. However, once I turn the jar, I lose the only original presence I might have been thought to have. Clearly, full perceptual presence is impossible for presence is, to a degree, always a function of deferral. As Derrida puts it, "the presence of the perceived present can appear as such only in as much as it is *continuously compounded* with a nonpresence and a nonperception." Furthermore, these absences, these deferrals "are neither added to, nor do they *occasionally* accompany, the actually perceived now; they are essentially and indispensably involved in its possibility" (Derrida 1973, p. 64). This seems to me perfectly true, but not of any profound import. After all, very few people would assert that 'objects are fully perceptually present to us,' once the rather odd notion of 'full perceptual presence' is made clear to them. The only thing that follows from perceptual 'deferral' is that we should be open to controversion of our assumed facts as well as our theories. But this should have been obvious to everyone to begin with—even if it was not.

There is another sense of 'perceptual presence,' however, which is more interesting. Derrida explains that, in his usage, "Perception is . . . a concept of an intuition or of a given originating from the thing itself, present itself in its meaning, independently from language. . . . I don't believe that there is any perception" (Derrida 1972, p. 272). In this sense, Derrida appears to claim that our perception of the world is always organized by our linguistic system. Perception is certainly limited and structured by numerous factors, some biological, some 'social' (see, for example, Marr 1982). Of course, there is perception independent of language. Animals and infants clearly perceive. But both humans and animals begin very early to constitute types—"primal institutings" (*Urstiftungen*) in Husserl's terminology (Husserl 1977, pp. 79ff.), "schemata" in Piaget's (see Piaget 1971), and so on. These types are in part biologically grounded, in part the result of social or socially common environmental conditions, and in part merely idiosyncratic. They function, in what Holland, et al., term "default hierarchies" (Holland, et al. 1986, pp. 18f.), to ease the identification and characterization of objects which are important to the aims of the person or animal in question. Thus, for example, I may form a type or schema for dogs. Then, given relatively little perceptual information of the relevant sort, I can identify a given object as a dog.

For obvious reasons, the development of one's idiolect—one's 'acquisition of language'—will contribute importantly to this process. In developing an idiolect, we seek to conform our own rules of speech to those of others. Part of this conformity involves referential vocabulary items—such as 'dog.' We seek to use 'dog' to refer to the same sorts of things as are referred to by those about us when they use the word 'dog.' In most cases, this sort of conformity, in turn, involves conforming our constitutions, our schemata—for example, that of *dogs*—to those of others. (Exceptions occur in cases of "the division of linguistic labor," as discussed by Putnam [see Putnam 1975, pp. 227ff.]. But these are not really important in the present context.) In this way, 'language' (in the sense of 'idiolect' or of Chomsky's "I-language" [see Chomsky 1986, pp. 19ff.]) enters significantly into perception, and Derrida's claim, though overstated and ill defended, is not entirely off the mark.

On the other hand, I, like others, suspect that Derrida has still more in mind than this—especially when he speaks of the presence of an object "in its meaning." Specifically, I take it that Derrida's anti-perceptualism is closely related to his ultra-relativism, discussed in the preceding section, and that he is here responding to, and once again assuming, a traditional metaphysical position associated with that of semantic presence—essentialism. As John Ellis points out, in a somewhat different context, logocentrism is, in many ways, "much the same as essentialism" (Ellis 1989, p. 35). For the essentialist, my perception—at least insofar as it enters into cognition—is, crucially, the perception of an essence instantiated, the perception of an object present "in its meaning," in Derrida's phrase. As Aristotle puts it in "On the Soul" (II 12), "By a 'sense' is meant what has the power of receiving into itself the sensible forms [τῶν αἰσθήσωσ εἰδῶν] of things without the matter. This must be conceived of as taking place in the way in which a piece of wax takes on the impress of a signet-ring without the iron or gold" (p. 674). A similar notion is discussed and dialectically superseded in Hegel's *Phenomenology of Spirit*: "Perception . . . takes what is present to it as a universal" (p. 67). Indeed, Hegel's dialectic of perception is no doubt one source of Derrida's deconstruction of perception.

In this view of things, my perception of an orange, if accurate, is (at least in part) a perception of an instantiation of orangeness. I see the thing *as an orange*, and not as something else, because that is precisely what it is essentially . (Of course, the views of writers such as Aristotle are far more complex than this, but we need not concern ourselves with that here.) Clearly, as my knowledge deals with universals (see "On the Soul" II 5), perception contributes to knowledge by providing instances of essences. Thought is true, knowledge is knowledge, then, precisely to the degree that it conforms to the facts, which is to say, precisely to the degree that the universals of thought conform to the essences of things—as, in the most fundamental and simplest cases, these are given, through particulars (καθ᾽ἕκαστον—II 5), in perception.

In contrast, Derrida, I take it, is claiming that I see the thing as an orange *not* because that is what it is essentially, but rather because that is how my "system of reference" (1972, p. 272) defines it. Thus there can be no question of conformity between any cognitive universal and any objective essence, because the cognitive 'universal' is merely the effect of an arbitrary linguistic system. As Derrida put it in another context, there is no "transcendental signified" which "would not refer to any signifier" (Derrida 1981a, pp. 19–20). In other words, "[t]here is nothing but text, there is nothing but extratext, in sum an 'unceasing preface' that undoes the philosophical representation of the text, the received opposition between the text and what exceeds it" (Derrida 1981, p. 43). Thus, as there is no possibility of our deriving universals from instantiated essences, as our universals are dictated by our "text" or "system of reference" and not by the nature of things, there can be no question of truth, of knowledge (even of the tentative empirical variety), or of anything else founded upon perception. And thus, it seems, Derrida arrives at his ultra-relativism.

But there are numerous reasons why Derrida's conclusions are erroneous here. First of all, we do in fact perceive particulars in a way which is at least partially independent of our "system of reference." Indeed, if we did not, we would never be able to acquire our "system of reference" in the first place, to correct initial mistakes in that acquisition, etc. It just is not the case that there is nothing but text. Our experience of objects goes beyond our knowledge of language, and objects themselves 'transcend' our signifiers. (Though it is, of course, trivially true that there is no "transcendental signified" in the sense of an object which we do not connect with any 'signifier' or schema whatsoever, if only that of 'thing' or 'event' or whatever.)

But still 'systems of reference' differ from society to society. Does this mean that we must either choose one such 'system' as the right one, and thus preserve essential truth, or accept the arbitrariness of all, the absence of any essence, and thus give up the very notion of truth? Are our options, so to speak, limited to ethnocentrism and relativism?

Not at all. In fact, cultural diversity and other phenomena thought to lead to relativism have absolutely no bearing on our ordinary notion of referential truth. The fact that different societies have different predicates is no more problematic than the fact that one society has different predicates. We may say of a given object that 'It is a rat' or that 'It is grey' or that 'It is an organism' or whatever. But clearly none of these statements inhibits the truth-claims of any of the others. All are as absolutely true or false as anyone could desire. The same holds for predicates across languages. If a given society has a term 'q' which refers to grey mice and a term 'p' which refers to all other rodents, this does not mean that a given object is or is not a q only 'relative to the system of reference of that society,' or the like. Nor does it mean that a given object is or is not a rat only 'relative to our system of reference.' Our predicates in no way hinder the truth-claims of the propositions of the other society; and their predicates in no way hinder the truth-claims of our propositions. An object is or is not a q or a rat in as absolute a sense as we ever imagined.

Thus, in the ordinary conception of truth, there is no question of the matching of predicates with essences. Essences are much like autonomous meanings. They are ontologically redundant, and epistemologically opaque. They are obscure entities which we have no reason to believe exist and no reason to believe we could come to know even if they did exist. Though I cannot argue the point here, ordinary considerations of evidence and simplicity—though not, necessarily, Derridaean deconstruction—lead us to deny essences. But this has no bearing whatsoever on a referential and non-relativist conception of truth. For there is absolutely no reason for us to assume that truth necessarily involves essences, that, so to speak, the truth of our propositions in some way involves the truth of our "system of reference" as well. Indeed, in our ordinary understanding of truth, this does not even make sense, for it amounts to saying that not only might *propositions* be true or false, but *terms* might be true or false also.

Furthermore, the redundancy and opacity of essences have no consequences regarding the possibility of perception, its function in contributing to rational adjudication of empirical truth or falsity, and so on. For perception in this sense need not be taken as essential presence, as understood and eschewed by Derrida. It may equally be understood as what perception in fact is—aim-oriented, schema-governed constitution. If I see something as an orange, this has nothing to do with essences, but means only that I construe certain experiences in relation to a schematic hierarchy and in the context of present interests and practices. (This is not only the commonsense view, but that of most recent cognitive science—see Holland, et al. 1986, p. 9. I take it that Wittgenstein's comments on the relation between language, 'reidentification,' and forms of life [see Wittgenstein 1958, throughout] have a similar point, though my differences from Wittgenstein should be evident.) Thus, there is not really any question of presence or absence here—in the sense of *essential* presence or absence—but only one of interest, belief, etc., along with rule-governed perceptual constitution in the ordinary cognitive psychological sense outlined above.[6]

Perception in this sense is all we have available to us in evaluating the empirical truth or falsity of propositions, but it is all we need. Our constitutions are not infallible, but they are corrigible. They are not determined by a "system of reference"; nor are they indubitable representations of a supposed essence. They are, most often, partially accurate and partially inaccurate understandings of the world. They are based upon our previous understandings, including those codified in our linguistic competence, but they are not confined to these. And their accuracy is a matter of the way relevant intentionally discriminated things happen to be, and not of the way supposedly essentially discriminated things are (or are necessarily).

In connection with this, it is worth returning for a moment to Derrida's critique of semantic presence and looking in conclusion at Rodolphe Gasché's construal of the autonomist basis of deconstruction. In his *The Tain of the Mirror: Derrida and the Philosophy of Reflection*, Gasché examines Derrida's thought in the context of German idealist philosophy, especially that of Hegel, whose idealism is, as I have argued elsewhere, an extreme version of linguistic autonomism (see Hogan 1980), and whose arguments concerning perception bear a clear similarity to those of Derrida, as already mentioned. In this context, Gasché presents four "ways in which the teleological value of the homogeneity of concepts is disproved by the very process of the formations of concepts." These are:

> First, since a concept is not a simple point but a structure of predicates clustered around one central predicate, the determining predicate is itself conditioned by the backdrop of the others. Second, each concept is part of a conceptual binary opposition in which each term is believed to be simply exterior to the other. Yet the interval that separates each from its opposite and from what it is not also makes each concept what it is. . . . Third, concepts are always (by right and in fact) inscribed within systems or conceptual chains in which they constantly relate to a plurality of other concepts and conceptual oppositions from which they receive their meaning by virtue of the differential play of sense constitution, and which thus affect them in their very core. And fourth, one single concept may be subject to different functions within a text or a corpus of texts. (Gasché 1986, pp. 128–29)

We see in numbers two, three, and four, the Saussurean/structuralist conception of differantial semantics discussed above—numbers two and three dealing with difference or paradigmaticity, and number four dealing with deferral or syntagmaticity. One thing different about Gasché's discussion here is that he concerns himself not only with signs (numbers two, three, and four), but also with predicates (number one).

However, insofar as I understand Gasché's conception of concepts as clusters of predicates, it indicates an important flaw in deconstructive thought or, more generally, thought in the Idealist tradition—and one particularly relevant to the supposed impossibility of a transcendental signified (or Kantian noumenon, the philosophical precursor of Derrida's transcendental signified; recall that German Idealism was really initiated by the rejection of the noumenon). Specifically, even in discussing predicates, the Idealist/autonomist notion of concepts is a *dictionary* notion—a notion of concepts as defined entirely by other concepts, in the manner of terms and definitions in a dictionary.

Confining ourselves to referential terms (the most relevant in this context), it is certainly true that such terms have predicative definitions. In other words, they may be defined by predicates, themselves defined by further predicates, and so on. In this way, all signifieds—which is to say, all concepts—are signifiers also. But, as we have already remarked, besides a definition of this sort—and for Gasché the concept appears to be nothing but such a definition—terms also have an *extension*, or rather, the terms to which these concepts correspond have an extension, a set of objects to which people use them to refer. (Moreover, they usually have perceptual types, or constitutions, or schemata, as discussed above—I will leave these aside for the present discussion, in part because they are intersubjectively accessible only by way of definitions or extensions.) It is this extension—delimited in our individual ability to use terms to refer to specific objects; our capacity to reconcile our individual references in communication, etc.—it is this extension which prevents meaning from leading off into an endless chain of predicates, an endless play of difference and deferral.

Indeed, on this topic my view is again more extreme than Derrida's. As I have already remarked, Derrida believes or seems to believe that intentional access to autonomous meaning is limited, while I believe that were there autonomous meaning, there would be no clear way in which it would be accessible at all. Similarly, Derrida believes, or seems to believe, that a differantial conception of meaning renders concepts nonhomogenous—not *meaningless*, but disrupted and deferred in the specificity of their meanings. However, it seems clear that a dictionary conception of meaning, removed from reference or extension and the individual intending subjects who do the referring, leads to absolute meaninglessness. If 'a' is defined in terms of 'b,' and 'b' in terms of 'c,' and so on, individual use, reference, etc., never entering, then meaning is not deferred, but simply absent. If we define a 'drik' as a 'flib,' and a 'flib' as a 'snu,' we have not given 'drik' a deferred meaning, a 'trace' of a meaning—we have not given 'drik' any meaning at all. This is *always* the situation of definition without extension.

Thus, Derrida is certainly correct that there is, throughout the history of metaphysics, something akin to what he calls "logocentrism." However, this logocentrism is not most importantly a function of a belief in presence, semantic or perceptual. Rather it is crucially a function of a belief that there is something which might or might not be present—the autonomous meanings in the first case, the correlate essences in the second—and that these define knowledge and truth. The proper response to logocentrism and the metaphysics of presence is not to deny the presence of the two, but rather to deny the very premise of the argument—that there is such a thing as autonomous meaning, that there are any such things as essences, and that essences (or autonomous meanings) do or could have any bearing on truth or perception or perceptual knowledge. As far as I am able to tell, Derrida denies only the full presence of autonomous meaning and the existence of essences. He does not deny the existence of autonomous meaning or, evidently, the contingency of perceptual knowledge and predicative truth on essences. (Or, if he does deny this contingency, then his sceptical conclusions regarding perception simply do not follow from his in many ways correct, if somewhat obscure and for the most part unsupported, account of perceptual constitution, as discussed above.) Thus, despite his engaging and sometimes brilliant exposition and critique of 'logocentrism,' Derrida remains a metaphysician in the sense he rightly urges us to eschew.

2. *Phonocentrism: 'Overturning the Hierarchies'* of Speech and Writing

For some reason, Derrida's critique of phonocentrim has been, at least superficially, more influential than his critique of logocentrism. This critique is especially noteworthy for its clear use and presentation of the specifically deconstructive *method* in which, as I have noted, the contradiction of an asserted—i.e., intentional—position is sought in the autonomous, disseminative, differantial language of that assertion *per se*. Principally due to the widely read summaries of deconstruction by Barbara Johnson and Jonathan Culler, this method is most often understood specifically as an 'overturning of hierarchies.' It is claimed that, as Helène Cixous puts it, "Thought [i.e., Western metaphysics] has always worked by opposition. . . . By dual, *hierarchized* oppositions" (Cixous 1980, pp. 90–91), and that what Derrida does in his deconstructions is to demonstrate that the very 'language' which defines and purports to maintain the hierarchy of any given opposition does so in such a way as to undermine that hierarchy.

This seems to me a fair enough characterization of some of the presuppositions and some of the results of deconstructive method. Certainly Derrida is quite clear that the overturning of hierarchies is crucial to deconstruction. First of all, Derrida claims that "an opposition of metaphysical concepts (for example, speech/writing, presence/absence, etc.) is never the face-to-face of two terms, but a hierarchy and an order of subordination" (Derrida 1982, p. 329). In other words, the *paradigmatic differences* most crucial to metaphysics are always formed into hierarchies. Thus, Derrida claims, given the presence of these hierarchies, "we must traverse a phase of *overturning*. To do justice to this necessity is to recognize in a classical philosophical opposition we are not dealing with the peaceful coexistence of a *vis-à-vis*, but rather with a violent hierarchy. One of the two terms governs the other. . . . To deconstruct the opposition, first of all, is to overturn the hierarchy at a given moment" (Derrida 1981a, p. 41). Of course, Derrida admits, "Nor does it suffice to overturn the hierarchy" (Derrida 1982, p. 108). "To remain content with reversal is of course to operate within the immanence of the system to be destroyed," he explains (Derrida 1981, p. 6). However, he emphasizes that overturning is ethically critical—"But to sit back, in order to go *further*, in order to be more radical and more daring, and take an attitude of neutralizing indifference with respect to the classical oppositions would be to give free rein to the existing forces that effectively and historically dominate the field. It would be, for not having seized the means to *intervene*, to confirm the established equilibrium" (Derrida 1981, p. 6).

Thus there can be no dispute as to the importance of overturning hierarchies in deconstruction. But to reduce deconstructive method to such an overturning would make the deconstructive procedure appear to be more mechanical than it is, at least in Derrida's works, and would leave it open to some obvious objections. For example, as John Searle has pointed out, what happens to the "dual, *hierarchized* opposition*" of deconstruction/logocentrism in such a scheme (Searle 1983)? I take it that Derrida's claim that deconstructive reversal serves to displace the entire "conceptual order" (1982,

p. 329) indicates the manner in which problems such as this may be resolved, at least at one level. In this context, what I see Derrida doing is overturning only a particular set of hierarchies, specifically those hierarchies which might be identified with the metaphysical system governing our "conceptual order," the hierarchies of the metaphysics of presence, which is to say, ultimately, the hierarchy present/differant and its permutations.

In other words, it seems to be widely assumed that Derrida means to take all oppositions as rigidly hierarchized and thus open to deconstruction. But this is, I think, a gross error. It is, at least, an ungenerous and uninteresting way of interpreting deconstruction, in that the thesis it proposes for deconstruction is self-evidently ridiculous. For example, is beard/moustache a hierarchized opposition requiring deconstruction? or how about green chili/red chili? Moreover, are these simply and univocally bi-polar?[7] Is whole red chili opposed only to whole green chili, or is it opposed to ground red chili, or even tabasco sauce, as well and concurrently? Or how about table and chair or tree and shrub, or bush and shrub, or table and desk? Indeed, even of those oppositions which we can count as simply dual—though there certainly are none such, strictly speaking—and hierarchized, are they always hierarchized as is usually claimed? For example, do we not in general consider the identical bad, 'deviant,' 'secondary,' etc., when it comes to sexuality (cf. the insightful recent coinage, "homophobia"—fear of 'same,' which is to say 'same' or identity in sex), and do we not consider difference primary, definitive, etc., in this area? Or on the topic of presence/ deferral, do we not consider deferral of pleasure in many ways primary for health, or intellectual achievement, or even sexual enjoyment? (Isn't that why Epicureanism ends up sounding a good deal like Stoicism when its principles are laid out in detail?) Or to take presence/absence, with which Derrida himself often enough identifies presence/differance, do we not consider the presence of cancer or body lice or malarial fever or household rodents to be the secondary and deprecable phenomenon, and absence thereof to be the primary and laudable phenomenon?

Thus it cannot be a simple matter of setting up all the hierarchies elbow to elbow and reversing them willy-nilly. Similarly, it cannot be a matter of assuming that *all* thought, even all *Western metaphysical* thought, operates in terms of hierarchized oppositions which even *might* be lined up elbow to elbow. Of course, for any given term we will always be able to choose another to which it might be opposed. Indeed we should almost certainly be able to find some such term with which it would stand in a hierarchized opposition. But this is only to make the trivial claim that we have more than one word, that at least two words have different meanings, and that we don't value all things at the same rate. This triviality is almost certainly not what Derrida has in mind. That we can find some 'hierarchized opposition' into which to force our terms does not at all imply that our thought, or those terms, are defined in such oppositions. Indeed, blatantly, for the most part they are not.

Thus it seems Derrida must limit the 'hierarchized oppositions' which might be the object of a deconstruction to those oppositions directly assimilable to the hierarchized terms which define logocentrism. Moreover, he must limit deconstruction to such oppositions *insofar as* they are so assimilable. In other words, he must be sure that he does not deconstruct in one meaning an opposition which is assimilable to the logocentric oppositions in another meaning.

Of course, this does not really eliminate Searle's objections, which I for one find compelling, as far as they go. It merely pushes back the question to what is, in my view, the appropriate level. The problem becomes, then, not how to account for or justify the hierarchization deconstruction/logocentrism, but how to establish criteria which will map 'present/differant' onto 'speech/writing,' and perhaps 'heterosexual/homosexual' as well as other difficult cases, but will not map 'present/differant' onto 'deconstruction/ logocentrism'—or 'freedom/slavery,' 'respect/abuse,' 'feminism/ misogyny,' and so on, some of which seem to fit the present/ differant paradigm quite well. Indeed, even independent of the other problems treated above in connection with autonomism and essentialism in the critique of logocentrism, problems which undermine the present/differant paradigm anyway—I suspect that establishing appropriate criteria is a difficulty impossible of a resolution which is not merely arbitrary or *ad hoc*. Of course, Derrida does manage at least to characterize phonocentric and phallocentric oppositions in logocentric terms. However, as we will see, even this is less a rigorous assimilation of the former to the logocentric opposition than a rather trivial manifestation of the fact that, starting from one term, any other term may be demonstrated to be deferred and different. The entire 'assimilation' is a matter of circularity on the one hand and invalid inference on the other.

Returning to the deconstructive method, Derrida's 'overturnings' generally proceed in three stages. He begins by examining what it is that characterizes the 'secondary' term of the hierarchy as secondary to or derivative of the first term. He then demonstrates that precisely the same properties mark the primary and definitive term as determine the secondary term to be secondary. From here, Derrida concludes that the primary term is itself secondary and derivative with respect to the the secondary term. Thus Derrida reverses the hierarchy. (And from here the disseminative free play of the entire system is engaged.)

Let us turn to the specific deconstruction of speech/writing, to which Derrida attends principally in *Of Grammatology*. Already in *Speech and Phenomena*, Derrida had argued that the semantic presence posited in logocentric metaphysics is always associated with speech. Moreover, he had maintained that the perceptual presence posited therein is most completely manifest, for the metaphysician of presence, in the voice which utters that speech. Similarly, Derrida had indicated that difference and deferral, as well as absence and inaccessibility, are classically linked to writing. Specifically, for the metaphysician of presence, it is only in oral speech that meaning is fully accessible and fully present, whereas in writing it is, precisely, made *different* from intent; its presence is *deferred*. Thus, clearly, writing is identified with differance, and speech with presence. Of course, writing may also be associated with presence in that it remains and, however imperfectly, communicates an authorial intent when the writer is absent and even when he or she has died. Moreover, speech may be associated with absence because it vanishes, because it fades like the life of the speaker. Had it suited his purposes, Derrida would perhaps have emphasized these aspects of speech and writing, rather than their contraries.

In any case, as we have already remarked, it is quite predictable that notions of linguistic autonomy and semantic inaccessibility are frequently associated with writing (see references cited above). Though writing is not in fact any more semantically autonomous than speech, it is certainly more *physically* autonomous and thus it presents an image—a misleading image—of language isolated from speakers and hearers, isolated, indeed, from the entire community, from all 'users' of that language. Moreover, though if anything writing extends rather than inhibits presence, the common confusion of physical and semantic autonomy here does in fact concern a type of 'language' which has been rendered at least partially opaque—hence partially semantically inaccessible—through the necessary loss of the clarifying contextual and dialogic aspects of oral speech. Given these connections, it should come as no surprise that Derrida, theorist of linguistic autonomy and partial semantic inaccessibility, may be found fighting on the side of writing and endeavoring to overturn the supposed hierarchy of speech/writing. As Paul de Man puts it "Derrida's main theme [is] the recurrent repression, in Western thought, of all written forms of language, their degradation to a mere adjunct or supplement to the live presence of the spoken word" (de Man 1983, p. 115). It is this repression which Derrida opposes by shattering the domination of speech over writing.

To effect this shattering, reversal, and, ultimately, free play, however, deconstructive method requires a text, for it proceeds by examining the 'language' of the assertion of hierarchy. Thus on this topic Derrida turns, in *Of Grammatology*, to several writers who have treated speech and writing—crucially, de Saussure, Lévi-Strauss, and Rousseau. The arguments of all three are much the same. First we have speech, which represents things—or more properly, which we use to 'represent' or refer to things, though unfortunately this is not the way any of the three writers in question conceives of reference or 'representation.' Subsequent and subordinate to this, we have writing, which represents speech—or, more accurately, which we use to 'represent' or refer to speech. Now there is a clear and straightforward sense in which de Saussure, Lévi-Strauss, and Rousseau are all correct. For all the time humans have been speaking, only a small fraction of that time have people been writing. Even since the invention of writing only a tiny number of people have ever written anything, and even those who have written have in general written far less than they have spoken. Moreover they too spoke first and learned writing only many years after speaking and *precisely as a method for representing spoken words* (and this is the case whether the writing is 'ideographic' or phonetic). There simply is no such thing as a society which has not been, at some time, a society without writing but with speech. Similarly there is virtually no such thing as a writer who was physically capable of speaking before writing, but did not become competent in oral speech before achieving competence in writing (i.e., written speech). Indeed, if I understand correctly, in many, possibly most cases, what mute and deaf-mute children learn first is more clearly assimilable to speech than to writing. (Similar points have been made by others responding to Derrida—cf., for example Ellis 1989, p. 21.)

But, as I understand him, Derrida wishes to remain entirely at the 'level of the signifier.' History, society, developmental psychology, are not really important for him in this context. Specifically, Derrida wishes to argue that, in an abstract sense, there is in the metaphysics of presence an attempted hierarchization of speech and writing, but that any expression of this hierarchization is necessarily undermined by the very (autonomous) language which defines it. This, I take it, is due principally to the inherently differantial nature of language, which Derrida sees as disruptive of hierarchies evidently because difference is necessarily 'bi-directional.' In other words, a term 'a' is defined by its difference from a term 'b'—but 'b' is thus equally defined by its difference from 'a,' and thus neither can be taken to be the standard.

Even at this general level, however, Derrida's argument does not stand up. First, there are some clear ways in which at least some definitions cannot be considered fully bi-directional—as will become clear below in our discussion of the hierarchical structure of theories, where historically and practically the definitions of certain terms (e.g., those naming recent and controversial posits) rest on those of other terms (e.g., those naming older and more widely accepted posits). Thus when, say, pre-quarks are initially and controversially posited as the constituents of quarks, *quark* is and remains the basic concept in the scientific community (i.e., there is no definitional bi-directionality here), at least until the positing of pre-quarks becomes widely accepted and a characterization of pre-quarks—which does not rely on the notion of quarks—becomes standardized.

Beyond this, even in cases where bi-directionality is possible, we are free to set standards in definition as we see fit, for we are the ones free to define the terms as we see fit—and in this way there is no reason we cannot simply decide on a hierarchy to which 'the language itself' is indifferent. For example, in international trade, we may wish to stipulate one national currency as the standard in terms of which other national currencies are defined—as in effect occurred in the Bretton Woods system. In principle, the definitions of all national currencies might be bi-directional; given such a stipulation, however, they are not—at least in certain legal contexts relating to international trade.

Finally, and most important, considerations of definition have nothing to do with hierarchization in the vast majority of cases. For example, in the case under consideration, speech and writing, the hierarchization is historical and developmental, not definitional. In a like manner, but perhaps more obviously, we do not consider health superior to illness because we fail to realize that 'health' may be defined as 'the absence of illness,' with illness thereby established as the standard. Hence, this evidently basic principle of deconstructive method is mistaken; bi-directionality in definition is not unchallangable—and even if it were, it would be irrelevant to any of the cases under consideration, or any other cases of importance.

I take it that, by concentrating his analyses on the language of specific texts, texts in which *non*-semantic criteria are brought to bear on hierarchization, Derrida is seeking to bolster his semantic or definitional or differantial analysis—not relying merely on the supposed general bi-directionality of definition. But here too, in these specific analyses, Derrida's arguments fail. They fail in the first place because of his linguistic bias, because he treats empirical, social, historical, and other non-semantic characterizations of objects as definitions of terms, because he commits the same sort of error in his concrete analyses as he commits in his more general arguments. They fail also because, in transforming characterizations into definitions, Derrida arbitrarily truncates the characterizations, and thereby constructs definitions which falsely appear to be mutual.

Returning to the particular case at hand, let us take our own immediately preceding outline of the primacy of speech. Our outline could, I think, be considered a sort of better informed and unsentimental version of Rousseau and others on the primacy of speech over writing. Rousseau especially is an easy target for Derrida's attacks in that he tends to romanticize the 'primitive' and thereby sentimentalize the oral. In doing this, Rousseau combines two logically separate claims about speech and writing—that speech is primary and writing derivative, and that speech is Edenic and writing fallen—with some unrelated, and quite implausible ethnographic conjectures. More exactly, for Rousseau, speech involves some sort of systemic articulation and some sort of spontaneous or direct personal expression. As time progresses, the former increases and the latter decreases—a regrettable situation, from Rousseau's point of view. Worse still, in writing, the expressive is pretty much eliminated in favor of the systemic. But not everyone is equally badly off. Primitives and savages are, according to Rousseau, blessed with simple languages, lacking in extensive articulation and filled with pure expression, languages farther removed from writing, more purely speech, than the languages of civilized people. In this way, primitives and savages are closer to the happy state of nature.

I am in complete agreement with Derrida that there is no uncorrupted nature or pure origin in the mystical/romantic sense of Rousseau. I also agree that there is a painfully clear ethnocentric element in Rousseau's discussions—indeed, a painfully clear racist element, despite Rousseau's obvious liking for 'primitives' and 'savages.' Moreover, I find Derrida's careful scrutiny of Rousseau's essay frequently illuminating. However, I disagree with Rousseau because I believe that he was historically and linguistically mistaken—egregiously so, in fact. Thus, what is at issue here is not whether or not Rousseau was right in all his views related to speech and writing, but whether or not Derrida's particularly deconstructive arguments concerning Rousseau are valid and generalizable. These apply most importantly to those claims of Rousseau—as well as de Saussure, Lévi-Strauss, and others—which concern the primacy of speech. Thus, in considering the deconstructive analysis of Rousseau, I will consider Rousseau's very common and quite plausible claims about the primacy of speech in isolation from his more culturally limited and quite implausible claims about articulation and expression.

Just as Rousseau did not think writing was present *ab origine*, neither does he think speech was, and neither do I, and neither does anyone else. For the purposes of argument, let's say that speech derives from perception, memory, expectation, and desire. Possibly we could give an account relying on a Lewis-type notion of convention (see Lewis 1969) in which 'cooperation' relative to perception, etc., issued in speech. This would not, I think, be far from the spirit of the contractualism Rousseau espoused elsewhere, and would be at least plausible on its own. In any event, it is clear that every individual has perceptions (though not, of course, in Derrida's sense), etc., and that the person learns language through these. To take the most obvious sort of example, a child cannot learn that Mommy is called 'Mommy' unless he or she hears or otherwise perceives the word 'Mommy' and, usually, has some perception of Mommy with which to associate the word as well. Moreover, it is clear that perception, etc., were common to our ancestors well before any even rudimentary speech arose, by Lewis-type convention or otherwise. Thus we have a sort of modified Rousseauean position here. But, at least according to David Norris (1982, pp. 32ff.), Derrida says of Rousseau and, I assume, would say of us, that now we have reached the moment of the deconstructive reversal. What did we say 'defined' writing if not *secondariness*? Now we see that speech itself is defined by *secondariness*. Thus we find that speech, far from being the primary and definitive phenomenon we thought it, is merely secondary and derivative, which is to say, a sort of writing. The deconstructive method reveals to us that the very signifiers themselves have effected the reversal of the hierarchy of writing and speech.

But this is clearly spurious reasoning. First of all, we never *defined* writing or speech in terms of secondariness. Rather we *characterized* them as such. That characterization is quite distinct from any *definition* we might propose (for a plausible definition of writing most particularly, see Ong 1982, p. 84). Furthermore, our characterization was not merely in terms of secondariness, but of secondariness *with respect to. . . .* It was not that we found 'secondariness *per se*' (whatever that might be) in writing, then found the same thing in speech, but rather that we found writing secondary *with respect to speech* in a fairly clearly definable way and speech secondary *with respect to experience*, etc., again in a fairly clearly definable way. Note that the same holds for Rousseau's claims about articulation and expression in speech and writing. Writing is,

for Rousseau, more fully systemic than the speech which it represents, but that speech is more fully systemic than the earlier speech
from which it itself derives. The situation would be the same with a
Biblical account in which writing is viewed as secondary with
respect to contemporary speech and contemporary speech is viewed
as secondary with respect to pre-Babel speech, or whatever. Indeed,
many other 'onto-theological' views are immune to deconstruction
in precisely the same manner. All these speech/writing hierarchies
could be reversed only if their 'deconstruction' led to the conclusion
that speech is *secondary with respect to writing*. But this has in no
way been demonstrated, or, as far as I can tell, even defended as a
thesis. By argumentation such as this, one could conclude from my
assertions that my gall bladder is inside me and that I am inside my
apartment, that, in fact, *I* am defined by 'insideness' and thus the
hierarchy which puts my gall bladder inside me can be decon-
structed and overturned so as to demonstrate that I am, rather,
inside my own gall bladder—a conclusion with profoundly liberatory ramifications, no doubt.

   Of course, Derrida is not as absurd as Norris makes him out to
be. In the detail of his argument, as presented in *Of Grammatology*,
he attends more carefully to the questions of identity and presence
which occupied him in his critique of logocentrism. Thus, he presents an argument which in many ways concerns 'writing' in a sense
quite distinct from, though not unrelated to, that with which we
have concerned ourselves. Specifically, as we have already remarked, Derrida argues that writing is phonocentrically characterized in precisely the terms of *differance*—of difference and deferral—which he 'revalorized' in his critique of logocentrism. In this
context, phonocentrism might be best summarized as the complex
of beliefs surrounding an understanding of oral speech as fully
present and positively self-identical. Now this in fact works well
enough with Rousseau. Moreover, Rousseau does come rather
close to repeating this characterization with respect to experience or
life or nature and speech. In other words, for Rousseau, it is
experience or feeling which is fully present and positively self-
identical and speech is, thus, deferred and different or 'differantial.'
The plenitude of my experience of nature is, thus, lost in my speech
about nature. Here, then, the deconstructive 'overturning' functions
precisely as before. Far from being fully present and definitive of

identity, speech is itself deferred and different, mere differance. As de Man puts it:

> Whenever Rousseau designates the moment of unity that exists at the beginning of things, when desire coincides with enjoyment, the self and the other are united in the maternal warmth of their common origin, and consciousness speaks with the voice of truth [actually something more like unreflective, emotional effusion], Derrida's interpretation shows, without leaving the text, that what is thus designated as a moment of presence always has to posit another, prior moment and so implicitly loses its privileged status as a point of origin. Rousseau defines voice as the origin of written language, but his description of oral speech . . . can be shown to possess, from the start, all the elements of distance and negation that prevent written language from ever achieving a condition of unmediated presence. All attempts to trace writing back to a more original form of vocal utterance lead to the repetition of the disruptive process that alienated the written word from experience in the first place. (de Man 1983, p. 115)

Thus it is not so much that writing precedes and determines speech (though Derrida often at least seems to claim such), but that there really is no such thing as speech, that speech is 'always already' a 'form' of writing—or "arche-writing" understood as "loss of the proper, of absolute proximity, of self-presence, in truth the loss of what has never taken place, of a self-presence which has never been given but only dreamed of and always already split, repeated, incapable of appearing to itself except in its own disappearance" (Derrida 1976, p. 112). In other words, the only speech is writing, defined as the autonomous play of *differance* (see Derrida 1976, pp. 7, 14, and elsewhere).

Rousseau certainly does characterize writing in terms of systemic articulation. But, although Derrida's notion of differance does not provide the only possible account of systemic articulation, Derrida evidently assumes it does. Thus he assimilates Rousseau's notion of writing to his own notion of differantial language. Moreover, from here, Derrida points out that there are, according to Rousseau, elements of systemic articulation in all speech, and concludes from this that speech is always already a form of writing, understood as a system of differance (see Derrida 1976, p. 315). This is a patent non sequitur, even granted the reduction of systemic articulation to differance. While Derrida is right to point out the element of articulation in Rousseau's notion of speech, he is wrong to conclude that the existence of an element common to speech and writing in any way undermines the speech/writing hierarchy. More important, even if Derrida were right in that Rousseau did characterize speech and writing in identically systemic terms, then his conclusions—minus their differantial presuppositions—would follow for purely intentionalist and non-deconstructive reasons. There would be no dehiscence between intent and language but, if anything, between intent and intent. There would not be dissemination, but just confusion. Thus, even if Derrida's relevant conclusions were correct, they would not be generalizable or contribute in any way to a case for deconstruction. Moreover, those related claims which are, indeed, correct—for example, that there is no pure experential presence—are correct for entirely non-deconstructive reasons, as discussed in the preceding section.

Finally, Derrida's arguments, whatever their status, could not prove anything as regards *speech* and *writing* in any usual sense of those terms, anyway. In one respect, Derrida's argument here is simply circular. It proceeds from an assumption that language is autonomous to the conclusion that, if we call autonomous language 'writing,' all language is writing and hence all speech is a form of writing. Derrida does not really present any argument on this point, but a substitution of synonyms misleadingly fixed in their meaning by concealed stipulations—which furthermore presuppose a, once again, untenable semantic theory.[8]

I emphasize this last point less because of its theoretical importance—which is really not great—than because of its political importance. Though it is often at least implicitly claimed revolutionary to alter the meanings of 'writing' and 'speech' as Derrida has done in his partially circular and partially invalid 'deconstructions,' if anything the thrust of this distortion is to the contrary. Not only is it misleading, circular, and based on invalid presuppositions, it actually supports what is *de facto* a pervasive and politically pernicious valorization of writing over speech. Specifically, while Derrida is scrutinizing the innocuous claims that speech precedes and determines writing and the admittedly ridiculous claims that speech and writing are lapsarian, the latter more so than the former, he is—typically—ignoring the tacit beliefs and normative principles surrounding speech and writing and the concrete political, social, and moral effects of these beliefs. Thus while Derrida decries a pervasive phonocentrism in Western society he himself expresses precisely the ideology of 'grammacentrism' which does pervade Western, and other highly literate societies. As Deborah Cameron explains, in a slightly different vocabulary, "'Scriptism'—a prejudice against speech as compared to writing—is ingrained in the western tradition" (Cameron 1985, p. 166). Let me give just two brief examples.

First, it has been true historically that entirely *written* languages have dominated intellectual and literary work to the detriment of the primarily spoken vernaculars. This is most spectacularly evident with regard to learned Latin in the European Middle Ages and early Renaissance, but has been true to a lesser degree of classical Chinese, Hebrew, Sanskrit, and Arabic. To take the first case only, as written, scholarly Latin, constrained by the vocabulary and syntax of classical authors, remained relatively static, while its spoken dialects developed and diverged quickly, Latin and the various vernaculars derivative therefrom became mutually incomprehensible languages. But they were not of equal value. Latin became a language controlled and maintained entirely by writing. Eventually, no one grew up speaking it and everyone who could speak it could read it and write it as well. The vernaculars, on the other hand, were first *spoken* by the children learning them—as is always the case with first languages—and most often not written at all, sometimes even by those who wrote Latin. Now, it was precisely the *written* language of Latin which was lauded as being of the proper nobility for philosophy and, less so, for elevated literature. Thus it was in writing-controlled Latin that serious work was, in general, undertaken. There are, of course, exceptions to this, but quite generally, the spoken vernaculars were conceived of as inferior and unsuited to the grave matters of philosophy, as well as medicine, law, and natural science. The situation was complicated in the case of literature as it was often composed in the vernaculars, but even then required knowledge of Latin for its composition. As to the theater, for example, those who knew no Latin (e.g., women) had no access to the principles of rhetoric or to the commonplace tradition so crucial to dramatic composition, as evidenced massively in Shakespeare's writings. Thus, to be excluded from (written) Latin and confined to a (spoken) vernacular was to be excluded from all intellectual debate and in effect from literature as well. As we will discuss momentarily, in the context of Derrida's critique of phallocentrism, while most men were thus excluded, virtually *all* women were thus excluded, for virtually no women were taught learned Latin (or classical Arabic, Hebrew, or Chinese). Women have almost invariably been confined to the *spoken* languages, the vernaculars. It is precisely grammacentrism, not supposed phonocentrism, which has helped foster and maintain male dominance.[9]

For a second example, we might look to the present. Again, Derrida claims that writing has been 'degraded' and 'repressed' in Western metaphysics and that it has been conceived of as not only secondary, but somehow deviant. However, Derrida's valorization of writing is itself more in keeping with the real and effective attitudes of 'Western metaphysicians,' as well as politicians, pedagogues, news reporters, and men and women on the street today. It is in fact *speech* which has been degraded and repressed and judged not merely secondary, but deviant as well. Specifically, it is the *grapholect* of a language which establishes *normative* principles for all the *spoken dialects*. Prior to the spread of literacy, there simply is no prescriptive grammar which differs from the tacit descriptive grammars of the speakers of the language in question. What makes cockney, Hiberno-English, Black English, and Southern English 'wrong' is the grapholect of imperial power—British and White American—or other political, military, or economic supremacy (e.g., Northern U.S.). It is the grapholect which *defers* the 'dialects' or their grammars and it is in contrast with the grapholect that these dialects are judged *different*. To valorize writing is to reenforce a prejudice which tends to or has in the past tended to exclude Blacks, as well as Southerners, Irish, lower class English, and others, from intellectual dialogue. (For a complementary discussion of the manner in which the traditional valorization of writing is allied with ethnocentrism, see Ellis 1989, pp. 19ff.)

3. Phallocentrism and the Claims
of Hierarchical Identities

As just remarked, women have historically been excluded from training in the written languages such as learned Latin. They have been associated with and confined to a somewhat limited oral speech and, with still greater limitations, the written forms of their vernaculars. This has been in part responsible for the virtual absence, prior to this century, of women in science and philosophy, as well as in the more rhetorical literary genres, especially drama (again, training in rhetoric was classically a training in *Latin oratory*). Moreover, I rather suspect that the stereotype of women as intuitive and illogical, as well as certain related prejudices, derive in part from women's 'lack' of training in the artificial logical forms of syllogistic reasoning, as codified and taught in Latin, and the (Latin) vocabulary of disputation. In any event, it is quite clear that writing tends to be in the control and service of the dominant group or groups, and speech associated with the 'oppressed.'

However, again, Derrida is not concerned with mundane reality, but with the sign or concept. What Derrida finds when he interrogates the crucial sign is that before Freud and after Lacan logocentrism and phonocentrism have been *phallocentrism*. Specifically, like speech, man, Adam, is thought of as primary and definitive, presence and identity, as well as activity, reason, and so on, whereas woman, Eve, is conceived to be secondary and derivative, a deferral (of another man, her son), a mere difference, as well as palpable passivity and unreason. By an argument of the same variety as he employed to 'overturn' the hierarchy of speech/writing, Derrida effects an overturning of the hierarchies of man/woman, active/ passive, phallus/hymen, which he identifies with that of speech/ writing and, ultimately, those of presence/deferral and identity/ difference. I do not wish to examine Derrida's arguments in any detail here as I have already treated much of this in connection with the deconstruction of speech/writing. The sort of argument Derrida employs is no more valid with regard to male/female than to speech/writing. Moreover, I will be attending to feminist developments of Derrida's arguments in the next chapter.

However, I should remark several things here. In their most obvious senses, the assertion of chirographic secondariness and the assertion of female secondariness make empirical claims. I take it that the claim is correct in the first case and, not being a 'creationist' or other biblical literalist, I take it that the claim is false in the second case. The first problem here is simply that we have some very bad science going on. The difficulty with the claim that women are secondary *is not* that it is somehow similar to the claim that writing is secondary, but that it is wrong. Or rather the difficulty with this claim is that all the evidence we have goes to indicate that men and women *must* be coeval and no more evidence indicates that women are secondary than indicates men are secondary. Indeed, granted the general outlines of contemporary evolutionary biology, it is difficult to say what a thesis of secondariness of either sort would even mean and what *could* count as evidence toward it. Once again, the proper response to this bad science is not, I think, faulty argumentation based on linguistic autonomism, but, ideally, *good* science.

As to the characteristics of difference and deferral, these involve assertions of quite another order from those made concerning writing. Writing is different from speech because the intending subject is most often not present in the literal and mundane sense of being right there uttering the thing and meaning it. Moreover, it is a deferral of speech in the straightforward sense that one means what one writes and it is only subsequently that that writing is read, even by the author him or herself. Thus meaning is expressed and deferred. But in the case of women, the assertions are another thing entirely. If women are considered *different*, that is to say that men define the 'standard'—a notion which either makes no sense or is just wrong. It is impossible for a rational person to claim, for example, that the male genitalia are the 'standard.' Clearly, the male genitalia are reproductively incomplete without the female genitalia and when two things are required to fulfill the functions of either, it just makes no sense to refer to one as standard and the other as deviant. Again, if women are conceived to be a mere deferral of men then women are conceived as mere means, and, thus, not as ends in themselves. This is not a question of facts but of ethics—and the relevant claims and acts are clearly unethical. Of course, were someone to claim that 'God made woman to be the servant of man' and thereby endeavor to justify the conception of woman as a deferral of man, there would be a question of fact at issue beyond the ethical question. I would reject the ontological presuppositions of any such assertion and thus would dismiss it as in tacit violation of the Principle of Minimal Interpretation before any more particular empirical question arose. On the other hand, I should think anyone with religious leanings would question a picture of God as so fundamentally unethical.

Thus again we have a complex empirical claim along with one ethical assertion. What is objectionable in the empirical claim about women is not its, in this case wrongly supposed, identity with a common claim about writing, but its simple falsity (or nonsensicality). What is objectionable in the ethical assertion is its ethical perversity—in our case, its contradiction of judgments conducive to the establishment of a kingdom of ends. Once more, it seems clear that the most appropriate response to these claims is a concern for truth along with a concern for ethics—here, again, a concern for the systematic and individual treatment of all subjects as ends in themselves—and not 'disseminative free play,' the 'setting in motion' of autonomous linguistic hierarchies, and so on.

Clearly, the status and relations of Derrida's three principle 'centrisms' are dubious at best. His arguments are quite generally invalid or circular, his claims implausible—or plausible only for non-deconstructive reasons—and the political implications of his 'valorizations' either nil or, in the case of writing, mildly supportive of the dominant ideologies. Liberation, for colonized peoples, for minorities, for women, certainly lies elsewhere. However, as we have remarked, a great deal of feminist literary theory and non-literary feminist theory important to feminist literary theorists and, especially, the most avowedly 'sophisticated' of these theorists, has drawn extensively and enthusiastically upon Derrida's work. In the following chapter, I will turn to a discussion of some trends in recent feminism and feminist literary theory, concentrating most particularly on the 'new French feminisms' which to such a degree derive their fundamental theoretical principles from deconstruction and related post-structuralisms, as well as Lacanian psychoanalysis. However, before going on to this, I would like to make a few brief comments on the putative relations between Marxism and deconstruction as presented in Michael Ryan's important volume on this topic, for Ryan's book presents one of the few clear and systematic attempts to develop deconstruction in the context of more obviously and traditionally political and revolutionary theory.

4. Marxism and Deconstruction

I should begin by remarking that to my mind Michael Ryan is one of the finest American deconstructive theorists. His work is both

lucid and erudite. He is also one of the few truly politically committed theorists writing today. I would like, then, to take this opportunity to express my respect and political solidarity.

That said, it should be clear from the preceding that Ryan and I
hold rather different views on the validity and political expediency
of deconstruction. More important, I take the preceding arguments
to hold (or not to hold) independently of any connection which
might be drawn between deconstruction and Marxism. However,
due both to the importance of Ryan's book and the relevance of
Marxist analysis to the present study, I feel that it is important to
say a few things about Ryan's analysis.

Principally, I would maintain that Ryan's arguments connecting
deconstruction and 'critical,' anti-authoritarian Marxism for the
most part fail on one of two counts: (1) They are based not on
logical argument but on very loose analogy or, what is worse, a
coincidence of metaphors. Or, less frequently, (2) they are based
upon a too narrow or simply erroneous view of the function of
certain technical concepts, particularly concepts of logic and empirical science. There are also occasional historical lapses, sometimes
quite significant.

Many examples of each sort of argument may be found in Ryan's
book. Ryan's discussion of Hobbes, for example, well illustrates the
first (see Ryan 1982, pp. 3ff.). Here, Ryan identifies Hobbes' notion
that all enquiry must be organized into a deductive system with
Hobbes' political absolutism. He then goes on to find logocentrism
in Hobbes' preference for unequivocal language in deductive systems and in law. He finally determines that "Hobbes associates
ambiguity, equivocation, and improper metaphor with sedition"
due to his logocentrism (p. 3), because metaphor, etc., break the
"law of identity," question "absoluteness" (p. 4), and generally engage a disseminative economy which denies a transcendental signified. Of course, even if Hobbes compared the two, his notion of the
construction of a deductive system and his political absolutism are
not related by logical necessity—after all, Chomsky sees some
general connections between his own similar rationalism and *anarchism*, quite the contrary of absolutism, as do I. More important,
the two notions derive from different principles and enquiries in
Hobbes' work. The function of a deductive system is to avoid

inferential error through the rigorous statement of premises and the painstaking deduction of conclusions. One can well believe that Hobbes made errors nonetheless, and often enough errors of a politically unfortunate variety. However, there is nothing at all inherently absolutistic about an attempt at the construction of a deductive system for any given enquiry. Now, once one has decided to do this, unequivocal language is absolutely crucial. The whole point of the construction is to avoid errors in reasoning to as great an extent as possible. One frequent sort of error in reasoning involves ambiguity. In our premises a term has one meaning, then we draw conclusions involving the term in another sense. Let us take a rather silly and obvious example:

1. Socrates is a bachelor (sense 1 = unmarried man)
2. All bachelors (sense 2 = a young male fur seal kept from the breeding territory by older males) are fur seals.
3. Therefore, Socrates is a fur seal.

The use of unequivocal terminology is an attempt to avoid subtler forms of this sort of fallacy. There is not anything very revolutionary—any opposition to "absoluteness"—in reasoning of this sort. Rather, there is only confusion which we should all seek to avoid. Reasoning of this variety may harm the master—but it also harms the slave.

Hobbes' political principles are another matter entirely. These derive from his scepticism about human nature and have, no doubt, deep ideological roots. In any event, the dictatorship of an absolute chief of state is by no means related to a deductive system, except in the loosest and most unrevealing sort of analogy. As to unequivocal diction in laws, I will only say that, whatever Hobbes' reasons for urging this, I myself would certainly prefer clear and straightforward laws to their metaphorical and disruptive relations. Clear and straightforward laws allow us to have clear knowledge of the constraints to which we are subjected. Clear and straightforward phrasing of laws tends to inhibit capricious interpretations of those laws by the police or the judiciary. Were the laws highly metaphorical, the police or judiciary could interpret them as they pleased, and thus we could have no clear idea of the constraints imposed upon us. Imagine, for example, a law which, instead of or in addition to forbidding the importation of specified items or types of items, forbade the importation of 'objects which might darken the light of our spirit' or simply 'evil objects.' Clearly the possibilities for legal repression are far greater in the second or third case than in the first.

Finally, as to Hobbes' identification of equivocation with sedition—this has absolutely nothing whatsoever to do with a logocentric fear of the disruptive, disseminative force of metaphor. Rather, it has to do with Hobbes' awareness of the actual, systematic, literally seditious use of equivocation by certain English Jesuits—most particularly Father Garnet—in connection with purportedly treasonous activities in the seventeenth century, most particularly the 'Gunpowder Plot.' (Father Garnet claimed the right to make ambiguous statements in order not to incriminate himself.) For much of the seventeenth century the term 'equivocation' was linked directly with this incident in the minds of literary and philosophical authors and, it seems, in the popular imagination as well. Of course, Ryan may claim that equivocation is still revolutionary in this case. And it may be revolutionary, but this would not be due to its differantial efficacy. It would merely be due to circumstance. Anything from murder to dancing, from pursuing empirical science to wearing red clothing may be revolutionary in a given circumstance. That equivocation is not somehow exempted from having revolutionary potential is really quite insignificant for Ryan's thesis.

Possibly a more interesting example, this time one relying principally upon a coincidence of metaphors, may be found later in the book. Here Ryan rightly denounces the centralism and dogmatism of orthodox Leninist Marxism. Then, rather than opposing these on ethical and rational grounds respectively, he invokes disseminative, de-centered deconstruction with its 'deprivileging' of "the centrality of the logos" (see p. 187). Reconstructing somewhat, the argument would go something like this: Lenin believes that he has the true science which yields the ultimate truth and thus he centers any 'discourse of truth' about himself as subject of this knowledge. Furthermore, believing himself the center of the discourse of truth, he makes himself the center of power. This centering of power and 'truth' in the person of Lenin entails a centering of the economy, and so on. Deconstruction, on the other hand is *de*-centering and disseminative, and opposes the history of Western metaphysics which is entirely centrist, specifically logo[phonophallo]centric. Ergo, a deconstructive anti-metaphysics will oust logocentric Leninism and make way for decentered Marxism. As Ryan puts it, "Once the centrality of the logos or cogito is deprivileged . . . [t]he planned society would not be conceived of as an integrated system with a central nervous system" or the product of a "central planning body" but would democratically accept different elements (p. 187; see also p. 172 on Lenin's interpretive and political practices).

Now, as we have indicated, logocentrism is a sort of tacit metaphysical doctrine which asserts that we have direct introspective or intuitive access to meaning and similar direct access to the world (of/through perception). The deconstructionist who argues for a disseminative conception of meaning argues that meaning is always 'beyond' introspection or intuition and can never be 'captured' thereby. Thus logocentrism is 'centrist' in enshrining presence as the supreme metaphysical principle, and deconstruction is 'decentrist' in disputing the very possibility of such presence. (For simplicity, I leave aside the asserted links with phono- and phallo-centrism, which are partially metaphorical themselves.) Now it should be clear that Lenin is 'centrist' in one sense of the term and deconstruction is *de*-'centrist' in quite another sense. Similarly, participatory democracy accepts difference in one sense (i.e., difference in the approaches, points of view, origins, etc., of citizens), while deconstruction accepts difference in a completely unrelated sense (i.e., difference between signifiers in a linguistic system). Decentered Marxism and decentered deconstruction are linked in their metaphors alone. Ryan's 'argument' is not actually an argument but a coincidence of such metaphors. We might metaphorize totalitarian control as 'centrism' and metaphorize belief in direct semantic introspection (or full perceptual presence) as 'centrism,' but this does not make the two identical or even similar, or even vaguely connected. Ryan manages to style these two phenomena in similar metaphorics and concludes therefrom that a deconstructive undermining of the latter is necessarily a deconstructive undermining of the former. Clearly, this does not follow at all.

Of course, it is no doubt true that the terror promulgated by Lenin and his successors was in *some* degree the result of their lack of scepticism regarding particular doctrines. It is also no doubt true that deconstructionists—like many others—tend to counsel scepticism on a broad range of issues. Unfortunately, as we have seen, deconstructionists tend to do this by way of a dogmatic insistence upon a highly implausible doctrine concerning, in the first place, semantics and perception. Clearly, the ordinary guarded and sceptical methods of rational enquiry—so disparaged by deconstructionists—are far more germane to forging an anti-Leninist or anti-Stalinist left, especially if these are combined with a Kantian ethics which grants to individuals their rights as ends in themselves.

For an example of the second sort of problem I see in Ryan's analysis—that involving technical concepts—we might turn to Ryan's attack upon the notion of "'objective' law [in the classical Marxist sense of an economic law determinatively governing social development], sanctioned by an absolutist conception of 'science,'" which, Ryan tells us, "is merely a theoretical version of the unquestioned self-empowerment of the male" (p. 100). There are several issues involved in the argument Ryan is making. First there is an exegetical question concerning Marx's position on the place and function of economic laws—for Ryan, Marx's position was more or less deconstructive and disseminative, as we will see. Second, there is a question of the nature of descriptive laws in general and most particularly in the study of society. Finally, there is a question concerning the validity of privileging specifically *economic* laws in Marxist social analysis.

Referring to Althusser's discussion of economic determination "in the last instance" (see Althusser 1965, pp. 111ff.), Ryan claims that deconstruction demonstrates that there is no "origin" and therefore no such thing as a determinative instance (pp. 100f.). It is unclear whether Ryan wishes to debunk all deterministic law, all social law, economism (i.e., the privileging of economic law), or what. In any event, he maintains that a theoretical commitment to the notion of a determinative instance "sustains currently existing structures of sexual domination" (p. 101). As to Marx's view on this topic, Ryan regards deterministic economism as "premarxian" (p. 101) and, following Engels, sees Marx's notion of material production as including not only economic production, but biological reproduction as well (p. 100).

As to our first question, there seems to me quite certainly an adequate number of texts to indicate that Marx's writing is not "deconstructive of the metaphysical opposition" between economy and politics, still less that a supposed "confusion of the two categories in his political journalism" (p. 99) could count as such a deconstruction. One need only instance the famous analysis of the *Manifesto of the Communist Party* that "the history of all hitherto existing society is the history of class struggles" (Marx and Engels 1975, p. 32) and the consequent claim that "The executive of the modern state is but a committee for managing the common affairs of the whole bourgeoisie" (p. 35)—or any number of other texts from Marx's canon. As to the connection with economic laws, we need only look at the opening pages of *Capital*, vol 1, where Marx speaks of the "natural laws of capitalist production . . . working with iron necessity towards inevitable results" (Marx 1967, p. 8) and a few paragraphs later directly identifies the "natural laws" of the "movement" of "a society" with "economic law" which cannot be changed. This immutable economic law destines society to a particular development in which our only part can be to "shorten and lessen the birth-pangs" of any new system which might arise out of its "iron necessity" (p. 10). Indeed, Marx goes on to explain that in *Capital* "individuals are dealt with only in so far as they are the personifications of economic categories, embodiments of particular class-relations and class-interests. My standpoint, from which *the evolution of the economic formation of society is viewed as a process of natural history*, can less than any other make the individual responsible for relations whose creature he[/she] socially remains, however much he[/she] may subjectively raise him[/her]self above them" (p. 10, my emphasis). Thus it seems odd to claim that Marx's "confusion" of the political and economic in some journalistic writing—a confusion which is actually not evidenced in the passages Ryan quotes—indicates a deconstruction of the classical conception of strictly nomological and specifically economic determination of the social. Moreover, the notion of 'material production' is not nearly so vague as Ryan supposes and does not reduce to a bland notion of "material life" with an emphasis on "its nature as activity" with deconstructive implications (p. 101). Thus I think that Ryan is quite wrong on the exigetical question.

Turning to the other question, I am, again, unsure as to whether Ryan wishes to oppose all causal analyses, only those concerning society, only those which are deterministic with respect to society, only Marxist economism, or what. In fact, I myself am sceptical of economism and am not very sanguine about the possibility of discovering useful deterministic laws concerning society. Without undertaking definitively to decide Ryan's view, I should like to say a few words about each, indicating my diasagreements with a deconstructive critique in each case and my own positive views as well.

At various points, Ryan seems to object to any notion of an 'objective' law. By speaking of 'objective' laws, Marx and later Marxists intended primarily to indicate that these are not merely laws of mind. They are not ideal, but material. They are not Kantian categories of the understanding or Hegelian developments of *Geist*; they are categories of material reality and the development of material—specifically economic/productive—conditions. This may seem a trivial point in an age not inclined to idealism, but it has some important consequences, and consequences relevant to a Marxist evaluation of deconstruction. Most important, it indicates that any claims about production, cognition, etc., must be the result of concrete, empirical, economic, and historical research. No claim can validly be put forward *a priori*. For example, in a famous passage of the *Phenomenology of Spirit*, Hegel relies upon a bit of word-play to explicate and develop his presentation of the self-cognition of spirit. Specifically, he justifies his conception of a dialectical development from sensation to perception in part by reference to the evident etymology of the German term for perception—*Wahrnehmung*—which, unlike sensation, he tells us, must be *taken* as *true* (*wahr* = true, *nehmung* = taking; see Hegel 1973, p. 73). This is, of course, perfectly comprehensible in the context of Hegel's linguistic idealism (on which, see Hogan 1980). What is relevant here is that it is precisely this sort of 'argument by pun' that we find repeatedly in deconstructive writing. Ryan is, I think, right in seeing a conflict between deconstructive practice and Marxian 'objectivity.' It is a modern version of conflict between idealism and materialism.

Unfortunately, however, a mystical understanding of objective laws or laws of nature is not confined to idealists. Laws of nature are, it seems, widely conceived of as some mysterious entities that intervene in the material world like invisible sprites and make things happen. In fact, laws of nature are simply generalizations concerning causal patterns to be found in nature. Laws do not *explain* these patterns. They just state that such patterns exist. The only thing that explains one causal pattern is another causal pattern. Thus when Newton connected the patterns of planetary motion and the patterns of falling bodies on the earth's surface, he 'explained' both by reference to another, larger pattern, one generalized in the so-called 'Law of Universal Gravitation.' Such laws are entirely descriptive. They merely say, 'This is the way things happen: . . .' Thus they are unrelated to the *normative* laws which might be laid down in connection with "the unquestioned self-empowerment of the male" (p. 100). Of course, people have used the notion of a natural law towards ideological ends, claiming, for example, that certain races are superior by natural law. But this is a perversion of the notion, a use which relies on bias and ideology rather than reason and scientific method. That a notion has been misused indicates nothing about its general validity. Indeed, Ryan himself remarks at various points that deconstruction has been put to reactionary uses, as has Marxism.

Given the preceding conception of a law, it should be clear that we have social laws whenever we have causal patterns of social behavior. Let us take a simple example from economics. The complement of a good is something people buy with that good. For example, bacon is a complement of eggs. A simple law of economics is that when the price of a good increases, the demand for its complements will decrease, all other things being equal. In other words, if the price of eggs goes up, people will buy less bacon. The law is simply a statement of a certain causal pattern. Now, in its concern for the 'objective,' classical Marxist analysis is merely aiming to isolate laws of this sort. Again, I see no way in which deconstruction can rationally be used to oppose this. Certainly no one would wish to claim that an increase in the price of a good does *not* have this consequence or does not *regularly* have this consequence. Once one has accepted this, however, one has accepted the in principle validity of social laws.

But here our next question arises—can such social laws be deterministic? More specifically, can economic laws be deterministic in the way Marx evidently envisioned? The first thing to say here is that there is not some grand ontological division between probabilistic laws and deterministic laws. A deterministic law is merely a probabilistic law with a probability of 1. The second thing to say is that there are, no doubt, deterministic social laws. This is because probabilistic laws can usually—perhaps always—be rewritten as deterministic laws by fixing certain variables. For example, quite generally people who have taken math courses do better on math tests than people who have not taken math courses. This is true 'quite generally'—that is, often but not always—because many other variables enter. However, holding those variables fixed would produce a deterministic law. Thus, given two people with identical genetic endowments and identical experiences, except that one took and passed a competently taught math course while the other never did anything related to math, the one who took the math course would do better on relevant math tests. More generally, everything else being equal, it will always be true that someone who has taken and passed a competently taught math course will do better on relevant math tests than someone who has studied no math. Now, there are obviously social laws like this and such laws are as deterministic as laws can get. The real question, then, is whether or not there are deterministic laws which are of any use, deterministic laws which apply to real conditions. While this is an empirical question and thus cannot be definitively decided, my own view is that there are not any truly worthwhile deterministic social laws, because in actual social conditions the relevant variables are not ever fixed. Thus, I disagree with Marx on the "iron necessity" of the economic laws of social development.

On the other hand, the power of Marx's economic analyses cannot be denied and their revision as probabilistic laws does not for the most part diminish their force. For example, his analysis of the crises of world capitalism seems to have been quite accurate at least in its general outline (see Chapter XVII of Marx's *Theories of Surplus Value*; see also Kolko 1984, pp. 100–56) and it is really a matter of indifference whether it is phrased deterministically or probabilistically—*except* in terms of the crucial final crisis. Marx appears not to have suspected the possibility of the rise of state-managed capitalism and thus could not have envisioned the sort of relative stabilization of capitalism that has occurred in the last half-century (as discussed by Kolko). Had he conceived of this or other relevant variables, he no doubt would have recognized that the laws he was seeking to isolate were, in the context of real social conditions, (non-deterministically) probabilistic at best.

Finally, we should turn to the problem of specifically economic determination or economism. I take it that economic determination can have at least three meanings: (1) Each and every social event has a direct economic cause or directly instantiates an economic law. (2) Any non-economic social laws are at some level explicable by reference to economic laws. (3) Economic laws define, at the very least, necessary conditions contributory to the operation of any particular social laws which are of direct consequence for the structural development of a given society.

I list these possible construals in order of increasing subtlety, and hence increasing plausibility. The first represents the crudest form of base/superstructure determinism. In this model, causality is conceived to be entirely and completely a matter of economy and it is understood as fully deterministic. Thus, for example, the election of a president would be explained *entirely* in economic terms, with no reference to personality or visual presence, group psychology, etc. Similarly, the genesis of a particular philosophy would be simply and solely an economic matter, unrelated to precedent or concurrent philosophical or, more generally, intellectual developments. I assume we may dismiss this view without further consideration.

The second construal is more suggestive. First of all, it does not require that economic laws be *deterministic* simply because they are *determinative*. More important, it allows for the 'relative autonomy' of non-economic social phenomena. However, it qualifies this autonomy in one of two ways. It claims either: (1) The autonomous non-economic events, etc., enter only as *random* phenomena, ungoverned by social laws, and thus function only to alter, within limits, the specification of the economic laws and the initial conditions to which the economic laws apply. Or, (2) the autonomous non-economic events, etc., are patterned, do instantiate laws, but these patterns are themselves to be explained by reference to other, *solely economic* patterns. Adopting this view, one might, for example, allow that there are many reasons for a given work being published, but insist that any systematic, rule-governed reasons for publication be explained economically. Suppose—as is in fact the case—that one's institutional affiliation systematically influences the likelihood of one's articles being published. In and of itself, this is a non-economic law. But, according to the view we are examining, the explanation for such a (probabilistic) law must ultimately be sought in economic factors—class divisions within the professions, salability of the journals, etc.—and not, say, in a supposedly widespread and economy-independent 'recognition' of institution-related professional quality.

The final construal of economism is much the same as the second construal, but loosens the condition on non-social events, etc., so that we might add the final alternative: Or, (3) the autonomous, non-economic events, etc., are patterened and are not explicable in terms of larger, economic patterns, *but* they can directly govern structural developments of society only when economic laws provide necessary conditions for such developments and only such developments. Suppose, for example, we accept that transference, in the psychoanalytic sense of the term, was a relevant factor in the development and success of German fascism, and not merely a peripheral factor, germane only to certain more or less unimportant details. Clearly, transference is not, in itself, economic. Moreover, it is not fully explicable economically. However, this psychoanalytic view could be reconciled with our third form of economic determination if, say, we take the authoritarian/patriarchal family to be at the root of any transference which is specifically politically authoritarian and we take economic inequality (between parents and children and between husbands and wives) to be a necessary condition for that authoritarian/patriarchal family. In this way, the transference phenomena would have an independent causal role, and one relevant to structural developments of society, but only because certain necessary economic conditions obtained.

It should be clear that at least some version of these last two principles is basically in accord with the (extremely vague) Althusserian notion that economic determination is determination "in the last instance" (see Althusser 1965, pp. 111ff.). In any event, they are far looser and more plausible than the initial construal. The first thing to say, then, is that these seem hardly the pernicious, logocentric statements Ryan indicates talk of economic determination must be. Even were deconstruction an at all plausible sort of political 'intervention,' I see no reason why we would wish to deconstruct these principles. We would, of course, want to scrutinize the data in an effort to judge their validity and may come to judge that even in its weakest form a claim of economic determination is implausible, but this is quite a different thing. Moreover, the use of principles of this sort as a rule of thumb has undeniable advantages, especially for the sort of critical analysis most Marxists and socialist libertarians would wish to encourage. An excellent example of this may be found in Gabriel Kolko's *Anatomy of a War* (Kolko 1985). In this history of the war in Vietnam, Kolko adopts classical Marxist techniques to uncover precisely the 'economic determination in the last instance' of which we have been speaking. Specifically, Kolko acknowledges the relative autonomy of, for example, ideological and even narrowly personal factors, but then goes on to uncover *economic* principles which sustained the non-economic factors and, as the necessary conditions of their efficacy, allowed them to play the independent role they did. There are relatively few historians capable of this sort of rigorous analysis of economic determination. However, when one, such as Kolko, appears, the power of the method, and the theory which underlies it, become obvious.

Yet, despite all this, I remain highly sceptical of the universality of economic determination. Or rather, I strongly disagree with two of its supposed corollaries: (1) That our analysis of economic laws will allow or does allow us to *predict* future *structural* developments—for Marx, changes in the dominant mode of production, principally the necessary development of socialist production out of capitalist production. And (2) that the abolition of private ownership of the means of production—or even of *state* ownership of the means of production—would in and of itself terminate oppression. In fact, neither of these theses is necessarily implied by the notion of economic determination, as should be clear, but both are without a doubt frequently associated with such determination.

As to the first 'corollary,' then, without necessarily endorsing his broader program or accepting his more general conclusions, we might develop and specify Karl Popper's argument against "historicism" (see Popper 1961, pp. vi–vii) in the following manner: Surely, the nature of the dominant mode of production must be determined at least to some significant degree by scientific discoveries and technological inventions—this was certainly true in the past and will presumably be true in the future also. Now, we cannot predict the precise nature of scientific discoveries or of technological inventions. This non-predictability is, after all, what makes the former count as discoveries and the latter count as inventions. To predict the precise nature of a discovery or an invention is, in effect, to make the discovery or invention. Thus it follows that, as discoveries, etc., cannot be predicted and as these are of crucial importance to the determination of the dominant mode of production, the precise nature of changes in the dominant mode of production also cannot be predicted.

This argument appears to me quite cogent, with a few possible qualifications of little consequence. I would add only that, as already mentioned, there are large numbers of variables which limit the certainty of social or economic predictions even outside of areas in which innovation is crucial. For both these reasons, it seems that while new relations in production, new social structures, etc., can be envisioned, struggled for, and so on, the genesis and precise nature of a new mode of production, along with all that this entails, are unpredictable. Thus it would appear that the claims of positive predictive capacity of Marxist analysis—concerning most particularly the necessity of the development of communism out of capitalism—are, unhappily, unfounded.

As to the second 'corollary,' it should be relatively clear that various sorts of oppression could easily persist even in a democratic, socialist community. For example, in any democracy, a majority can, with greater or lesser ease, tyrannize a minority. Similarly, the elimination of private and state ownership of the means of production (in, for example, an anarchist or "council communist" society [on which, see Pannekoek 1975]) would not in and of itself guarantee the elimination of even the sexual division of labor, not to mind unrelated forms of sexual oppression.

Thus I am in agreement with Ryan that certain doctrines correlated with the principles of economic determination are quite wrong. However, it seems clear that Ryan's recourse to deconstruction in this context is mistaken. It involves the use of the sorts of metaphysical, anti-historical, and anti-rationalist principles criticized above; moreover, it employs these principles in arguments which frequently involve confusion on technical points and which are otherwise weakly analogical or worse.

On the whole, then, deconstruction, whether or not it is linked with Marxism, is a theory mired in implausible metaphysical presuppo-

sitions and developed in frequently dubious and often straightfor-
wardly invalid arguments, in many cases combined with an intimi-
dating rhetoric. It does not seem in any way a suitable replacement
for or even a worthwhile adjunct to ideological critique in the
simple sense of an enquiry into validity, morality, and function, as
explained at the outset of the present chapter.

3

Language, Gender, and Reason: A Critical Analysis of Some Feminisms of Difference

Undoubtedly, the most influential challenge to the sort of political interpretation proposed above—with its emphasis on rational inference and empirical enquiry and its downplaying of language as a determinative entity—is the recent wave of 'new French feminisms,' prominently those of Luce Irigaray and Helène Cixous. Developed out of a critique of Lacanian 'phallocentrism,' while maintaining many of the presuppositions of the Lacanian position, the writings of both Irigaray and Cixous oppose the ordinary inferential and empirical principles of natural science as patriarchal and locate patriarchal oppression and phallocentrism fundamentally in these principles as well as in the system of language. In my view, these claims are very wrong—and, if seriously acted upon, would be very harmful. In the following pages, I will seek to explicate and criticize some of the relevant theses of these and related thinkers.

Because much of the work of such post-structuralist feminists or 'feminists of difference' has its basis (positively or negatively) in psychoanalytic theories of gender, and most particularly in Lacan's writings on this topic, I will briefly discuss these also. Before going on to any of this, however, I should like to make a few introductory comments on what I will call "gender essentialism" and "textualism," particularly influential versions of the general essentialism and linguistic autonomism discussed above.

The women's movement in its various historical stages and its different social manifestations is probably the most laudable and significant liberation movement in the history of humankind, the movement which has done most to reconcile actual society to the ideal of a kingdom of ends. Though it has much still to accomplish, its achievements have already been remarkable, both practically and ideologically. However, due in part to the history and severity of women's oppression, there has arisen on the left an ethic of non-criticism in regard to the women's movement. To my mind this is both unjust, and harmful to the interests of women as an oppressed class. However great its overall importance in liberation and enlighten-ment, the women's movement, like all human things—including, of course, my critique—is not perfect in all its expressions. I believe that its work can only be furthered by theoretical scrutiny and criticism. I hope my comments below will be understood in this context.

Feminism, Essentialism, and Textualism

1. Essences of Gender

In the case of gender, race, etc., I take essentialism to encompass the belief that people are to be understood not by reference to individual and unique complexes of properties, but rather, first of all, by reference to one or another putatively definitive property—in these cases, gender or race. This property serves to identify any individual as, in the first place, a member of a certain group, which is understood to be widely uniform in affective, moral, and cogni-tive tendencies and potentials. This view is clearly stated by Mar-guerite Duras, in her claim that, "before everything else, before being Duras, I am—simply—a woman" (p. 175).

For many years, essentialism was associated with sexism and racism. However, it has recently become a prominent feature of certain sorts of feminism—if under different names. As Gisela Ecker explains in her excellent introduction to a collection of essays in aesthetics by contemporary German feminists, "traces of essen-tialism . . . can be found everywhere in the feminist debate on the artistic expression of women" (Ecker 1986, p. 15) and thus in "feminist criticism of art . . . it often happens that what starts off as a description of historical phenomena ends up in essentialist statements" which list 'definitive' features of 'truly' feminine writing (p. 16). Hence, while "It is perfectly true that many of these features can be found in women's writing . . . when they are generalised they lead to new exclusions of . . . forms of writing" practiced by individual women (p. 17). Thus women whose writing is 'rational and objective' can be and are vilified for spurious masculinity. Indeed, I know of numerous cases of this in my own extremely limited personal experience, cases in which, for example, women Ph.D. students were urged to rewrite dissertation chapters in a more 'intuitive and feminine' style. In an essentialist context, women are encouraged not to develop their *own* capacities, but the putative capacities of their gender-essence, not, for example, the capacities of their own individual brains, but, rather, the capacities of their supposed Essential Woman's Brain.

But here, as elsewhere, essentialism is implausible. Individual capacities are, precisely, individual and must be accounted for as such. My intellectual limitations are precisely the limitations of *my* brain, *my* mind, etc. The positing of some sort of 'male cognition' has no bearing on this. A putative masculine essence could have no causal role in my thought or in the thought of any other man. The same holds, of course, for women, and putative feminine essences.

Certainly, empirical study *could* determine that there are gender-related patterns in cognitive potential or in actual cognition. Then, one might object, we have the same situation. But this would be a misguided objection. Empirical study could indicate that women's brains *tend* to be structured so as to inhibit reason, or the reverse, or that men's brains tend to be structured so as to inhibit reason, or the reverse. However, one's own individual brain would still provide the only norm for one's behavior. Let us take a clearer example. Women tend to be less muscular than men. However, women's strengths are still purely individual matters and their relevant aspirations should be governed *not* by some fantasy of Essential Female Weakness, but by an understanding of their own individual strength. If a particular woman is not capable of succeeding at a particular sort of vigorous physical labor, it is not because she is female, but because she, as an individual, is too weak; in the same situation, a man of equal strength would also fail, while another, stronger woman would succeed. The point here is that precisely the same holds for cognition as for strength. Even if we discovered strict covariance between certain cognitive capacities and gender, these capacities would *still* be individual. Even when patterns are discovered, capacities cannot be *defined* and *delimited* by gender, race, or any other putatively essential property. As Chomsky puts it, with regard to questions of race and cognitive capacities: "[I]n a decent society there would be no social consequences to any discovery that might be made about this question. Individuals are what they are; it is only on racist assumptions that they are to be regarded as an instance of their race category [or on sexist assumptions that they are to be regarded as an instance of their gender category], so that social consequences ensue from the discovery that the mean for a certain racial [or gender] category with respect to some capacity is such and such. Eliminating racist [and sexist] assumptions, the facts have no social consequences whatever they may be" (Chomsky 1987, pp. 199–200).

Moreover, there do not seem to be any significant patterns anyway, as, for example, Ann Fausto-Sterling has argued in her powerful study of the literature on male/female cognitive difference (or non-difference), *Myths of Gender*. Fausto-Sterling summarizes the conclusions of her research by noting that some writers "believe that males and females are equally intelligent while entertaining the possibility that the two sexes have somewhat different cognitive skills." "Although the possibility is admissible," she continues, "I have tried to show both that any such differences are very small and that there is no basis for assuming a priori that these small variations have innate biological origins" (pp. 59–60). In other words, there are very few cognitive differences between men and women. Moreover, these few differences are very slight and are explicable by reference to social factors. Fausto-Sterling goes on to cite Nobel laureate Roger Sperry, agreeing with his suggestion that "each person's brain may have more physical individuality than do the person's fingerprints" and thus that "attempts to lump people together according to broad categories such as sex or race are doomed to failure" (p. 60).

Fausto-Sterling draws her conclusions from a careful consideration of the data used to support various sorts of claims for cognitive difference. In verbal ability, "gender differences . . . are small and often statistically insignificant, and, in fact, many of the studies show no sex-related differences at all" (p. 26). More recent methods of analysis make claims of difference in this area teeter "on the brink of oblivion" (p. 30), though "when there *are* sex-related differences in verbal reasoning," contrary to the claims of anti-empirical theorists such as Irigaray and Cixous, "females usually come out ahead" (pp. 28–29). In visual capacities, again contrary to the post-structural feminist claims, Fausto-Sterling found little difference, and that fully explicable by social factors (pp. 33–36). Furthermore, the supposed tactility of women, much urged by Irigaray, as we will discuss, is undermined by tests designed by H. A. Witkin. In such tests, no significant gender-based differences in tactile cognition were discerned (pp. 31–32). Finally, the neurophysiological claims often used to support cognitive difference seem for the most part baseless or insignificant (pp. 37ff.).

Other writers who have recently undertaken a review of relevant research—for example, Beryl Lieff Benderly (see Benderly 1987) and Cynthia Fuchs Epstein (see Epstein 1988)—tend to draw the same conclusions. In fact, in addition to addressing cognitive and affective issues, Epstein's work contains a cogent critique of supposed moral differences between men and women, particularly those affirmed in recent years by feminists of difference such as Carol Gilligan (see Epstein 1988, pp. 81f. and 181–86). Moreover, Epstein emphasizes the real costs of gender-essentialist thinking in this and other areas—its inhibiting effect on freedom, self-worth, the possibility of human fulfillment, and so on (see, for example, p. 233).

In sum, gender essentialisms appear to lead toward ethically objectionable constraints upon individual aspiration, expression, action, etc., and they do this on the basis of generalizations which evidently lack empirical and logical foundation.

2. Feminism and Textualism

Prima facie, it might seem that, however gender is understood, the oppression of women is a matter of human behavior and the institutional structures by reference to which humans justify or constrain or motivate that behavior. Recently, however, certain groups of feminists have come increasingly to view language, conceived of as an autonomous and extra-intentional entity, as the most crucial locus of sexist oppression. This is what I call 'textualism' or 'ethical autonomism.'

A good example of this is to be found in an essay by Wayne Booth, by no means a new French feminist, entitled "Freedom of Interpretation: Bakhtin and the challenge of Feminist Criticism." In this essay, which is in part a critique of sexism in Rabelais' writings, Booth eschews deciding whether he is evaluationg the author's beliefs or the works' effects. As he puts it, what he is doing is "both author-criticism and reader-criticism" (p. 66). This does *not* mean that he first adjudicates the ethical value of the author's beliefs and aims as expressed in the work and subsequently adjudicates the ethical value of the readers' acts or the readers' beliefs and aims insofar as these are fostered by the work. Rather, it means or appears to mean that, like many ethical-evaluative critics, Booth fails to be clear about what sorts of things might or might not properly be termed ethical and, responding to the seeming-autonomy of the text, decides to attach his ethical evaluations to it.

More generally, Booth, like many contemporary writers, assumes the existence of an autonomous language which is itself somehow open to ethical evaluation, and is, indeed, the primary object of any such evaluation. Booth elaborates this ethical autonomism elsewhere in the same essay. For example, he cites a famous passage from *Huckleberry Finn* as an example of a work exhibiting something morally objectionable in order to critique it. As Booth puts it, "Mark Twain sometimes used Huck Finn and others to expose *racist language* ironically. 'Anybody hurt?' asks Aunt Sally. 'No'm,' Huck replies. 'Killed a nigger'" (p. 65, my italics). Now some people may have thought that it was *racist beliefs* or *attitudes* which were criticized or ironized in this passage, but for Booth this seems not to be the case. For Booth, it would seem, the principal evil is not the belief that blacks are not human, but rather the language in which the belief is expressed. But this is an almost indefensible position, for it implies that such dialogues as the following should be inoffensive, or at least less offensive: "Anybody hurt?" "No'm. Killed a black man" or "Anybody hurt?" "No'm. Killed an Afro-American." Of course, we do conventionally use certain words with derogatory intent and thus there is reason to avoid those words. The point is that it is still the belief which is the culprit, not the word. Though changing the word may help change the belief, changing the belief is the proper goal, and once the belief is changed, changing the word is, in general, irrelevant.

The most obviously problematic feature of ethical autonomism is its autonomism, its, usually Derridaean, assumptions about the systemic and extra-intentional status of language. As we saw in the preceding chapter, there are fundamental difficulties with any such conception of language. Ultimately the positing of autonomous language is unnecessary and the status of any such posit, as well as its relation to intent, would be inscrutable anyway. Rather than speaking vaguely about a purportedly autonomous language, we should speak specifically and clearly about speech patterns and the beliefs and aims that go to account for those patterns.

Now, ethical autonomists claim that language in their sense is sexist. I claim that there is no such thing as language in their sense. However, it is possible that their claim might remain relatively unmolested if merely altered so as to assert that language *in my sense* is sexist. But what does this mean? Well, first of all it cannot mean that language is entirely, or even for the most part, or even in large part, or even significantly sexist. It is clear that the overpowering majority of everything that constitutes language in this sense is simply irrelevant to sexism. Rules for the formation of simple past tense, semantic redundancy rules for pluralization, phonological rules for length of vowels before '-tion' nominalizations, vocabulary items like 'roof,' 'quickly,' 'laugh,' and 'yellow,' simply cannot plausibly be claimed sexist in any way. This leaves a few semantic conventions and a few vocabulary items open to the charge of sexism. In some cases, in a very limited sense, the charge may well be true. For the most part, however, it is not.

For example, there is some evidence that supposedly 'unmarked' 'he'/'him'/'his' is in fact interpreted by speakers as masculine (see Crawford and English 1984). Though the inference is based on very small differences in male and female recollections of a passage about a political scientist (hence a member of a stereotypically male profession)—and no comparable studies are cited dealing with, say, (stereotypically female) nurses or (male and female) parents—the conclusion seems plausible. Indeed, we should have been able to predict it. The use of the masculine pronoun as the 'unmarked form' is very nearly a myth. As James McCawley has indicated, this convention is followed inconsistently at best; thus an unknown doctor is referred to as 'he,' but an unknown nurse as 'she' (see McCawley 1979a, pp. 177–78). Specifically, we do not use 'he' for an unknown person if empirical considerations or gender typing indicates that the person is more likely to be female or 'should' be female. Thus there are three uses for 'he'—one specific and masculine ('John . . . he . . .'), a second 'general' and masculine ('A doctor . . . he . . .'), and a third general and generic ('Someone . . . he . . .'). Moreover, some people use 'he or she' or 'they' for generic third person. Given all this, it would be very surprising if people spontaneously interpreted 'he' as generic. Of course, there are many ambiguities in any language, and some may impede understanding for certain meanings in certain contexts. This is not necessarily pernicious in and of itself. However, in the context of a sexist society, the use of a 'generic' masculine, which is likely to be interpreted non-generically, appears to be at least mildly objectionable.[1]

But it should be clear that the real context of sexism, the sets of beliefs, desires, and practices which constitute a sexist society and make the 'generic' masculine sexist, are far more objectionable than the 'generic' masculine itself could possibly be. In the case of the preceding example, we tend to say 'he' in referring to some particular but unknown doctor because the majority of doctors are male, and we tend to say 'she' in referring to some particular but unknown nurse because the majority of nurses are female. The problem here is not primarily with language. The problem here is the world—our beliefs, desires, and practices. What is oppressive is not so much the fact that we say 'he' for an unknown pedestrian, or even that we say 'he' for doctors, seeing as most doctors are male, and 'she' for nurses, seeing as most nurses are female. The crucial problem here is that, indeed, most doctors *are* male and most nurses *are* female and many people believe that things *should* be like this.

None of this is to say, of course, that we should not change certain conventions of speech. We certainly should. First of all, in a sexist society, certain conventions are, or seem to be, sexist in the manner already discussed. Secondly, changing such conventions might allow readier change in beliefs by making people aware of the issues. In other words, the use of he or she or the like as the generic form in English might discourage spontaneous tendencies to view medicine as a necessarily male profession (through phrases of the form, 'some doctor . . . he or she . . .'), clerical work as a necessarily female profession (through phrases of the form, 'his or her secretary . . . he or she . . .'), and so on. It seems to me therefore extremely valuable to alter certain speech-practices—even though the 'sexism of language' *per se* is very limited and dependent.

As to vocabulary, much the same seems to me true. Of course, there are certain dissymmetries in any vocabulary with regard to the sexes, but there are dissymmetries everywhere. No language has a single word for everything under every description under which we would like to refer to it. If it did, then we would never have occasion to create new words, or, for that matter, to use adjectives or adverbs. But these dissymmetries seem to me less significant than they are usually taken to be. For example, it is often asserted that for an unmarried man we have the word 'bachelor,' but for a woman we have no such term, unless she is older, in which case we term her a 'spinster' (the older man being a mere 'confirmed bachelor'). But of a young, unmarried woman we merely say that she is 'single,' or 'unmarried.' We have no noun for her in this state. However, those terms we do possess seem to me to serve well enough and without bias. Moreover, the opprobrium surrounding the term 'spinster' is again clearly a matter of belief and not of 'the language.' After all it is a *belief*, held by many men and women, that women over, say, forty are not desirable spouses. It is a *belief* that women only 'fulfill' their 'function' by marrying and bearing children, and hence that spinsters are mildly deplorable. Again, it is the people and their beliefs which are to blame, and not 'the language.' In all of these cases, it seems to follow that if our beliefs are changed, the language will not matter, or will matter very, very little.

As Robin Lakoff puts it, "The presence of the words is a *signal* that something is wrong, rather than (as too often interpreted by well-meaning reformers) the problem itself" (Lakoff 1975, p. 21, my emphasis) and "Linguistic imbalances are worthy of study because they bring into sharper focus real-world imbalances and inequities. They are clues that some external situation needs changing, rather than items that one *should* seek to change. A competent doctor tries to eliminate the germs that cause measles, rather than trying to bleach the red out with peroxide" (p. 43)—though, as we have indicated, linguistic reform, unlike measles-blanching, can have a slight, but possibly significant 'therapeutic effect.' Similarly, as

Victoria Fromkin and Robert Rodman put it, "Language cannot be sexist in itself . . . but it can reflect sexist attitudes . . . the language is not responsible for the sexism; it merely reflects. . . . There is nothing inherently pejorative about the word *spinster*. The connotations reflect the different views society has about an unmarried woman as opposed to an unmarried man. It isn't the language that is sexist; it is society" (Fromkin and Rodman 1983, pp. 270–71). Indeed, very much in keeping with the preceding analysis, Fromkin and Rodman point out that while for the most part "Changes in the language follow changes in society," it might still be the case that they "also affect . . . attitudes toward women" (p. 271), concluding that "When everyone in society is indeed created equal, and treated as such, there will be little concern for the sexual asymmetries which exist in language" (p. 272).

To take a simple example of this last point, suppose that one-half of the 'postmen,' 'chairmen,' 'congressmen,' etc., seen by a young child were female. It is hard for me to believe that in that case the child would be inclined to believe mail delivery, administration, and representation in government are male activities, that men are the 'norm' for such activities, etc. Indeed, the use and interpretation of words such as 'Freshman' would seem to indicate this even now. Again, I wholeheartedly support the use of 'mail carrier,' 'chairperson,' and 'congressional representative,' due to the mild, contingent 'sexism' of the earlier terms, their tendency to evoke solely "male imagery" (see Sorrels 1983, p. 25, and citations). In fact, 'mailman/woman,' 'chairman/woman,' and 'congressman/woman' would probably be better still in that they might encourage us explicitly to bring women into our "mental landscape," in Deborah Cameron's phrase (1985, p. 85). However, it seems to me quite clear that, whatever we do in these cases, the truly crucial issue is not the (secondary and mild) sexism of language, but the (primary and severe) sexism of beliefs, desires, and practices which constitute society.

Reason, Language, and Cognition in Feminisms of Difference

As I have already indicated, by 'feminists of difference,' I intend those theorists who assume and value fundamental, indeed essential, cognitive and affective differences between men and women. Again, new French feminists or post-structuralist feminists such as Luce Irigaray and Helène Cixous combine essentialist feminism of difference and ethical autonomism with modified Lacanian views on gender and language; moreover, in doing so, they adopt an explicitly anti-rational stance. I should like to concentrate on the position of these writers with regard to the general nature of the supposed sexual difference, paying particular attention to their conception of language and writing and the relation of these to logical principles, truth, and scientific enquiry.

One theme that seems to run through the writings of the post-structural feminists is that women have been denied a voice, prevented from speaking, from expressing themselves and recounting their experiences. Therefore women must begin to talk. This talking, it is claimed, is crucial to the liberation of women, possibly more crucial than economic independence, and other traditional goals of the less theoretically oriented feminisms. At the outset, I wish to express my own wholehearted agreement with the assertion of women's discursive oppression and the need to overcome this. But while agreeing, I would like to extend the claims of this assertion. Women have been in part publicly and privately silenced, but they have equally been economically, politically, and ideologically forced to speak *not* as themselves, but as types, as 'women.' Similarly, men have been ideologically forced to speak as types, as 'men,' though in this case the typing has certainly been less oppressive. In this context, it seems clear that the task of a 'praxis of speech' is first of all to get individual women—and men—speaking *themselves*, and not speaking their *types*. It is at this relatively early point that I diverge with the post-structural French feminists. In their view, women must break the silence *not* by speaking as individuals whose grievances and aims are partially identical and who have joined together in a solidarity. Rather, they must break the silence by speaking precisely '*as women*.' I take this to be a mere revision of the problem rather than any sort of solution.

I am in large part in agreement with the editors of *Questions Féministes* who assert that "the present trend of 'neo-femininity,' which attracts many women [and men] because it appears to be constructive [and, as we will see, because it does not challenge the fundamental, essentialist thinking, the problematic which has defined the limits of all possible discourse on sexuality], can be interpreted as a return to anti-feminist classicism." The authors continue, "Under the pretext that we are 'women,' 'different,' we are prevented from fully leading the life of free and independent individuals. . . . It is the patriarchal system which prescribes the idea of a feminine 'nature' or 'essence'" (p. 214). While I share their scepticism about any possible feminist 'biologism,' I do not go along with these writers when they claim that we should *refuse* "any concept of 'woman' that would be unrelated to a social context" (p. 214), as there are empirical questions here which simply cannot be decided *a priori.*

I am in unqualified agreement with them once again, however, when they argue that the first tasks of a *radical feminism* are the achieving of autonomy for women and of "each person's right to her or his singularity outside of any reference to sexual identity." They explain the latter thus: "This does not mean that 'we wish to become men,' for at the same time as we destroy the idea of a generic 'Woman,' we also destroy the idea of 'Man'" (p. 215). Then subsequently, following the principles enunciated by Simone de Beauvoir in *The Second Sex*, "We must reclaim for ourselves all human potentials, including those unduly established as masculine, that is to say, those monopolized by men in order to enslave us more thoroughly. For instance rational discourse: it's up to us to change its content. . . . More than women, we are individuals. . . . From our position as oppressed persons, we do not demand a 'feminine' society but a society where men and women would share the same values, those being necessarily anti-phallocratic and anti-hierarchical" (pp. 222–23; cf. de Beauvoir 1974, pp. xiv and xxvii). These are precisely the consequences of the moral and rational principles I sought to outline in the opening chapter.

1. The Sexual Difference: Luce Irigaray

Luce Irigaray is a psychoanalyst with doctoral degrees in Philosophy and Linguistics. She is a scholar and a clinician, an activist and a poet. She is justly disturbed and angered by the male bias she correctly perceives in psychoanalytic theory and practice, most particularly as this was developed by Jacques Lacan, especially in his later writings. I share Irigaray's dissatisfaction—indeed adamant rejection—of Lacan's conception of the castration complex and more important the conclusions he draws from this. Indeed, I reject not only Lacan's conclusions, but many of his relevant premises also. Irigaray, however, for the most part accepts Lacan's premises while rejecting his conclusions.

Lacan's first principle with regard to gender is that there is but one signifier of desire and it is the phallus (see, for example, Lacan 1966, p. 694—see also the anonymous article from *Scilicet*, the official publication of Lacan's École freudienne, in Mitchell and Rose 1983, p. 110). The reaction of most people to this statement is—well, why can't the yoni be a signifier of desire also? Possibly I am simply being naive, but both assertions seem to me entirely incomprehensible. First of all, the phallus is a thing, not a signifier. Now 'phallus' is a signifier; however, it refers not to desire, but to the phallus, the thing itself. The signifier of desire, it would seem, is, precisely, 'desire.' Hence, the signifier of masculine desire is 'masculine desire' and the signifier of feminine desire is 'feminine desire.' This all seems quite obvious.

Of course, Lacan might claim that, yes, these are the signifiers in English—and there are parallel signifiers in French ('phallus,' 'désir,' and so on). However, the point is that for the individual subject, the signifier of desire, and most particularly the desire which is inaccessible to the signifiers of English, French, etc., the *unconcious* desire, is the phallus. But once again this seems just wrong. The unconscious desire of any particular subject is entirely particular, is expressed in a particular manner, and must be interpreted precisely in its particularity—as, in fact, Lacan and his followers have repeatedly emphasized (see, for example, Schneiderman 1980, pp. 14–15). Moreover, the apparition of the phallus is not univocal; indeed, as Lacan himself pointed out in one of his famous dicta, when examining dreams we are often told to interpret a church steeple as a phallus, but it is wrong to infer from this that we cannot therefore interpret a phallus as a church steeple (see Lacan 1966, p. 709).

Lacan defends his notion of the privilege of the phallus as signifier by reference to *lack*. The frustration of demand, the recognition that we are not everything for the one—archetypically, the mother—to whom we address our demands, gives rise to a feeling of a "lack in being" which is the source of desire and which is itself "symbolized by the phallus" (Lacan 1966, p. 730, my translation here and throughout). This occurs because we come to view the phallus as the cause of the mother's desire and thus come to see ourselves as lacking insofar as we are not the phallus, the cause of the mother's desire. As Lacan puts it, "If the desire of the mother *is* the phallus, the child wants to be the phallus" (Lacan 1966, p. 693).

This is certainly a comprehensible argument, but: (1) It in no way shows that there is one signifier of desire, or lack, or that the phallus is it. If the argument is correct, then it indicates only that children construe the cause of the *mother*'s desire to be the phallus. The argument implies that their own desire is not the phallus, but the mother, and that the phallus is, for them, merely a means to that end. Now, of course, this means *could* become the signifier of all desire, but the argument in no way necessitates this. (2) In one crucial respect, the argument is almost certainly incorrect anyway. Specifically, it seems very unlikely that any child infers that the cause of the mother's desire is the phallus *per se*. Rather, the child presumably desires the devotion of the mother and finds that the devotion of the mother is caused by many different things with many different traits. The child then forms a composite of these traits, which goes to constitute an ideal, and the child's lack is, then, a lack with respect to the ideal. Now, this ideal may include a phallus. If so, *having* the phallus would be *part* of that which the child wishes to be. But this is quite another thing than wishing to *be* the phallus *itself*. And it certainly does not imply that the phallus will be the sole signifier of desire.

In any event, Lacan built upon this thesis, maintaining in later work that, "Jouissance, insofar as it is sexual, is phallic, which is to say that it does not enter into a relation with the Other as such" (Lacan 1975, p. 14). As women 'lack' the phallus, then, they must fall under the category of what Lacan terms the "not all" (the "pas tout")—indeed, it is their "essence" to be such (Lacan 1975, p. 68). Thus as "there is no other but phallic jouissance" (Lacan 1975, p. 56), woman, who is defined as "not all," has no jouissance which is her own. Thus Lacan speaks of "the jouissance of which it is not possible to say whether woman might say something about it" (Lacan 1975, p. 82), even going so far as to say that "If what I am proposing is true, namely that woman is not-all, there is always something about her which escapes expression" (Lacan 1975, p. 34), and, worse still, that "Nothing can be said about woman" (Lacan 1975, p. 75).

Moreover, Lacan locates the privilege of the phallus in *language* and invokes formal *logic*—specifically predicate calculus—in defense of his point (see especially Lacan 1975, pp. 73ff.). As Lacan puts it, "The sexed being of these not-all women does not pass through the body, but through that which results from a logical exigency in speech" (Lacan 1975, p. 15). Finally, he identifies woman with *truth* in an androcentric system, saying, "the truth . . . woman . . . both are, at least for man, the same thing" (Lacan 1975, p. 108).

I myself can make no sense out of the last statement and believe the former statements to be simply and obviously false. It seems clear that there is no such linguistic constraint as Lacan proposes. Certainly Lacan provides us with no reason to think otherwise—beyond his unsupported insistence that the phallus is the sole signifier of desire. Moreover, the logic which Lacan invokes is so simply and obviously irrelevant to his conclusions that it is not even worth discussing. Thus I reject not only Lacan's privileging of the phallus, but his claims about logic, language, and truth also. However, Irigaray, and to a somewhat lesser extent Cixous, reject Lacan's privileging of the phallus, but accept his other claims, the premises which allow his privileging of the phallus. Thus, Irigaray's rejection of the privileging of the phallus becomes, necessarily, a rejection of logic, ('male') language, and truth. Because Irigaray, and Cixous, accept the premises of Lacan's arguments on these points—as well as the premises of deconstruction discussed above—their work crucially involves the elaboration of a generic, genital-modelled notion of feminine essence which denounces logic, language, and truth as patriarchal, ethically repugnant, and oppressive.

Before going on to criticize Irigaray's claims and arguments, however, I should like to express my admiration for several points in Irigaray's work. As to intellectual analyses, Irigaray undertakes several insightful and revealing examinations—for example, of the importance of paternal and patriarchal fantasies in the life of the young girl (Irigaray 1985a, pp. 34ff) or of the relation between Freud's conception of the female oedipus complex and his conception of mourning (pp. 66ff.). More important, as to ethical judgment, Irigaray deplores precisely the treatment of women as mere means, which we also have condemned, if in Kantian, rather than Marxian terms. As Irigaray puts it, "woman is traditionally a use-value for man" (Irigaray 1985b, p. 31). Woman has suffered a "consignment to passivity" and thus been reduced to a mere "beautiful object of contemplation" (Irigaray 1985b, p. 26). And finally "Woman in [the] sexual imaginary [of patriarchal society] is only a more or less obliging prop for the enactment of man's fantasies" (Irigaray 1985b, p. 25) because "the female imaginary" has been "repressed" (Irigaray 1985b, p. 28).

My only disagreement here is that I would say that *women are* traditionally treated as use-values for men, etc., not that *woman is* so treated. More crucially, I would say that there is no "female imaginary" to be repressed or not to be repressed. There are only the various imaginaries of various women—and it is these which have been repressed. Though perhaps not greatly significant in themselves, these points are quite relevant for the general criticism of Irigaray's work, to which we should now turn.

The first thing to remark in this context is that Irigaray explicitly rejects the notion of *essence* in the sense of the Platonic *eidos*. However, as Gisela Ecker points out (Ecker 1986, p. 18), an explicit denial of essences is often accompanied by an implicit acceptance of them as well. In Irigaray's case, the notion of essence is linked to the Lacanian notion thereof and to the consequent definition of woman in terms of *lack*, specifically *lack of the phallus*, as mentioned above. Alluding to the etymology of *eidos*, Irigaray takes essence to be a sort of *visual form*. Thus, she claims, men conceive of the female genitalia as a *lack* because they do not constitute a visible object (see, for example, Irigaray 1985a, pp. 47f.). As Irigaray puts it, "*Nothing to be seen is equivalent to having no thing*" (Irigaray 1985a, p. 48).

There are a couple of problems here already. First, the notion of *essence*, as discussed above, is most often one of a *definitive property*. If the essence of that green leafy thing outside my window is its *treeness*, that means that what is 'definitive' of the thing's 'being' is its treeness and whatever that entails. All its *particular* and *individual* features are merely 'accidental.' They may even be judged *deviant*, in fact, if they do not conform to the essence. Now it seems to me clear that Irigaray takes the property of *female* (or male) to be definitive in precisely this sense. In other words, Irigaray implicitly takes the cognitive and affective mentality of individual women to be defined by the single property which defines them as women— their 'femaleness'—and thus this becomes an essence. As we have already indicated, assumptions of this sort are not only implausible, but may lead to prescriptive views of femininity which condemn as deviant any cognition or affection of women which does not conform to the essential criteria of femininity. Thus, Irigaray's conception of *essence* is such as to allow the condemnation of essence in one sense and yet permit its acceptance and use in another, in my view far more pernicious sense. Moreover, the sense in which Irigaray uses the term *essence* has little if any relation to the contemporary use of the term. For example, essentialists such as Saul Kripke most often speak of the essences of various 'mass' items such as water, rather than those of 'count' items such as *trees* (see, for example, Kripke 1980). The notion of essence as visible form might apply to certain essentialist construals of the latter, but it will not apply to any construal of the former. The molecular structure of water, for example, just is not the visible form of water.

The second problem with Irigaray's contentions here is that supposed male visualism cannot account for the positing of the castration complex. Irigaray opposes male visualism to female tactility (Irigaray 1985b, p. 79). However, the vagina and vulva are just as sensible to sight as to touch. If three- to five-year-old children (male or female) judge the female genitalia as lacking, it is difficult to understand how this error might be rectified by touch, or how greater tactility might disincline a child to understand the female genitalia in this way. Moreover, Irigaray's claim that tactility is a female and her assertion that "The idea that a 'nothing to be seen,' a something not subject to the rule of visibility or of specula(riza)-tion, might yet have some reality, would indeed be intolerable to man" (Irigaray 1985a, p. 50) are both almost certainly false. One has only to think of contemporary physics—and not merely or even primarily that of female physicists—to find the latter claim almost totally indefensible, not to mention the relevant perceptual studies discussed by Fausto-Sterling.

Upon the basis of her tacit essentialism and her opposition to supposed 'male visualism and formalism,' Irigaray argues to rather sweeping conclusions about mind and language from observations concerning the structure of the female genitals. Specifically, Irigaray maintains that "Woman is neither open nor closed. She is indefinite, in-finite, *form is never complete in her*. She is not infinite but neither is she a unit(y)" (1985a, p. 229). Rather, in opposition to the "*one* of form . . . of the (male) sexual organ" (1985b, p. 26), "within herself" woman "is already two—but not divisible into one(s)—that caress each other" because "her genitals are formed of two lips in continuous contact" (1985b, p. 24). Thus the (formless, essential) form of the subjectivity of 'woman' is, for Irigaray, a function of 'her' genital form. However, Irigaray's claim—that woman *is two*—makes no sense insofar it does not tell us of what somethings 'she' is two. Moreover, it seems the argument invites only the conclusion that women have a bipartite genital, not that they *are* two anything. How can Irigaray or anyone else be said to be dual? If she is two, she is two somethings, in the same way that if she is one, she is one something. Just like everything (except, possibly, pre-quarks), Irigaray is indeed both one something and many somethings. Number is entirely and solely a function of description (and intention), as such writers as Frege and Geach have pointed out (see, for example, Frege's critique of Husserl's *Philosophie der Arithmetik*, excerpted in Frege 1980, pp. 79ff., and Geach 1980, pp. 238ff.), but Irigaray does not indicate what description is relevant to her claim.

The problems are only increased when Irigaray subsequently expands woman's duality into a multiplicity and indicates that the relevant term of plurality here is 'person.' As Irigaray puts it, woman's "sexuality, always at least double, goes even further: it is *plural*," because "*woman has sex organs more or less everywhere*" (1985b, p. 28). Moreover, woman's sexual pleasure is "*never . . . simply one*" (1985b, p. 31). Indeed, woman "*is neither one nor two. Rigorously speaking, she cannot be identified as either one person, or as two*" (1985b, p. 26). In other words, women have a multipartite organ and therefore cannot be counted individually as single persons (or even as dual persons)! But of course individual women must be in some sense singular, which is to say individual, persons, or one would not be able to isolate and distinguish them as individual women and then claim their non-singularity. Clearly, for example, Irigaray is, in some sense, one, even if she is also two, or three, or whatever. Now normally we would say that she is *one person*. But Irigaray claims that she, and each other woman, is *not* one person. However, as they must be one *something*, it is incumbent upon Irigaray to explain what makes Irigaray, and other women, *one* and what makes her, and other women, not one *person*—that does not make men such as well. Moreover, she must explain how the thesis of multiple personhood can be said to follow from the premises of genital structure and erogeneity. Finally, she must further explain her opinion of the revolutionary consequences of this formless multi-personhood. "Ownership and property," Irigaray tells us, "are doubtless quite foreign to the feminine. At least sexually. But not *nearness*. Nearness so pronounced that it makes all discrimination of identity, and thus all forms of property, impossible . . . She herself enters into a ceaseless exchange of herself with the other without any possibility of identifying either. This puts into question all prevailing economies; their calculations are irremediably stymied by woman's pleasure" (1985b, p. 31).

Irigaray extends her conclusions to language, identifying the "multiplicity of female desire" with a comparable multiplicity of "female language" (1985b, p. 30). In "her language," woman "sets off in all directions" leaving man "unable to discern the coherence of any meaning. Hers are contradictory words, somewhat mad from the standpoint of reason. . . . For in what she says, too . . . woman is constantly touching herself" (1985b, p. 29). It should be clear that these are the standard clichés to the effect that women are chatterboxes with no point to their deluge of vain or narcissistic ('self-touching') speech. The difference here is, of course, that Irigaray condemns the principles which oppose vain, pointless, narcissistic speech. In her characterization of women she is at one with the patriarchs. It is only in their evaluations that they diverge. This becomes even clearer subsequently, when Irigaray identifies all female speech with the female "body-sex," claiming that "if 'she' says something, it is not, it is already no longer, identical with what she means. What she says is never identical with anything." From this, Irigaray concludes that "if you ask [women] insistently what they are thinking [or, evidently, speaking] about, they can only reply: Nothing. Everything" (1985b, p. 29).

Irigaray's conclusions here may, I think, be taken in two ways: (1) She herself means nothing/everything by her assertions—is thinking of nothing/everything making these assertions. In this case, they have no stable meaning or truth-value and, indeed, are not, strictly speaking, asserting that women think/mean nothing/ everything. Rather they are claims of *nothing* and/or of *everything*, including their own denial. (2) She means/thinks some specific thing—for example, that women mean/think nothing/everything— and thus falsifies her own specific claim about what women do.

But of course Irigaray would denounce this argument as patriarchal as it accepts sexist language and logic. Thus Irigaray claims that "woman does not have access to language, except through recourse to 'masculine' systems of representation which disappropriate her from her relation to herself and to other women" (1985b, p. 85). Unfortunately, she never makes clear precisely what she has in mind, but it is obvious that her complaints concern far more than the peripheral pragmatic and lexical considerations discussed above. Irigaray goes so far as to claim that there is no such notion as 'female libido' because of male *syntax* (1985a, p. 43) and in consequence calls upon women (woman?) to *"overthrow syntax"* (1985a, p. 142). Following Lacan, she claims that "The sexes are now defined only as they are determined in and through language" (1985b, p. 87). This leads Irigaray to assert "the impossibility of articulating such a statement" as "I am a woman" (1985b, p. 148; evidently the statement 'I am a woman' does not itself articulate the statement 'I am a woman'!). From this, Irigaray comes to the startling conclusion that "The choice [woman] faces would be between censoring her instincts completely—which would lead to death—or treating them as, converting them into, hysteria" (1985a, p. 72), thus echoing the 'liberatory' view of Marguerite Duras that "Neurosis in women is so ancient . . . —all women are neurotic in my opinion—that people are used to their behavior" (in Marks and de Courtivron 1980, p. 176). Once again, Irigaray presents no evidence that individual women are defined by a female essence, that this essence is one of irrationality and diffusion, even hysteria, and that syntactic principles—for example, those governing subject/verb agreement—are sexist in effect or in intent. We have absolutely no reason to accept these theses and much reason to deny them.

It is interesting to see what Irigaray proposes as a replacement for sexist language—what she calls "parler-femme" or "woman-speak" (with puns on "parlez, femmes," "speak, women," and "par les femmes," "by (the) women"). Irigaray explains:

> [W]hat a feminine syntax might be is not simple nor easy to state, because in that 'syntax' there would no longer be either subject or object, 'oneness' would no longer be privileged, there would no longer be proper meanings, proper names, 'proper' attributes. . . . Instead, that 'syntax' would involve nearness, proximity, but in such an extreme form that it would preclude any distinction of identities, any establishment of ownership, thus any form of appropriation. (Irigaray 1985b, p. 134)

We anxiously await true dialogue—rather than male monologue—in such a language. As for now, Irigaray tells us, we may find examples of such "syntax" in women's "suffering" and women's "laughter" (p. 34).

It is interesting to contrast with the intuitions of Irigaray concerning feminine cognition and her conjectures concerning womanspeak, the empirical studies of actual women's writing and speech done by American feminists, such as Mary Hiatt. Hiatt did extensive computer-based research on 100 books of various genres by men and women. There are some inherent biases in her work, of course. For example, a random seletion turns up many more books by women on sexual topics, and many more books by men on political topics, and thus introduces a sort of semi-concealed variable into the analysis. Questions might also be raised about the representativity of published works. However, Hiatt's work still seems to me extremely valuable in this context—and it directly controverts the implications of Irigaray's and, as we will see, Cixous' claims. For example, as to the unstructured, flowing speech imputed to women, Hiatt finds that women tend to write briefer sentences, interrupting themselves more frequently than men. Most interesting for our purposes, however, is that women's writing tends to be *more logically rigorous than men's writing*. Hiatt explains that "women . . . offer reasons and justifications for their arguments 50 percent more often than do men; they offer exemplification and conclusions 5 percent *less* often than the men" (Hiatt 1977, p. 124). This is to be explained in part by reference to publication decisions. It is also to be explained in part by reference to Hiatt's somewhat limited method of judging what is to count as a justification. But in any event, Hiatt's data—especially when considered in conjunction with related empirical work by researchers in other disciplines, such as that discussed by Fausto-Sterling, Benderly, Epstein, and others—most certainly go to controvert the post-structural and differential claims we have been examining; whatever problems there may be with these data, this much at least is clear.[2]

In a related vein, Deborah Cameron, a prominent feminist linguist, observes that many "feminists . . . make unwarranted statements about female speech style, and . . . believe in simplistic stereotypes" (Cameron 1985, p. 54). This is especially harmful as "stereotypes of women's talk are so inaccurate" (p. 32), or, as Dennis Baron observes, "In many cases, gender stereotypes prove to have no connection at all with actual language use. Close analysis suggests that men use 'women's' language and women use 'men's,' that there may be few real sex differences in the English language" (Baron 1986, p. 220). Moreover, as Cameron points out, "what is striking [about these stereotypes] . . . is the extent to which feminist beliefs resemble those put forward by linguists whose political views are the opposite of feminist" (p. 34). Thus, for example, "[t]here is little evidence that children's acquisition of language is significantly affected by their sex. Nor does there seem to be much evidence for the alleged marginality of women as speakers and writers" (Cameron 1985, p. 131).

Moreover, when gender-based differences in speech *are* discovered, it seems clear that these are not best understood as differences in male and female linguistic capacities and attitudes or as the effect of an oppressive language, as writers such as Irigaray indicate. Rather, they are the manifestation of more general dissymmetries in power, authority, etc. Thus, for example, Jacqueline Sachs has presented data that indicate young girls may be more likely to soften and qualify commands than young boys. Jean Berka Gleason has argued, similarly, that women use fewer direct imperatives than men, are less likely to interrupt in conversation, and so on. But these dissymmetries in speech are just what one would expect from the dissymmetries in power and authority of the speakers. Referring to studies of children's speech, such as that of Sachs, Susan U. Philips points out that "studies of language socialization . . . do not reveal differences in the forms controlled by boys and girls . . . [but] only differences in their frequency of use" (Philips 1987, p. 5). It appears, then, that such studies do not reveal *linguistic* differences at all, in the sense relevant to the claims of Irigaray. They merely point to social differences, in the manner discussed by Lakoff, Fromkin and Rodman, and others. Finally, the differences such studies reveal may be quite superficial (if they exist at all; in fact the data are not as unequivocal as it might seem even on these issues—see, for example, Cameron 1985, pp. 42–50, for relevant discussion). Thus, despite the dissymmetries just mentioned, Marjorie and Charles Goodwin argue that "the prevalent stereotype that female interaction is organized with reference to politeness and a dispreference for dispute" is mistaken (Goodwin and Goodwin 1987, p. 200), in that girls use "dispute structures quite similar to those of . . . boys both in their interaction with each other and in their interaction with boys" (pp. 239–40). Moreover, the girls in the Goodwins' study showed "considerable sophistication" and "skill in domains of talk, such as legalistic debate, traditionally associated with male concerns," and, in fact, they "frequently outmaneuvered . . . boys in more extended dispute sequences" (p. 240).

Given the nature of her conjectures on women's language, it should come as no surprise that, in sharp contrast with the Goodwins' study, as well as relevant work cited by Fausto-Sterling, and others, Irigaray concludes that woman's language and indeed woman's being are incompatible with logic. Logic, Irigaray claims, "is modeled . . . on the submission of one sex to the other" (1985b, p. 128). Woman or the feminine contradicts the principle of noncontradiction; it "is removed at least as the property of a subject, from the predicative mechanism that assures discursive coherence" (1985b, p. 149). Thus, "woman's desire has . . . been submerged by the logic that has dominated the West since the Greeks" (1985b, pp. 25–26). Logic necessary excludes woman, she claims (1985b, p. 90).

As is well known, the logic which has "dominated the West since the time of the Greeks" is a formalization of the logic that has "dominated" all human thought always—and it has nothing to do with the castration complex. It involves rather the principle of noncontradiction, which tells us that it cannot be true that this thing in your hand is a book and that, in the same sense at the same time, it is not a book. It involves inferential rules which allow us to conclude that (1) 'All of my wife's brothers and sisters are in India,'

(2) 'Girija is one of my wife's sisters,' and (3) 'Girija is in Nepal,' cannot all be true in the same sense at the same time. And so on. Logical principles are simply the principles we all *must* use, and indeed *do* use, however imperfectly, if we wish to engage reality in any but a phantasmatic manner. Moreover, as we have already indicated, they are the principles we must use and indeed do use (however imperfectly) if we wish to engage in a *dialogue* with others, recognizing, addressing, and attending to them in any but a narcissistic and dogmatic manner.

As to the incoherence of woman's being with respect to logic, this is expressed in Irigaray's claim that "(the/a) woman does not obey the principle of self-identity, however the variable x for self is defined. She is identified with every x variable" (1985a, p. 230). One can only conclude from this that Irigaray does not understand the function of the variable in the claim that for all x, x at the time $t = x$ at time t. To say that woman is to be identified with all variables just makes no sense—unless it means that woman is to be identified with the letter 'x' itself, a queer notion. To say that woman is to be identified with all *values* of the variable, on the other hand, does make sense, but can hardly be what Irigaray intends. To say that woman is to identified with all values of the variable is to say that this book is woman, that Ronald Reagan is woman, that Howard the Duck and the largest Kellogg's cornflake in the world are woman, and so on.

Finally, Irigaray claims that any notion of truth and any empirical science—not merely, for example, certain parts of contemporary medicine—repress woman. As Irigaray puts it, "the phallic economy . . . of course, goes hand in hand with the economy of truth" (1985b, p. 100). Indeed, "*speaking the truth constitutes the prohibition on woman's pleasure*" (1985b, p. 163). Thus she condemns "*the sexual indifference that underlies the truth of any science, the logic of every discourse*" (1985b, p. 69) and dismisses the notions of "cause" and "effect" as forming "a single system" with patriarchal law.

We have discussed the notions of truth and causality at some length in the preceding chapter. However, it is worth saying a few words in this context about scientific inquiry. Scientific inquiry can, for our purposes, be understood as the search for broad descriptive symmetries or causal patterns and widely applicable explanatory principles. Scientific method involves systematic observation (in the context of a theory, of course) and adherence to the principle of minimal interpretation. In other words, the scientist is fundamentally someone who looks at the world—in a systematic and selective manner—and seeks to explain what he or she sees by the simplest means possible. This involves the description of individual objects and the isolation of similarities across such objects—for example, the isolation of general principles of human physiology through the description and comparison of the physiologies of individual humans. Similarly, it involves the description of individual events and the isolation of correlations across such events—for example, the isolation of trajectories of planetary motion through the description and comparison of periodic changes in planetary position. Finally, it involves the construal and selection of the simplest principles which can be used to explain a given set of similarities or correlations.

It is very important to be clear about this last aspect of scientific inquiry—adjudication by reference to simplicity—especially as it is most often ignored or seriously misunderstood by literary critics. The simplest explanation is the explanation which accounts for the most patterns with the fewest posits, principles, etc. An obvious case of this is, again, Newton's reduction of two patterns—the pattern of falling bodies on the earth's surface and the pattern of planetary motion—to one pattern, expressed in a single set of explanatory principles, the Law of Universal Gravitation. Simplicity considerations are, however, more broadly relevant than this example might indicate. Indeed, even our formulation of what we consider to be data, even our decision that bodies do fall on the earth's surface or that they fall at such-and-such a rate, is guided by simplicity. We indicated earlier that explanation is a sort of generalization. To explain, say, an event of some sort is to find a causal pattern into which it fits and which, in the best circumstances, allows one to predict the recurrence of events of its type. Explaining one pattern, we have emphasized, means finding another pattern of broader applicability which the narrow pattern instantiates. We now see that it also means finding the *simplest* pattern; it means adhering to the principle of minimal interpretation when choosing among competing explanations—including those explanations that we come to call 'data.'

But why do we adhere to this principle and seek simplicity? Why don't we make our scientific decisions in some other way, following some other criteria? The fact of the matter is that there are not really any viable alternatives. There are quite literally infinitely many possible explanations of any given phenomenon. Clearly, it would be drastically inefficient merely to choose and test these explanations at random. To deal with them at all efficiently, we require an ordering principle. In cases of possible immediate danger, the wisest and most common ordering principle concerns worst possible outcomes and preparations for these. If we are in the forest and hear a certain sound, it may be a falling branch or it may be an unfriendly animal. We assume it is the animal and ready ourselves on the assumption that this is the safest choice. In other cases, however, our ordering principle must be the one which will allow us to find the correct explanation most quickly. Quite generally, this will be the simplest explanation because the simplest explanation will be the most easily falsified explanation and serial elimination of the most easily falsified explanations is the swiftest and most systematic way to arrive at a satisfactory hypothesis. For example, it will be easier to falsify an explanation that covers all cases of falling bodies on the earth's surface *and* all planetary motion than it will be to falsify an explanation of the former, or the latter, only. On the other hand, the simplest explanation is the most useful and the easiest to understand and apply—though not the easiest to derive—if it is not falsified.

Thus, to oppose scientific enquiry as a whole and in principle—rather than opposing particular contemporary doctrines—is to oppose observation, particular and relative description, the search for explanatory generalizations, and the principle of minimal interpretation. How these, or the principle of non-contradiction, *modus ponens*, and other principles of inference, are patriarchal or otherwise politically offensive is, to my mind, incomprehensible. Irigaray does, however, offer one reason for her assertions. It concerns the relation between solid and fluid mechanics. Irigaray identifies formless women, who continually "diffuse themselves," with fluids. On the basis of this identification, she argues that the relatively late and relatively limited development of a "'mechanics' of fluids" is part of the repression of the feminine (see "The 'Mechanics' of Fluids" in Irigaray 1985b, 106–18). Science, she claims, "grants *precedence to solids*" (1985b, p. 110) and thus represses the female fluid. This indicates "a complicity of long standing between rationality and a mechanics of solids alone" (p. 107).

Having spent so much time on Irigaray's claims about woman, it should be clear why I find her identification of *woman* and *fluid* indefensible. However, I should like to say a few words about her treatment of solid and fluid mechanics. Why did the former develop earlier and more fully? Sinister phallocratism and patriarchal reason? No. We explain solid mechanics better and did so earlier because they are easier to explain. Without going into the function of idealization in physics, the notion of the point-mass, and so on, it should be clear that one billiard ball hitting another is a simpler thing, a thing easier to describe and explain, than one one wave hitting another. Or compare tossing a ball in the air and tossing a handful of water. Claiming that patriarchy is to blame for the fact that we know more about the mechanics of solids and investigated these earlier is like claiming that patriarchy is to blame for the fact that most people learned to play "Fish" early and *still* cannot play 18 simultaneous games of 3-D chess while blindfolded. Irigaray's account clearly violates the principle of minimal interpretation.

Thus, Irigaray really presents no reason whatever to believe that the general principles of logic and scientific enquiry, the ordinary notion of truth, and the general 'structure' of language, are patriarchal, phallocratic, or otherwise biased and deserving of denunciation. Once again, all the evidence indicates that quite the contrary attitude is in order.

2. The Sexual Difference: Helène Cixous

I should now like to turn, more briefly, to the work of Helène Cixous. I should begin by remarking that there is much in Cixous' work with which I am in complete agreement. I share her repugnance concerning the Cinderella myths she anatomizes early in "Sorties" (Cixous 1986, pp. 66ff.), her dissatisfaction with the notion that "the female sex" "cannot be represented" (p. 69), her vision of "an antiland . . . where distinctions of races, classes, and origins would not be put to use without someone's rebelling. Where there are people who are ready for anything—to live, to die for the sake of ideas that are right and *just*" (1986, p. 72). I am moved by her recollections of a sensitive and isolated childhood in Algeria (1986, pp. 70f.). I most particularly agree with her in denouncing the unjust treatment of women, where injustice here has its Kantian sense—as Cixous puts it, "Every woman is a means" in patriarchal society (1986, p. 76). Moreover, in this regard, I share with her the "demand that love struggle within the master against the will for power" (1986, p. 140), if 'love' is understood as the attitude with which one attends to those one treats as ends in themselves.

However, Cixous, like Irigaray, presents an essentialist, ethical autonomist, and anti-rationalist construal of 'woman.' It is this to which I now turn.

Like Irigaray, Cixous denounces essentialist thinking. She adjures her reader "to be careful not to lapse smugly or blindly into an essentialist ideological interpretation" (1986, p. 81). She asserts the historical relativity of all gender concepts (1986, p. 83) and claims that "There is 'destiny' no more than there is 'nature' or 'essence' as such" (1986, p. 83). However, as Gisela Ecker points out, "Although the idea of 'essence' is frowned upon in post-structuralist theory, [Helène Cixous'] programme of *écriture féminine* which is based on the same grounds of thinking does occasionally move towards essentialist positions" (1986, p. 18). Again like Irigaray, Cixous holds to a narrow conception of *essence* which allows her to assume that gender is the property definitive of individuals, that gender is an essence, and yet deny the concept of essence. In Cixous' case, essence seems to be a matter of desire. As Cixous asserts, *"For [Ernest] Jones:* femininity is an autonomous 'essence.' From the beginning . . . the girl has a 'feminine' desire for her father" (1986, p. 81). This seems to indicate that for Cixous the notion of essence is confined to a notion of heterosexual desire—to which Cixous opposes a sort of bisexual desire (see, e.g., Cixous 1986, p. 85). In any event, all that is crucial is that her conception of essence is not one of definitive property, in the sense discussed above. This she does not repudiate, but, implicitly, embraces.

Cixous concurs with Irigaray in identifying 'woman' as principally *body* and 'her' speech and writing as bodily. As Cixous puts it, "Woman must write her body" (1986, p. 94). She urges women, "Write yourself: your body must be heard," explaining "To write" is "the act that will 'realize' the uncensored relationship of woman to her sexuality" (p. 97). "Woman," Cixous claims "is body more than man is. . . . More body hence more writing" (1986, p. 95). When woman speaks it is the "body speaking" (1986, pp. 87–88). Evidently Cixous—and Irigaray—accept the patriarchal commonplace that while the cognition of men can, in some degree, go 'beyond' mere experience, the cognition of women, like all else in their lives, is a mere function of gross physiology. Once again, the difference between the classical sexists and such feminists of difference lies only in their evaluative judgments.

This notion of the bodily character of woman leads Cixous to her own critique of language and her own apocalyptic development of woman-speak. In one way, Cixous goes well beyond Irigaray in her critical claims, even condemning any concern with intentional meaning as patriarchal. As Cixous puts it, presumably seeking to communicate an intention of her own, "intended meaning. Intention: desire, authority—examine them and you are led right back . . . to the father" (1986, p. 67).

Like Irigaray, Cixous claims that woman has "more than one language." Clearly, Cixous does not intend 'language' in any ordinary sense—for example, in the sense of 'autonomous language' or in our sense in which it is an abstraction from speech or speech competence. Thus, it is very difficult to argue or even disagree with this point. Nor does the context clarify, for these multiple languages "will make the old single-grooved mother tongue reverberate" and derive from "woman's . . . thousand and one thresholds of ardor." Cixous elaborates obscurely, with rule-governed syntax, that "the strength of women . . . sweep[s] away syntax," which is somehow to be identified with male oedipal attachments! (Cixous 1980, p. 256). Again, it is precisely because we have some relatively uniform principles of syntax that we can communicate, hence debate, etc., at all. To sweep away syntax is not to sweep away male domination, but rather to sweep away any possible articulation of opposition to oppression, or anything else. Syntax is not "a surrogate umbilical cord" (1980, p. 256) but a series of principles that allows 'Men oppress women' to mean that men oppress women rather than women oppress men, or anything else, or nothing at all.

Continuing, Cixous reiterates the tired cliché that women "have not sublimated" (1986, p. 95). Irigaray makes similar claims in "Psychoanalytic Theory: Another Look" (see Irigaray 1985b, p. 66). But this claim is self-evidently false. It derives ultimately from Freud's theorization of supposed dissymmetries in male/female development because of differences in the male and female 'castration complex.' Specifically, Freud maintains that due to her disappointment and, in effect, mourning for what she perceives as a physical inadequacy (her 'lack' of a penis), a girl develops a less severe super-ego (or conscience) than a boy and thus has less of a tendency to sublimate, to substitute cultural and social service and achievement for basic instinctual gratification. This claim is mistaken on two counts.

1. Clearly the super-ego, or, more generally, conscience, is formed by many rewards and punishments and is by no means a simple function of the castration complex even if we accept the crucial importance of this rather dubious complex in childhood psychosexual development. This should be evident not only from behavioral researches, but from the nature of the super-ego or conscience, which is not simply an internalized taboo on incest and matricide or patricide, and which is only partially unconscious, only partially involved with oedipal repressions. Even accepting Freud's theory of psycho-sexual development, one is not justified in drawing sweeping conclusions about the super-ego or conscience from gender-based dissymmetries in the castration complex. Moreover, the whole notion of the castration complex is highly suspect anyway.

2. It is simply wrong to say that women have not sublimated, that they have not foregone instinctual gratification for social and cultural service and achievement. There are painfully obvious social reasons why there have been more important male artists, etc., than female artists, etc., but they have nothing to do with the relative degree of sublimation of the members of the two groups. Indeed, we have, if anything, reason to believe that women have sublimated *more*, not less, than men. That is one of the consequences of being oppressed. Indeed, as it is widely acknowledged that in most societies and in most classes the labor of women is of longer duration and greater frequency and is less gratifying than the work of men and that women are quite generally allowed less sexual freedom and even less food than men (see, for example, *Grassroots* 1986, pp. 4–6; see also the summary of research from the "United Nations Decade for Women" by Debbie Taylor [1985, esp. pp. 3–5, 61f, and 70ff.]), it is baffling that the stereotype is not precisely the reverse.

A woman in rural Africa today puts in a 17-hour work day every day of the year. Describing the sexual division of labour in rural Bengal at the turn of the century, J. C. Jack discussed the considerable leisure of Bengali men, then contrasted this with the life of women. "The women-folk in the family have a much less varied time," he wrote. "They have no seasons of work and seasons of idleness, but must work throughout the year at duties that are always the same." They must wake up before the men in order to begin their arduous chores, which continue well into the evening or night. "No woman is ever . . . allowed to take any rest while husband or brother or father is in the house; or is ever allowed to eat until all the male members of the family . . . have finished their meal" (Jack 1916, p. 48)—at which time little might be left. The men, in contrast, spend some time in the fields—with frequent breaks for smoking—and the rest of the time napping, gossiping, or going to the market. Certainly, under such circumstance, the men would be more likely to create great art—*not* because of a fictive capacity for greater sublimation, but because of greater real leisure. Overall, it should be clear that in this and like cases it is the work of the *women* which requires greater sublimation, greater deferral of instinctual gratification or transformation of instinctual energy in the service of social values. Unfortunately, both Cixous and Irigaray accept without question the absurd Freudian dogma which claims the opposite.

(Mainstream feminist theory has, of course, always suffered from ethno-centrism as well as class- and race-bias—witness the unquestioned assumption of specifically Western stereotypes of femininity by Irigaray and Cixous. This bias is certainly part of the reason such absurd theses as that concerning sublimation continue dogmatically to be set forth. For one admirable attempt to rectify the general biases outside of this particular question, I refer the reader to bell hooks' *Feminist Theory: From Margin to Center*. For a discussion of some differences between European stereotypes and Indian views, see Borthwick 1984.)

From here, Cixous goes on to identify her essence as 'woman.' Referring to herself as "I-woman," Cixous opposes *body*, that is, woman, to *language*, that is, law (!), that is, man, and vows "Now, I-woman am going to blow up the Law" (1980, p. 257). Here, Cixous attacks "the language of men and their grammar," presenting the ethical autonomist position we have already discussed, but here with a twist. Ultimately, Cixous wishes to advocate a sort of erotic anarchism where all constraints are destroyed and the "cosmos [is] tirelessly traversed by Eros," becoming "an immense astral space not organized around any one sun" in the way the male body "gravitates around the penis," which centered penis "engender[s] that centralized body (in political anatomy) under the dictatorship of its parts" (p. 259).

Thus Cixous appears to be claiming that all constraints of whatever sort are male, phallocentric impediments to libertarian, sexual utopia. Moreover, as dictatorial political authority is "engendered" by the centering of the male body around the penis, this utopia must be female because the female body is not centered but diffuse. But the 'centering' of the male body around the penis, insofar as there is such a centering, is quite clearly a different sort of centering from that of governments. The central dictatorship monitors and controls against the will of the periphery, and it does so as one or several individuals controlling other individuals, whereas the central penis, not a separate individual, merely concentrates a pleasure and focusses a desire of the entire, singular body. Indeed, if Masters and Johnson are at all correct, the clitoris does much the same thing for the woman, if less fully (see, e.g., Masters and Johnson 1966, p. 63: "the clitoris, serving as a receptor and transformer organ, has a role as the center of female sensual focus"). But, of course, there is nothing more than a coincidence of metaphors relating the male body to the totalitarian state anyway. Cixous has posited a causal connection of such obscurity that it is impossible to puzzle out how one might even imagine it to work. She has given us no reason to believe that her loose analogies bear on anything real or have any relation to real ethical and political concerns.

As to the attack on rules of all sorts, including those of syntax, the absurdity of this notion should be clear on a moment's reflection. While it is certainly true that many rules or principles are inhibiting, not all are limitative, and even of those which are limitative, many are liberating rather than truly confining. Just as we must be limited by the resistance of the ground if we are to walk on it, or limited by the laws governing the coherence of our own skins and laws of surface tension if we are not to drip out onto the floor, just as we must accept certain physical constraints if we are to

have any physical freedom, so too there are certain social constraints we must accept if we are to have any social freedom.
Syntactic principles are clearly among these. Again it is only by way
of syntactic and other, related principles that by 'Men oppress
women' I can mean, and communicate what I mean, that men
oppress women. Indeed, principles such as those of syntax are
different from physical laws in that I have a choice to follow the
former, but not the latter. I can, if I wish, violate principles of
syntax. In this way, such principles do not limit me in any way.
They merely create freedoms and abrogate none.

As to juridical law and syntax, there is only this one relation:
without syntax we could create no laws. But this is only because
without syntax we could communicate little, probably nothing, of
complexity. Beyond this, however, there is no clear connection
between law and syntax. If laws are unjust they are unjust as they
do not foster actions tending toward the establishment of a kingdom of ends. If Cixous wishes to maintain that there is some
necessary injustice in laws which flows directly from principles of
syntax or syntactical properties of certain sentences, or whatever,
she must explain how this might be the case. Of course, Cixous
might find laws so pernicious that she would be willing to do away
with any possibility of complex communication to be rid of juridical laws. If so, her position seems rather impractical, but not
indefensible. It is fundamentally a Rousseauean position, urging a
return to nature—a notion which does not lack some charm from a
cozy apartment, but becomes less enticing when meals of rotting
tree bark come to mind. In any event, there is absolutely no reason
to believe that legality *per se* has anything to do with 'masculinity,'
though, of course, the specific set of laws we now have has a great
deal to do with the desires and beliefs of many individuals almost
all of whom were men. Similarly, we have no reason to believe that
legislation as such is necessarily unjust or pernicious.

Thus, Cixous presents us with no reason to alter our rational and
empirical approach to ideological critique or to switch our focus
from intents, effects, beliefs, and so on, to syntax or other aspects
of (autonomous) language. Far from presenting a new and more
powerful critique of sexist ideology, Cixous and Irigaray, it seems,
merely repeat that ideology with a change in the value of its terms.

What they provide is not a substitute for rational and empirical investigation and criticism but rather an object for such investigation and criticism.

Sexual Relativism: Conceptual Framework, Historical Period, and Gender

There is one further issue concerning gender, ideology, and ideological critique that it is very important to address in this context, an issue raised by such theorists as Irigaray and Cixous, but also by such writers as Ecker. Both Cixous and Irigaray denounce gender "indifference" as a form of bias, claiming that knowledge is, at least to some degree, relative to one's gender. Men are necessarily men and thus limited by their gender 'perspective.' Ecker, while opposing the essentialism of these thinkers, makes similar claims (see Ecker 1986, pp. 21–22). We might refer to this position as 'gender relativism.' Clearly, gender relativism bears many similarities to the historical and conceptual relativisms of theorists such as Stanley Fish. Fish claims that we cannot "rise above [our] historical situation" (Fish 1985, p. 100) and thus achieve a knowledge which is not historically relative. Fish and others raise similar objections to 'rising above' one's 'conceptual scheme.' The question then is—are we so bound by constraints of history, conceptual scheme, and gender, that our knowledge must be relativized thereto?

Let us look for a moment at conceptual relativism. There are two varieties of conceptual relativism—one cultural, one scientific. The cultural conceptual relativist claims that we operate within the conceptual frame provided by our society. This conceptual frame is incommensurable with the frames of other societies and, moreover, incomprehensible from their points of view. Thus our assertions are true or false only *relatively* and our knowledge is necessarily limited. We cannot escape the prison of our concepts and understand others or assert a non-relative truth.

The related, scientific version of conceptual relativism (most often associated with the work of Thomas Kuhn—see Kuhn 1970) runs something like this: When we undertake scientific enquiry and explanation, we do so on the basis of a network of presuppositions, many of them explicitly formulated as part of the theory or discipline in which we are working. Thus the very statement of our *data* involves theoretical presuppositions. Thus different theories are incommensurable because their presuppositions diverge to such a degree that they share no data. For example, we run certain experiments and from these we conclude that atoms behave in certain ways. This inferred atom behavior constitutes our data. We then seek to explain this data by positing a certain atomic structure involving a nucleus and an electron shell, for example. Now clearly when we speak of *atom* behaviors as *data*, we are presupposing a considerable mass of physical theory. Atom behaviors are hardly immediate and indisputable givens. They are, rather, highly theoretical constructs.

Thus we may isolate three problems of conceptual relativism: (1) The commensurability, and, ultimately, adjudicability of theories at one time in one place, in one culture, which is to say the commensurability of certain specialized conceptual—usually scientific—'sub-schemes' within a common, broadly social conceptual scheme. This is frequently taken to be a problem of truth and relativism within a conceptual frame, but, I will argue, in fact concerns only certain limitations on the principle of minimal interpretation and thus on the decidability of certain theses. (2) The commensurability of theories at different times and different places, in different cultures, which is to say the commensurability of diverse conceptual schemes which share no 'background scheme.' This is primarily taken to be a problem of relativist and absolutist conceptions of truth; I will maintain that it concerns, rather, essentialist and non-essentialist conceptions of truth. (3) The comprehensibility and accessibility of conceptual schemes which are not one's own. This is most frequently taken to be a question of whether we are all quite the same or are irreconcilably different by culture. I will maintain that of course there is such a thing as cultural difference—we are not all quite the same—but that it is a matter of degree, not of kind. As will become clear below, there is a similar division of questions in the cases of other relativisms, historical or sexual.

Beginning with the first, it is important to keep in mind the way in which theoretical terms are defined. Let us take again our atomic data. Should we posit a certain sort of atomic structure, naming the elements of our posit 'electrons,' 'protons,' and 'neutrons,' and claiming that the last two cluster together and the first circle, planet-like, around them, we are introducing terms which, insofar as they are meaningful, insofar as they could pick out an extension, are necessarily defined entirely in terms of precedently available concepts. Now suppose we do further experiments and gather data of proton behavior, which we then explain in terms of *quarks*. Then we gather quark data which we explain in terms of pre-quarks, and so on. When we posit the quarks, we necessarily do so upon the basis of a conceptual scheme which includes atoms and protons, but not quarks—that is, after all, the whole point of introducing a new posit. Similarly, when we posit the pre-quarks, we do so upon the basis of a conceptual scheme which includes atoms, protons, and quarks—as well as people, laboratories, particle accelerators, and so on—but not pre-quarks. Because of this, our data are always rephrasable in terms of earlier posits.

Suppose, for example, that we phrase a certain datum in terms of proton behavior. Someone may object that he or she does not accept the existence of protons and thus need not address this supposed datum. We may then regress to the level of *atom* data, rephrasing our findings in these terms. Moreover, we may present the atom data which led us to posit protons in the first place. Presumably, our interlocutor would be forced to accept these as data. If not, we could regress to molecules. Or possibly we could only get the person to accept that a large and complicated machine exists and that when certain switches are flipped, certain meters start moving in certain ways, etc. Thus in some cases we might have to regress quite a way to find a common phrasing for the data. However, there will always be some such point as long as there is some common conceptual scheme, even if it is only one of ordinary macroscopic objects and their motions and relations. (A similar point is made by V. A. Lektorsky; see Lektorsky 1984, pp. 204–5.)

Now, granted this degree of commensurability, there should be no problem with truth/falsity. To the degree that our characterization of posits is not vague—and it will certainly be vague to some degree—each theory either is or is not true in the ordinary sense (i.e., 'within' the shared conceptual scheme, as we will discuss) and there is no problem about it. Either the notion of 'nucleus' does in fact pick our bits of space-time or it does not; either the electron in a Helium atom is such-and-such a distance from the nucleus or it is not, and so on. Again, notions such as 'nucleus' and 'electron' will be vague, often to a remarkable degree, but this does not make statements involving these terms only *relatively* true or false. Rather it makes such statements neither true nor false *in certain cases* (those about which it is vague)—an ordinary thing for our ordinary vague terms and no less ordinary for vague scientific terms.

However, this determination of truth/falsity does not necessarily contribute to decidability. As we have indicated, any set of data is open to literally infinitely many explanatory accounts. There are infinitely many explanations of our proton data or atom data or gross machine-state data. Thus, to recur to the preceding example, we may present all our atom data to someone and that person may devise a perfectly adequate explanatory account that makes no reference to protons or proton-like entitites. As we have remarked, we seek to adjudicate rival, roughly empirically equivalent theories by criteria of simplicity. However, as the structural complexity of the theory increases—for example, as new posits accumulate—simplicity criteria apply less and less univocally. In other words, in relatively uncomplicated cases, simplicity criteria may provide us with clear theoretical preferences. However, as the theories develop, the question of their relative simplicity becomes far more difficult to answer. The complex and powerful theory which is simpler than a rival theory in one respect may be less simple in another respect, and we have no clear criterion to help us rationally to decide which sort of simplicity is preferable.

Thus, it would seem that the 'scientific' examples, the examples of *sub-schemes* which share a general or 'background' scheme, indicate *not* that there is any relativity of truth across individual theories, but that not all empirically undecidable claims within a scheme are equally open to adjudication by simplicity criteria, that, in general, the more deeply 'embedded' the sub-scheme, the less useful these criteria become. In other words, given a background theory along the lines of the commonsense, American, English-speaking conceptual frame, it is easier to adjudicate by reference to simplicity whether or not there are dogs than whether or not there are pre-quarks; however, granted the general conceptual scheme, the latter do or do not exist as non-relatively as the former. Once you have a common scheme, then there is no relativity of truth to given sub-schemes or theories; there is only increasing difficulty in adjudication of such sub-schemes or theories.

This, then, brings us to our second problem, for the question arises as to whether or not we should consider the claims of the particular theories, etc., true or false only relative to the background scheme or framework. Indeed, this may seem to follow from the preceding analysis. However, as I have already indicated, I do not believe that there is in fact any question whatsoever of relativity here. Rather, there is a question of essentialist versus quotidian, celestial versus mundane notions of truth. The essentialist and quotidian notions of truth both involve ordinary components—intended objects, relations, etc. The quotidian notion of truth involves nothing more. To say that the salt is next to the stove is to claim that a certain object which satisfies our criteria for counting as salt and which may be isolated as the specific object of our concerns stands in a certain relation to another object, and so on. And this is all there is to it. There is no relativism here whatsoever. The truth or falsity of the claim is as absolute as you like—within the limits of vagueness, of course—because there is nothing more absolute that truth could be.

The essentialist notion, on the other hand, involves all this *plus* essences. In other words, in the essentialist conception of truth, there are always, so to speak, two claims of truth: (1) the quotidian claim, just discussed, and (2) an essentialist claim to the effect that the objects in question 'really are' or 'are essentially' of the sort mentioned. Thus to claim that the salt is by the stove, or to claim that all humans are mortal, is to pick out an object or set of objects *as they really are defined independent of any language, intent, etc.* In other words, under the essentialist conception, the stove is a single entity independent of its intentional or descriptive isolation, and all humans form an essence-defined set again independent of the criteria we might devise to isolate any such set. For the essentialist, in other words, the world is divided into particulars and essences independent of any cognition and thus we must not only make claims which are true given our conceptual scheme, we must get our conceptual scheme right. We must talk of individuals only where there are individuals. We must make our concepts conform to objective essences.

Here and only here a question of relativism arises. A statement is *'relatively'* true if it is true in the quotidian sense, given the conceptual scheme in which it is made, *but this conceptual scheme does not or cannot be determined to correspond to the 'true' conceptual scheme*, that scheme of the already-individuated and essence-structured world. On the other hand, the *'absolute'* truth involves both the quotidian truth and the identity of its conceptual scheme with the 'true' conceptual scheme.

It is here that the problem of cultural relativism enters. To the extent that another culture employs a conceptual scheme which organizes the world differently from our own, and to the extent that we cannot adjudicate the rival organizations, it *appears* that we must surrender hope of absolute truth and confine ourselves to merely relative statements. However, the inadjudicability of such rival organizations, and numerous other phenomena also, indicate rather that, once again, the essentialist conception of truth makes no sense. There is and can be no question of a true or false conceptual scheme. In this context, a conceptual scheme is what orders the communicable, intentional meanings and references of our terms and there just can be no question of a claim being true or false before one means anything by its terms.

Thus, the cultural argument does not indicate any cultural relativism of truth. Rather, it provides us with a further impetus to abandon any essentialist conception of truth and to embrace the quotidian notion thereof. A claim which is true in one conceptual scheme—that is, a claim which is factually accurate within the terms of the scheme, and not necessarily a claim which is widely or firmly believed by members of the relevant society—is as absolutely true as a claim can be. And this is precisely because it makes no sense to speak of truth or falsity, correctness or error, prior to the development of a conceptual scheme. A conceptual scheme grounds the very possibility of truth or falsity.[3] Once again, the existence of different concepts across cultures provides no greater motive for accepting relativism than does the existence of different concepts within one culture.

This, then, brings us to our final question—are other conceptual schemes accessible? First, we should look at what a conceptual scheme might be. As I use the term, I intend it to be more or less equivalent to 'semantics' in the sense of the communicative rules any given community shares. Thus English speakers share a certain number of principles which determine 'normal' communicative speech that allow us to understand that 'salt' most often means *salt*, and not parsley, 'stove' means *stove*, and so on. In other words, the conceptual scheme is just the rules which govern the meaning and extension of terms in a given language community, along with perceptual schemata in relevant cases. What should be clear immediately, then, is that despite the preceding discussion, there is no such thing as a conceptual scheme. We speak of a semantics for English, but also for American English, and also for Southern English, and also for Kentucky English, and so on. And even then, where are the rules defining Southern English, or Kentucky English?—clearly these rules are nothing other than the rules of the individual speakers of Southern English or Kentucky English. Ultimately the semantics of a language is nothing more than an abstraction from the rules followed by individual speakers. It is merely what these individual speakers have in common. (This is, of course, the point of Chomsky's arguments against 'E-language,' mentioned above.)

Thus there is no question of our having or not having access to another conceptual scheme. There is no conceptual scheme, in this sense, to which we might or might not have access. Rather, there are only entirely individual principles. The real question is—how does one individual gain access to the principles of another individual, how do the individuals come to have common principles? This is relatively clear—through a desire to achieve common principles and extensive linguistic and other interaction. Thus through a 'form of life,' through 'sharing' life with others and interacting with them, we come to acquire semantic principles and adjust our principles to those of others. We also come to form certain very fundamental beliefs in this way, and so on.

But what of other cultures? The answer now seems clear. As conceptual schemes are entirely individual in any event, it is no less possible for us to adjust our principles to those of individuals in another culture than to those of individuals in our own. The fact of having acquired one set of principles can be a hindrance, but it can also be an aid. Certainly there are *pragmatical* difficulties, and these are sometimes insuperable. The point, however, is that there is no question of having access to or not having access to another conceptual scheme, of achieving a unity of one's mind with the structure of cognition in another culture. We never have any such unity. In our own culture we have only our own principles and the experiences which guide us in seeking to reconcile our principles with those of others. Clearly, the very same is true of our relation to other cultures. For various reasons it will be more difficult for us to adjust our principles to theirs, but the process is the same. The difference between our 'access' to 'our own' culture and our 'access' to other cultures is one of degree, not of kind. Once the possibility of the former is granted, the possibility of the latter is granted also.[4]

It should be clear that historical relativism raises precisely the same questions as cultural relativism and receives precisely the same answers. It may be somewhat less obvious, but it is nonetheless true, that the same applies to gender relativism as well. Staying with the final question, the one most relevant for the feminists of difference we have been examining, it should be evident that any given woman has no direct intuitive access to the experience of 'womankind.' She has only her own beliefs, desires, experiences, and so on. These form a quite literally statistically insignificant fraction of the beliefs, desires, experiences, etc., of women as a group. Moreover, in areas involving strong stereotypes—and gender differences are really the paradigm case of this—people's intuitions regarding both themselves and others are unreliable to a remarkable degree. As Deborah Cameron points out, referring in particular to speech practices, "It has been found that people consistently misreport their own behavior when they are asked to describe it. They report usages that owe more to the stereotype than to the truth" (Cameron 1985, p. 34). And as Cynthia Epstein explains, in more general terms, "individuals report feelings and 'traits' normatively prescribed as appropriate for their sex or group" rather than feelings or traits they actually possess (Epstein 1988, p. 88). As regards intuition about others, Epstein cites a number of studies which lead to the conclusion that "stereotypes create a self-fulfilling prophecy . . . in that others' behavior is mediated by the expectation created by the stereotype. . . . [B]ehavior consistent with what is expected is usually attributed to a characteristic of the actor, and behavior that departs from what is expected is attributed to a peculiarity of circumstance or other temporary causal factor" (pp. 84–85). For example, Epstein reports one shocking study in which "an infant's cry was interpreted as angry when subjects were told it was a boy and as fearful when they were told it was a girl" (p. 223). This phenomenon is sometimes referred to as "interpersonal expectancy effect" (see Rosenthal and Rubin 1978) and sometimes related to more general cognitive tendencies under the title "confirmatory bias." We will discuss the larger issue of confirmatory bias in the final chapter. For now, it is enough to note the relevant implication of this research—specifically that personal intuitions of individual women, no matter how firmly believed, simply do not involve special access to large-scale characteristics (feelings, experiences, etc.) of women as a group. Such intuitions are at best plausible but unsupported conjecture. At worst they are the mere reproduction of stereotypes.

The one way in which an individual woman can come to understand women as a group, then, is through self-conscious observation, discussion, and so on. Moreover, this observation and discussion must be as systematic and rigorous as possible to minimize the distorting effects of internalized stereotypes. Of course, a woman undertaking such a study may relate her observations, etc., to her own personal experiences, but her real knowledge is necessarily based upon the systematic, self-conscious observations, etc., and not her, once again, statistically insignificant personal experiences, unself-conscious stereotype-bound intuitions, and so on. Now, clearly, the same holds for men. It is only through rigorous and systematic, self-conscious empirical study that a man can achieve any worthwhile understanding of men as a group. Similarly—and this is the important point—it is only through such study that men can achieve any worthwhile understanding of *women* as a group. In other words, in understanding women (or men), women and men are in the same boat. They must pursue this understanding in precisely the same way. Of course, men will lack certain gender-specific experiences, etc., and this lack might affect their inferences in certain ways. More important, this lack, in combination with other factors, may inhibit men's willingness to try to achieve any serious understanding of women as a group or as individuals. But, nonetheless, men's mistaken—and usually stereotypic—intuitions about women (or men) will be open to correction in precisely the way as women's mistaken—and usually stereotypic—intuitions about women (or men)—that is, through systematic and rigorous observation, through study guided by the principles of general scientific method.

It should be clear, then, that there is no question of gender inaccessibility here, not to mind any relativity of truth. There is, again, only the problem of solipsism, the problem of intersubjectivity, the problem of individual human beings understanding one another and discerning patterns in the world in which they live. Truth and knowledge are no more relative to gender than to conceptual scheme or historical period. Truth is as absolute as can be. And knowledge is as tentative, inferential, and empirical as can be.

Thus, once again, writers such as Cixous and Irigaray provide us with no reason to abandon ordinary principles of rational inference and empirical investigation as the basis not only of natural science but of political action—including political interpretation—as well. Nor do they provide us with any reason to turn away from the world and toward the word. They accept highly dubious essentialist and textualist presuppositions and develop these in relation to implausible Lacanian hypotheses, without even undertaking their justification. They adopt without question a broad range of sexist stereotypes, which they regularly invoke and elaborate, but do not defend. They do not show us the way to a new, invigorated political practice and a new, deepened political understanding. Rather, they allow us to see more clearly the crucial importance of ordinary scientific method to *any* form of action or understanding, and the centrality, to any politics, of ideological critique—focussed not on language, but on beliefs and actions, and on the institutional practices which these define.

4

Dominations and Problematics: On Accepting Oppressive Ideologies

In the preceding chapters, I have sought to limit the realm of literary ideology to response, belief—both that which tends to foster action and that which does not—and, most crucially, effect, in the sense of effect on aims and behavior. Furthermore, I have urged a tri-partite approach to the critique of ideology, encompassing the analysis of validity, justice, and function. Now, let us suppose that we are dealing with an ideology in the strongest sense. Its claims are false, even palpably false, and its aims unjust. It functions to preserve and even extend domination. Indeed, its origin lies ultimately with the ruling elite. There are of course many examples of this sort of ideology—Ronald Reagan's vicious lies (delusions?) about Nicaragua being an obvious case in point. There is no real *descriptive* problem here. Our preceding, quite commonsensical analyses serve to allow us adequately to describe this ideology. The proffering of the ideology is easily enough addressed also. If the dominant groups put forth and even come to believe self-serving palpable falsities, this, I think, poses no problem for the *explanation* of this ideology. However, what is crucial about ideology is not its introduction, but its *acceptance* and what crucially must be explained is not the ideologically determined beliefs and acts of those who dominate, those who benefit from the ideology, those whose interests the ideology serves, but rather the ideologically determined beliefs and acts of those who are dominated, those who do not benefit, those whose interests are not only not served but concretely denied. It is this *explanatory* problem, then, to which I should like to attend in the following pages, not only because it is of such importance to us all as ethical subjects, but equally because it is, as I will argue, absolutely crucial to the functioning of the academy and to our functioning as teachers and scholars.

The first and most obvious reason why dominated groups accept ideology is that the ideology preserves the society's patterns of domination in which they, while dominated, also dominate. In other words, most dominated individuals, most particularly in an advanced capitalist and imperialist country such as the United States, have a stake in the system of domination; they have something to lose if that system is undermined. Thus to some degree they have the very same reason as the ruling elite to accept a given domination-preserving ideology—they receive a *primary gain.*

I would also argue, however, that in many cases dominated groups receive a *secondary gain* from their state of domination. "Secondary gain" is a term introduced by Freud (see Freud 1963, pp. 59ff., and elsewhere) to account for a patient's attachment to his or her symptom. Initially a symptom—for example, hysterical paralysis—is debilitating. However, as the neurotic lives with this symptom, he or she begins to draw benefits from the debilitation— for example, release from responsibility, increased familial affection and attention, even unconscious, guilt-relieving self-punishment. Freud terms these benefits "secondary gains." In and of itself a symptom such as paralysis provides no direct benefits; in and of itself, being unable to walk, for example, is only inhibiting. However, in a certain context, a symptom such as paralysis might provide indirect benefits to which the patient might then become attached. In this case, the patient would be inclined to accept the symptom and fear cure *not* because he or she received any direct or *primary* benefits from the symptom, not because the symptom did not directly cause suffering, but because the real indirect or *secondary* benefits have become for the patient more certain, more palpable, more reliable than the merely promised direct benefits of the cure.

Freud himself indicates that the notion of secondary gain is crucial for understanding many ordinary, non-neurotic behaviors. As Freud puts it:

> Let us imagine a workman, a bricklayer, let us say, who has fallen off a house and been crippled, and now earns his livelihood by begging at the street-corner. Let us then suppose that a miracle-worker comes along and promises him to make his crooked leg straight and capable of walking. It would be unwise, I think, to look forward to seeing an expression of peculiar bliss upon the man's features. No doubt at the time of the accident he felt he was extremely unlucky, when he realized that he would never be able to do any more work and would have to starve or live upon charity. But since then the very thing which in the first instance threw him out of employment has become his source of income: he lives by his disablement. If that is taken from him he may become totally helpless. (Freud 1963a, pp. 60–61)

I would argue that there are *secondary gains* which accrue to the members of any dominated group also and thus that an understanding of such gains is critical for an explanation of the acceptance by dominated peoples of ideologies which preserve and extend their domination.

Finally, I would maintain that there are various narrowly psychological factors, involving narcissism and 'transference' considerations in the technical, psychoanalytic senses of these terms. I would maintain, in other words, that there are profoundly unconscious reasons for the nature of our relation to authority and to the other members of the societies of which we are ourselves members.

I should like to consider these factors in turn, first briefly discussing the primary gains of dominated individuals—in the context of a further articulation of the notion of domination—continuing on to a more detailed examination of secondary gains, and concluding with a discussion of narcissism and transference in ideology. Before going on, however, I should note that the emphasis of the present chapter on affective and motivational considerations is not intended to imply that cognitive concerns are unimportant to an understanding of ideology. Indeed, we have already touched on what is perhaps the most important cognitive element in the acceptance, maintenance, and dissemination of ideology—confirmatory bias (see Nisbett and Ross 1980, pp. 238–42). Moreover, as the brief discussion of this topic in the following chapter should make clear, I take it that the anti-ideological practices proposed in the present chapter—for example, the practice of institutionally free dialectic— are relevant to cognitive factors in ideology, such as confirmatory bias, no less than they are to affective and motivational factors.

Domination, Wealth, and Primary Gain

Domination is, in the first place, the systematic facilitation of the treatment of one person or group of people as mere means by another person or group of people. Hence domination is antitheti- cal to the establishment of a kingdom of ends and is thus the general form of the unethical. Of course, for the most part, domina- tion is not complete for any group, but partial only. Men dominate women, but whites dominate blacks, and thus certain (white) women may dominate certain (black) men. The point in speaking of group or class domination is not that such domination is universal, but rather that it is regular under certain descriptions. Not all men dominate all women or all whites all blacks, but under these de- scriptions such patterns of domination are regular. Moreover, this domination need not be personal, at least in one sense. Ideology or law may put men into a position of dominance even when they do not wish to be complicitous with such domination and work not to be thus complicitous. In other words, a man may be in a position of economic dominance over his wife not because of any of his own acts or beliefs, but rather because she cannot find employment because of hiring biases, or because she does not wish to find a job due to her attachment to secondary gains or the ideological belief that men alone should work outside of the house, etc. Moreover, a man may be in a position of economic dominance (i.e., the 'means' may be all at his disposal as he is the one who has earned them) and yet treat his wife as an end in herself, thus not dominating his wife, not taking advantage of the privilege the situation offers him. Indeed a woman might readily enough take advantage of her hus- band's ethical behavior and use him as a mere means. Hence to say that men dominate women in this sense is not necessarily to say that particular men dominate particular women, or rather it is not to say that particular men actually treat particular women as mere means. Of course, particular men do treat particular women as mere means (and particular women treat particular men as mere means). However, it would not be inconsistent with the assertion that men dominate women were it to turn out that no men treat women as mere means, all men sacrificing their primary gains insofar as these would be to the cost of women. It will not turn out that way, of course, but it would not be inconsistent were it to so turn out. In grossly oversimple terms, male domination does not mean that men are unkind to women, but that women must rely on the kindness of men to a degree far beyond that to which men must rely on the kindness of women. That men are dominant means that men are privileged in various respects at the expense of women—whether they individually exploit their privileges or not.

Within the general category of domination, I should like to distinguish: (1) the sort of domination which is a function of ideology, the sort we have been discussing; (2) the sort of domination which is 'material' and, so to speak, 'official'—what might be called 'oppression'; and (3) the sort of domination which is 'material' and, so to speak, 'unofficial'—what might be called 'terrorism.' Of course, all three sorts of domination exist and interact in complex ways. Moreover, it is sometimes very difficult to say when one form of domination is ideological or official or unofficial. Usually it is all three. However, the three are in principle distinguishable. It is, in principle, possible to have a society in which any one form of domination exists with regard to two (or more) groups, but neither of the others exists.

The first sort of domination involves cases in which, say, women are limited as to employment due to beliefs—their own or those of prospective employers—to the effect that women are unfit for various sorts of work. There is no question of legal constraint or physical threat, but only beliefs and aims which constrain those who are dominated and help preserve the system of domination.

The second category encompasses, for example, actual legal restrictions which insure domination through the system of retribution operating within a state. When legally debarred from owning property, testifying in court, and so on, then women are *oppressed* in this sense—male domination is then 'official' in these areas. As to blacks, the slave system, apartheid, legal segregation, and so on, would be obvious examples of oppression. As to the Third World, we could cite U.S. foreign policy to that region almost in its entirety.

The third category comprises individual acts of subjugation, such as wife-beating and rape, cross-burning and lynching, and so on. These acts enforce domination by terrorizing the dominated group. To take an obvious example, it may be legal for a black family to settle in a white neighborhood, or for a black child to go to a white school, but at least in some cases if the family does move in, their house will be burned, and if the child goes to the school the child may be beaten, or his or her father may be kidnapped and whipped. Of course, the effectiveness of such terrorism relies at least in part on the complicity of the law enforcement agencies and the judicial system and thus at a certain point the distinction between oppression and terrorism blurs. At the risk of being accused of suffering from a mania for categorization, I might propose the name "oppressive corruption" for such complicity. Clearly this is more prominent in certain areas than in others. For example, in the Third-World countries the United States arms and operates, there often is no system of justice other than the system of oppressive corruption (thanks here to Uncle Sam, of course). Indeed, where there is dominant-group terrorism, there is usually at least some form of oppressive corruption, sometimes subtle and ideological, sometimes crude and economic or political.

What is in many ways most interesting in the present context is that, leaving aside ideology, these categories imply, or appear to imply, a certain absoluteness of domination. But this breaks down in at least one crucial area. Insofar as terrorism or oppression or oppressive corruption is a function of racial or sexual or other related considerations, there is little possibility for primary gain accruing to the dominated groups. Blacks simply achieve no direct, primary gains from a system in which they are enslaved, or imprisoned for seeking equality, or tortured by Klansmen. Women simply achieve no direct, primary gains from a system in which they are barred from owning land, raped, or forced to live with abusive husbands. In these and related cases—e.g., the case of hetero- and homo-sexuals—there are two and only two groups and members of any given group are all more or less equal with regard to their membership in that group. Though they may be drastically unequal in other ways, all blacks, *as* blacks, suffer and do not benefit from racist terrorism, etc., all women, *as* women, suffer and do not benefit from sexist terrorism, etc. However, what is in many ways the most crucial factor in determining status in a system of domination, wealth, involves everyone—blacks and whites, women and men, gays and straights—in a hierarchy which is not bi-polar, which is to a great extent not even usefully to be defined in terms of groups, and in which virtually everyone *both* suffers and benefits directly.

Up until now, we have in general avoided addressing the problem of *economic* domination, and have confined ourselves almost entirely to sexual and racial dominations, but as regards the distribution of primary gain, these two are quite misleading, for, once again, in these cases, unlike the case of economic domination, those who are dominated achieve no primary gain. Thus it is crucial to turn to economic domination in this context. Unlike most writers in the Marxist tradition, I take it that economic domination is more or less a function of wealth. In other words, it does not seem to me to matter whether or not one owns a factory so much as whether or not one owns *or could purchase and run* a factory, and where this places one in relation to the wealth of other members of the community. Of course, some distinctions need to be made here concerning liquidity of assets, etc., but these are of no great importance in the present context. Moreover, I take it that questions of this sort of domination are primary in one rather obvious sense. A sex-change operation or a blanching of the skin will probably not suffice to transform a woman or a black from a dominated to a dominating individual quite generally—though it may well relieve the person from racist or sexist terrorism, etc. On the other hand, a woman's or black's sudden inheritance of fifty million dollars will effect such a transformation immediately, even to a degree in the realm of racist and sexist terrorism. Certainly some societies have been so blindly racist or sexist as to refuse to honor the money of such an individual, or to legally disallow such inheritance, but ours is not, at least for the most part. Of course, our society is sexist and racist to the degree that women and blacks are less likely to become multi-millionaires, or even have very good incomes. However, if anything, this indicates the primacy of economic hierarchization all the more thoroughly, in that this economic discrimination is widely and, in my view, correctly considered the most pernicious aspect of sexual and racial discrimination, and for precisely the reason that economic advance by either group will tend to diminish domination of that group quite generally.

But, if domination is to a great extent a function of relative wealth, then domination is most often a more diffuse matter than, for example, certain forms of Marxist analysis would indicate. Specifically, economic domination, at least in the United States, is less a question of the domination of workers by capitalists, or even precisely the domination of the poor by the rich, than it is a question of the domination of those who are less wealthy by those who are more wealthy—and this across the board. Thus, for example, most of those we call 'poor' are not merely dominated, but also, with respect to those who are poorer still, dominant. Most of those we call 'wealthy' are not only dominant, but also, with respect to those who are wealthier still, dominated. Thus, again, rather than a merely dual and dichotomous hierarchy, we have a hierarchy in which virtually every individual is in a position of dominance with respect to some, while at once being dominated by others. This indicates one important motivation in the acceptance of the crucial ideologies originally proffered in justification of economic hierarchization. In a multi-tiered, hierarchical society, dominated individuals, say, workers, have quite palpable *primary* gains they wish to maintain, specifically gains of domination. Put crudely, everyone, or virtually everyone has or feels he or she has something to lose in an economic hierarchy such as our own (and unlike that of Marx's England, contemporary El Salvador, etc.). Thus pretty much everyone will be inclined in some degree to accept the ideology which reenforces and justifies the hierarchy in which he or she is, while dominated, dominant as well.

Thus while ideology functions to provide only dominant groups with primary gains, it turns out that in a society such as our own almost the entire population falls into the category of *dominant* relative to some other part of the population. Thus almost everyone receives primary gains from the system of domination and thus has reason to accept an ideology which sustains that system.

However, in accepting such ideologies, most individuals tacitly agree to sacrifice far more than they gain. Primary gain does not provide an adequate explanation of the acceptance of ideology by those who are drastically and unjustly economically limited. These reflections indicate at least some of the reasons why there is a women's liberation movement and a black liberation movement in this country, but no significant, broad-based socialist movement (for further, historical reasons, see Kolko 1984, Chapters 3 and 5). However, they do not explain the widespread opposition of women to the women's movement, the abject loyalty of many members of the working classes to leaders such as Reagan and Thatcher, whose policies run contrary to their interests, and so on. Similarly, it does not explain why sexist clichés, used for centuries to justify the oppression of women, have in recent years been raised on the banner of 'radical feminism.' To begin to understand such phenomena as these, we must, I think, turn to an examination of secondary gain, and of narcissism and transference.

Self-Serving Ideology, Other-Serving Ideology, and Secondary Gain

As we noted above, ideological beliefs are characterized by recalcitrance. Their adoption and/or promulgation are motivated in part by non-logical, non-empirical considerations and they are held despite contravention. This is, of course, a relatively common phenomenon outside of the 'political' realm. The student who insists that his or her teacher is unclear because the student is not able to grasp the material, or the teacher who insists that a student is a moron because the teacher is not able to communicate the material, is an obvious example. We might call this sort of thing 'personal ideology.' At this level, 'personal ideology' is what I will call 'self-serving.' The student's claim that the teacher is incompetent and the teacher's claim that the student is mentally deficient are both self-serving in obvious ways. But the student may convince the teacher that he or she is unable to teach, or the teacher may convince the student that he or she is not fit to study, and at that point the ideology ceases to be self-serving for all those who accept it. While remaining self-serving for one, the ideology becomes 'other-serving' and self-demeaning for the other. Thus, for example, the 'student Jones is incapable of learning'-ideology is self-serving for the teacher and other-serving for student Jones, should he or she adopt it.

Sticking to this example, however, it is clear that secondary gain will accrue to student Jones should he or she adopt this ideology. The student is said to be unfit—possibly stupid, possibly unprepared for a course at that level, possibly lacking skills in that particular area, or whatever. In any event, the student is relieved of responsibility for the course. If the student does not learn, does not receive good marks, he or she is not to blame. Rather the student's educational background, or genes, or upbringing is to blame. Thus when a student accepts a judgment that he or she is unfit, the student gains by it in much the same way he or she gains by accepting and having others accept that the teacher is unfit. Specifically, the student exonerates him/herself. In the one case, the student does so by exalting him/herself above the teacher. In the other case the student does so by demeaning him/herself below the teacher. In either case the goal of eradicating responsibility is achieved.

Let us turn to an example of more ethical and political consequence—the ideology of sexism. Sexist ideology benefits men in the first place. It benefits them at the level of political, social, and economic power. It allows men possibilities for intellectual, artistic, and other achievement denied women. This is obvious. Of course, this is not to claim that there have been no *real* constraints on women in these areas or that all men have had the real power or possibility for intellectual and other achievement. As to the first, historically the principle obstacle in the way of women's achievements was indisputably a matter of real, not ideological constraint. It was a matter of oppression, and, to a lesser degree, terrorism. At various times women could not attend school, vote, testify in court, own land, and so on. The point here is that women were oppressed in these ways and sexist ideology justified this oppression. That is precisely the way in which sexist ideology is, in the first place, a self-serving ideology for men and an other-serving ideology for women, the way in which its benefits are initially benefits to men. As to the dissemination of these benefits among men, this ideology did, in fact, benefit all men *as men*. (Of course, there are subtler ways in which it harmed them also, but they are not of direct concern here.) However, once again, beyond sexist ideology, there are racist ideologies, class ideologies, and so on, which work to benefit some women over some men, and so on. Ultimately, these other ideologies serve to exclude most men from any significant social, economic, or political power.

Returning to the issue at hand, it is clear that the ideology which makes of women infantile naifs, incapable of rigorous cognition, emotionally unstable, and tied to the body—hence the reproductive and nurturant functions thereof—is an ideology which serves to justify and preserve male domination in the academy, government, business, and so on. However, it should be equally clear that, placed in this position, women will, frequently, begin to draw a gain, however slight, out of it. As men succeed, they can fail also and thus be condemned. It must be the case that at least some women, not provided with the possibility of success, come to appreciate the fact that they are protected against failure also. As Cynthia Epstein puts it, "women . . . are lured by secondary gains . . . which remove them from the risks as well as the rewards of competition in the world of affairs in which men labor" (Epstein 1988, p. 234). This, no doubt, is especially true when women are taught, and themselves, it seems, often believe, that, being women, they *would* in fact fail.

Certainly, housewifery and other traditional women's occupations can be extremely difficult. However, *falsely but according to the ideology*, housewifery, etc., are simple jobs and if one finds them difficult, one must be entirely incompetent for 'greater' things. Moreover, the quite serious burden of financial responsibility does not usually lie with a housewife in an ordinary bourgeois family. Thus, although sexist ideology precludes many possible successes, much 'fulfillment' and even elementary autonomy for women, it limits the possibilities for certain forms of failure and humiliation, and it abrogates certain economic and related responsibilities as well, at least for many bourgeois women. While the primary gain of sexist ideology is to men, there is a genuine, if relatively far lesser, secondary gain which arises for women from this same ideology.

Now let us look back at the example of the teacher and student for a moment. Let us suppose that the student is unable to convince the teacher or the school administration that the teacher cannot teach. This student will still be successful in relieving him/herself from guilt and parental condemnation if the student succeeds in convincing him/herself and his or her parents *either* that the teacher cannot teach *or* that he or she is simply unfit as a student. In either case, the student suffers the same objective fate, which is to say he or she receives a poor mark. However, in either case the student also achieves the same gain—he or she loses responsibility for the grade and the ignorance which it implies. The student does not therefore need to exert him/herself and work to succeed and, thereby, risk failure. Failure is guaranteed. But so is exoneration. In one case the student may adopt a self-serving ideology and in another case an other-serving ideology, but in both cases the gain will be much the same—excepting, of course, that in the case of the self-serving ideology, the student is admired as well as relieved of responsibility.

Now beyond these two options there is a third, a sort of variant of both. The student may accept the adequacy of the teaching and assert his or her own inadequacy in comprehension and then go on to claim that in this case the inadequacy is, for various reasons, superior to adequacy. The self-serving ideology, the ideology which blames the teacher, achieves exoneration in the particular case, but allows for responsibility in other cases. The other-serving ideology, the ideology in which the student claims personal inadequacy, exonerates the student in *all* relevant cases, but is demeaning. In this third case, the other-serving ideology, with its secondary gain of complete abrogation of responsibility, is, so to speak, elevated to the level of a self-serving ideology by a simple trick of speech. Those who are unfit are now termed 'superior,' those who are fit, 'inferior.' I will hereafter call the *elevated* other-serving ideology, 'secondary ideology,' in contrast with the self-serving and *unelevated* other-serving 'primary ideologies.'

For those who find this notion of secondary ideology implausible, I should point out that not only is this a possible ideology, it is actual and active. In a class which requires much work and study, those who succeed are stereotyped as 'dexters,' nerds and rags, skags and geeks. Antithetical to the true ultimate party animal, they are unattractive, uncoordinated, uninteresting, unaware, unamerican—and altogether generally abnormal. Clearly, those who are 'unfit' in such a class and in similar classes are to be judged robust and sensible youths, attractive, athletic, engaging, informed—just some healthy, normal kinds of guys and gals, clearly preferable to their more successful peers.

It seems to me that something quite similar has occurred with some of the post-structural feminists and feminists of difference mentioned above. Furthermore, it seems to me it should be clear why this has occurred and why it is, therefore, ideological. Like the student who has been told he or she is unfit and comes to accept this and to enjoy the secondary benefits it brings, at least some women, endlessly told of their 'inferiority,' believe their detractors, accept the stereotypes, and begin to enjoy the secondary benefits, slight as these might be. Thus some women both believe the other-serving ideology of sexism and desire its preservation in some form. However, they also recognize that, like any other-serving ideology, it is demeaning. Much like the final ideology of the student, the new, post-structural feminism of difference provides a way of maintaining the secondary gain while eliminating the demeaning character imposed upon women by the other-serving ideology of sexism. Rather than claiming that men and women are overall of comparable, individual abilities—though women's *opportunities* have been drastically inhibited—it claims that women are indeed illogical, bodily, etc., but that *this is far superior to being logical, cognitive, and so on.* In other words, this feminism of difference in large part takes the other-serving ideology of sexism and turns it into a self-serving ideology merely by reversing what is most often termed 'superior' and what is most often termed 'inferior.'

Of course, this ideology preserves for men what had previously been their primary gain—a putative monopoly on logic, discipline, good sense, and so on. Certainly other feminisms have been, happily, challenging male monopoly in these areas, but such feminisms are not our present concern. Furthermore, if explicitly adopted as an other-serving ideology, the feminism of difference provides to the men who so adopt it the secondary gain of marking them 'progressive,' 'pro-woman,' deserving of lecture and defense, etc. It is little surprise that some of the most ardent advocates of the feminism of difference are men. Without sacrificing the primary gains of sexist ideology, they may accrue not insignificant secondary gains. Moreover, they can at once relax their logic and scholarship, and proclaim their new laxity a revolutionary 'gesture' which 'decenters' the androcentric 'economy.'

As we have already remarked, the new feminism of difference is, in large measure, the old sexism of difference revalorized (a point indicated by a number of writers—see, e.g., Cynthia Epstein 1988, p. 14). It is important to emphasize in this regard the very near identity of what are taken to be the two poles of thought on gender. Moreover, gender ideology is not at all peculiar in this regard. The assumptions of an other-serving ideology and those of such an ideology elevated to self-service are in all cases, by definition, identical. In this way, a dominant ideology may be said to determine its most 'radical' 'counter-ideology.'

By 'dominant ideology' I intend the ideology with respect to a certain number of groups—most often two—which is most widely held with respect to those groups and which 'reproduces' or justifies and thereby fosters the actual relations of domination between the groups. (If both these conditions do not obtain with respect to a single ideology, there is no dominant ideology with respect to the groups in question.) To say that the dominant ideology determines its most radical counter-ideology is to say that the latter is constrained by the *problematic* of the former. What is crucial here is that differences in position which appear to be grave may be such as to assume the same fundamental principles, principles which, in turn, guarantee *one* form of domination. It is clear that any discussion of such domination must address not only the individual ideologies—primary, secondary, other-serving, self-serving—but equally the problematic which underlies these.

The most common sense of 'problematic' is something along the lines of: that which constrains within a compass of 'reasonableness' answers to a particular set of questions. In this sense, a 'problematic' is a matter of doctrine. I will employ 'ideology' for this, seeing no reason to confine the reference of this term to univocal dogma. In other words, I take 'ideology' to encompass not merely 'singular' dogmas, such as 'Women are intuitive and illogical,' but also ranges of doctrine, such as 'The war in Vietnam was wrong because it was not planned and fought well, *or* because it was politically unnecessary, *or* because meddling administrators and newshound buttinskies were interfering with the work of the generals, *or* . . . but *not* because it was fundamentally an imperialist war of aggression.' As Chomsky has repeatedly pointed out, in academia and in the mainstream media what passes as 'reasonable' criticism of the Vietnam war is confined to practical and political questions. The morality of

U.S. intentions especially is beyond question for any 'reasonable' analyst. In other words, the morality of the war is *ideologically determinate*, while the value of its military tactics, its political motivation, etc., are open to dispute.

'Problematic,' on the other hand, I use in the more technical sense of: the set of assumptions common to self-serving primary ideology, other-serving primary ideology, and secondary ideology, or more generally the presuppositions common to an ideology and its permutations.

The sort of primary ideology which we have been examining might be conceived of as providing us with a set of ordered triples of the form: [{group₁, description₁, superior}, {group₂, description₂, inferior}]. For example, [{men; logical, etc.; superior}, {women; intuitive, etc.; inferior}]. This is a self-serving ideology when held by men and an other-serving ideology when held by women. It becomes a secondary ideology whenever there is a permutation, for example, when the values are reversed. Thus, for the preceding example of a primary ideology, the resultant secondary ideology would be: [{men; logical, etc.; inferior} {women; intuitive, etc.; superior}]. (I believe that this is the sort of thing Deborah Cameron has in mind when she criticizes "the inverted sexism which comes from keeping the same old categories and merely swapping round the positions of those who occupy them" [Cameron 1985, p. 127].) More generally, the elevation of a primary to a secondary ideology may be understood as a transformation of [{group₁, description₁, superior}, {group₂, description₂, inferior}] into [{group₁, description₁, inferior}, {group₂, description₂, superior}]. Here, the problematic might be understood to consist in the ordered pairs: [{group₁, description₁}, {group₂, description₂}]—[{male; logical, etc.}, {female; illogical, etc.}] in the particular case of gender.[1]

A problematic might equally encompass the presuppositions common to other permutations. For example, the gender ideology might be shifted such as to pair *female* with logic, etc., and *male* with illogic, etc. In this case, the problematic would involve the belief that the most general cognitive capacities are gender-determined, though it would not involve a fixed pairing of capacity and gender—these would vary with ideology. Such further permutations, however, seem in fact relatively uncommon. For this reason, I will use 'problematic' in the narrower sense, in which it encompasses the descriptive and referential parts, but not the evaluative part, of related ideologies.

To recapitulate, ideology, as we are using the term, is, in the first place, a range of beliefs, which are evidently empirically inadequate, logically invalid, or overinterpretive, and a range of aims which are unjust, that is, which are not coherent with the establishment of a kingdom of ends. Moreover, these beliefs and aims function to foster and preserve a certain sort of domination. Thus, those who dominate accrue primary gains through such ideology. But those who are dominated may themselves accrue secondary gains as well. 'Primary' ideologies, ideologies in their initial form, most often preserve evaluative judgments disagreeable to those who are dominated. The derived or permuted 'secondary' ideologies eliminate or reverse such judgments. It is often in this altered form that the oppressed accept the oppressive ideology; however, as the problematic is maintained in either case, the actual structure of domination remains fundamentally intact.

Psychoanalysis and Ideology

As noted above, beyond real material gains, primary or secondary, there appear to be further, psychological, indeed unconscious, propensities which may be of even greater importance to the acceptance of ideology. Quite generally, psychoanalytic theorists acknowledge two fundamental psychological relations: those to others and those to the self, *object relations* and *narcissism*. In the following pages, I should like to examine some of the ways in which each can be used to support and extend ideological beliefs and aims, particularly among the oppressed. Following this, I should like to examine the extent to which psychoanalytic theory, particularly that of Lacan, can furnish us with an effective response to unconsciously motivated ideology, without simply leading to further, oppressive, psychological manipulations.

1. Essentialism and Narcissism

Once again, essentialist thinking, as I am using the phrase, is thinking in which a particular property of an individual, a property relevant in certain contexts but not in others, is elevated to the level of a *definition* and hence is conceived to be relevant in *all* contexts. For example, the strength of one's arms is relevant in the context of manual labor, but not in the context of teaching—there it is, for example, knowledge and clarity of expression which are, or should be, important. One's skin color, or one's sex, may be relevant to what part one receives in a play, but it is not relevant to, say, teaching, or manual labor. Yet each of these properties is commonly elevated to the level of an essence, definitive of one's being, and hence relevant in all areas. Thus women are thought to be inadequate manual laborers because of their reproductive organs. Of course, there may be a significant statistical correlation between strength and sex, but that is irrelevant, as we have already discussed. When women are refused work in manual labor it is, or at least was, most often due to their sex, not their strength. Similarly, blacks are frequently considered inadequate physicists because of their skin color. Of course, in both cases this is less true than it was in the recent past. On the other hand, it might have reappeared in an insidious form—for example, in English departments, blacks are certainly deemed competent to teach black literature, but are they accepted as readily in Milton studies, or Beowulf, or even modern novel? I do not know, but I fear they are not.

Now, by narcissistic thinking, I refer to thinking whereby one 'identifies' oneself with some group to which one belongs and thereby rejoices in all the victories of that group, whether they are moral or not, whether they in fact benefit one or not, and so on. For example, the St. Louis University High School student cheers the "Junior Billikins" (!) to victory. The superiority of that team in, say, football implies some vague 'superiority' of the entire school and hence the superiority of each student. The victory of the football team is, for the student, in some sense his (all male school) victory, for he identifies his goals, etc., with those of 'the school.' The situation is obviously similar with regard to nationalism, one of the more pernicious forms of narcissistic thinking.

Clearly, when essentialist and narcissistic thinking are combined, the result is an identification with a group defined by a property—a "common quality" in Freud's term (Freud 1959, p. 40)—raised to an essence, such as 'male' or 'white.' (I choose the dominant groups for the reason that it is presumably they who first promulgate the problematic which involves such essentialist narcissism, though it is salient in secondary ideologies also, as the case of, for example, Cixous well illustrates.) The function of such thinking should be clear, but why is it so prominent? Why is it that people are so ready to define themselves and others by gender or race? Why are they so quick to identify their individual goals, etc., with the goals of one group defined particularly *against* one or more other groups? Why is morality or even personal advantage irrelevant? Not surprisingly, I suppose, I have no definitive answer here, though I do have a few suggestions.

First of all, it seems that people are inclined to think categorially. Quite generally, people seem to feel that they 'understand' something only when they have reduced it to a category or cliché which they have been told makes sense, whether *they* in fact make sense of it or not and whether it fits the data or not. In any event, they obscure the particularity of the individual, discourse, etc., by way of making the thing 'comprehensible.' This exclusively categorial thinking is especially pernicious when conjoined with the equally pervasive and equally unreflective acceptance of authority, which ranges from an acceptance of what the President says, 'because he's our president,' to an acceptance of what Derrida says, because he is so highly revered in the profession. For example, one student of mine concluded, with regard to an oral version of the above discussion of Derrida, that it *could* not be correct because if Derrida could be so controverted, he would not be so highly esteemed in the profession—not a far step to similar conclusions about Reagan, totalitarian Sandinist expansionism, and so on. Of course, my student should not simply have accepted what *I* said. The point is that she would not even *consider* my arguments as they did not fit the prevailing dogmas of disciplinary authority.

This prostration before authority starts very early, and innocuously enough. While I for one abhor 'Do it because I said so and I'm your Father [or Mother, or whatever]' 'arguments,' there simply is a point at which explanations and justifications must stop and the child must trust the parent, or the teacher, or whomever. If a child asks why he or she should not eat, say, floor polish, I may explain that it will make him or her sick, but at that point the child will probably just have to trust me—as I have trusted those who labelled the substance poison. No further justification can be offered, short of actually poisoning the dog, or oneself, or the child, I suppose, and thus authority enters in a non-pernicious manner.

In Chapter 2, I more or less dismissed arguments from authority, but that was unfair. Now that we have attended to some motivations of ideological assertions, we are in a position to modify this earlier dismissal. In fact, we are almost always in the position of relying on authority in some measure. If we wish to decide who is right about Nicaragua, we might listen to Ronald Reagan and Jerry Falwell or we might listen to Maryknoll missionary nuns, Amnesty International, members of the German Social Democratic Party, and so on. Even if we have been to Nicaragua ourselves, we are hardly in a position to make any definitive judgments, given necessary limitations on our experiences there. Thus, while we are making our logical arguments, we invoke arguments from authority at virtually all stages, often the specific arguments from authority termed 'testimony.' But, as in court, we must judge the legitimacy of such authority logically. Specifically, we must consider the *competence* of the speaker to observe and judge that of which he or she speaks, the *plausibility* of the speaker's claims internally and in relation to the claims of others, etc., the *motivations* the speaker might have to assert (or not to assert) what he or she claims, and so on. (For an example of this sort of analysis, I refer the reader to any one of Chomsky's books, particularly his *The Fateful Triangle*, in which he repeatedly considers criteria such as these in adjudicating conflicting testimonies.)

When I dismissed arguments from authority, I intended to dismiss those which either do not or cannot rely on any sort of logical argument for the establishment of that authority. This was the case in the two instances cited above in which logical arguments were in fact pushed aside in favor of an authority grounded solely upon popularity. That Reagan was president may indicate something about his popularity, but it does not in itself indicate anything about his competence, good will, etc., with respect to Nicaragua. Moreover, when we are asked to accept Reagan as an authority in the appropriate sense, we are asked to ignore the other evidence available to us—the compelling evidence of Amnesty International, the Permanent Tribunal of Peoples, Americas Watch, and so on. Indeed, Reagan did not ask us to consider his assertions as plausible testimony in the context of other plausible testimonies, etc. Rather, he asked us to ignore all other evidences and accept his testimonies, his 'analyses,' and his conclusions alone and in their entirety. Similarly, my student's complaint concerning my criticism of Derrida simply and without guile advised ignoring what Derrida says, how he argues it and to what extent his arguments are valid, what the empirical claims of his theory are and to what extent they are plausible, and so on, and attending, rather, to the relative status of Derrida and of myself. In other words, what this student found crucial was not Derrida's work, nor my construal or misconstrual thereof, nor the validity or invalidity of my arguments or Derrida's arguments. What was crucial was Derrida's exaltation among American English and Comparative Literature professors, most especially those at Yale—his popularity in a certain group.

Now, it is quite clear that arguments from authority are widely used by parents, teachers, clergy, and others in 'training' young children, and, as I have remarked, this is to a degree necessary. Moreover, it is to a degree necessary that children's earliest education involve a good deal of categorial thinking, toward the end of deriving empirical generalizations, and so on. However, ideology enters virtually at birth, and the authority of parents, educators, et al., goes to establish *definitive* and *essential* categories for the child, categories which, as I have remarked, are deemed relevant in *all* contexts. For example, in every way the male child and the female child are treated differently, spoken of differently, and so on. Each child is taught to identify others first by essential category—sex, race, religion, in some cases, or caste—and only secondarily by 'individual difference.' Moreover, narcissistic thinking is fostered in this context, for just as others are essentially defined, so is the child him/herself. The child first begins to form any notion of self largely upon the basis of what his or her parents say about the child, and these parents are almost certainly going to define any child as a boy or girl, as white or black, and so on, from the first. In a sense, the child cannot help but develop narcissistic patterns of thought for the very formation of his or her 'ego' (in roughly Lacan's sense of self-construal—on which, see Hogan forthcoming b) has been, to a very great extent, categorial and essentialist.

Thus we are faced with a dilemma. Narcissistic and essentialist thinking fit well into the categorial thinking in which the child is trained. They rely on a similar deference to authority, and are of a piece with the 'identifications' through which the child's ego gains definition. However, categorial thinking and deference to authority are to some degree necessary for any learning. Similarly, such 'identifications' as foster 'gender-identity' seem crucial for healthy sexual and emotional development (by 'healthy' here, I should note, I intend non-neurotic, not necessarily non-perverse, and certainly not necessarily heterosexual). So, how, then, are we to respond to this dilemma? In general it is at least clear that we should discourage essentialist and narcissistic thinking and encourage self-consciousness about the limitations of categorial thinking and of argument from authority; if we continue to think essentialistically and narcissistically, if we are unreflective and uncritical in categorial thinking, and if we proffer and accept arguments from authority other than those 'logical arguments from authority' mentioned above, we, *by these very acts*, promote ideological thinking, both in ourselves and in others. More concretely, there are a number of specific 'practices' we might undertake. For example, parents might work not to treat sex as germane in all contexts, either through speech or through practice—by, say, employing methods of dual parenting along the lines suggested by Nancy Chodorow in *The Reproduction of Mothering*.

However, before we can fully develop a specific response to the problems of essentialism, narcissism, prostration before authority, etc., a more detailed understanding of the transferential nature of these phenomena is crucial. Specifically, we see in the preceding cases two critical sorts of relation which contribute to an explanation of the acceptance of other-serving ideologies: (1) identification with a group by way of a property assumed essential, and (2) the elevation of some individual to a position of infallible authority, most often upon the basis of that person's position of dominance within an institution. Freud refers to the former as the identification of the ego with an object, analyzing the latter in terms of the replacement of the ego ideal by an object (see Freud 1959, pp. 46ff.). Similarly, but possibly more accurately, Heinz Kohut analyzes the former in terms of a narcissistic transference involving an archaic or infantile "grandiose self." He views the latter as a narcissistic transference involving an archaic or infantile "idealized parent imago" (see Kohut 1971, p. 27). Independent of the details of Freud's and Kohut's analyses, it should be clear to anyone of a psychoanalytic orientation that there is a significant transferential component involved in the acceptance of other-serving ideologies, most particularly insofar as these involve the sorts of narcissism and deference that we have been discussing. Thus I should like to conclude with an examination of what is to my mind the most insightful and most directly politically relevant conception of and response to the transference—that of Jacques Lacan. I will begin by examining the transference and the handling of the transference as specifically clinical phenomena and seek to extrapolate from there to some more general conclusions about ideology and the critique of ideology.

2. Lacan, the Constitution of the Transference, and the Constitution of Ideological Authority

As Lacan pointed out at various times, Freud's first serious practical and theoretical encounter with the transference, most particularly in its function as a resistance to analysis and in its relation to countertransference, came during his analysis of Ida Bauer, "Dora," and his subsequent reconsideration of that analysis in both editions of the *Bruchstück einer Hysterie-Analyse*. It is only fitting that Lacan, whose most renowned project was the engineering of a "return to Freud," should first address the problem of the transference in an essay dealing with Freud's analysis of Dora.

In the course of his "Intervention sur le transfert," Lacan undertakes to derive a general understanding of the nature and genesis of the transference by examining Freud's failure adequately to handle the transference in his analysis of Dora. I should like to look carefully at Lacan's notion of the transference as expressed in this essay, seeking to discern Lacan's answers to two practically and theoretically critical questions: (1) What is the transference? and (2) How does the transference arise?

2.1 WHAT IS THE TRANSFERENCE?

The first problem for any theorist seeking to re-articulate a fundamental theoretical concept is to establish for that concept some independent content which might allow it fruitfully to be compared with earlier articulations. Lacking that independent content, there is no way of assuring that the two articulations are in any usual sense articulations of one concept, formulations referring to one type of object. For example, Lacan argued forcefully against the common American practice of 'allying oneself with the healthy part of the analysand's ego.' I have on occasion heard people object to Lacan's arguments on the grounds that he and his antagonists are talking at cross purposes. Lacan, they say, objects to any sort of 'alliance with the ego' on the grounds that the ego is not the friend, but rather the enemy of analysis. However, they continue, this only goes to show that Lacan's conception of the ego is different from that of, say, Heinz Hartmann or Anna Freud. All three use the *word* 'ego,' but their *concepts* are crucially different. It is even possible, they conclude, that Heinz Hartmann or Anna Freud would agree with Lacan, if they understood his concept of the ego, and vice-versa. Now in fact I think this argument is wrong and that Lacan does establish independent content for the notion of the ego, but that is unimportant here. By this example, I wish only to illustrate the importance of establishing independent content for any concept which is to be reformulated. The point is simply that we need independent content to establish a common *concept*; otherwise we have only a common *term*.

In this regard, Lacan's focus upon Freud's *Bruchstück einer Hysterie-Analyse* is fortunate. Whether or not Lacan intended to employ Freud's case to this end, it serves to provide independent content for the notion of the transference and thus gives Lacan a common ground with his antagonists, a ground upon which meaningful debate can occur. Specifically, the transference is what results in the premature cessation of Dora's analysis. It involves Dora's feelings of hostility toward Freud, as well as her implicit assumption of the role of the governess in giving Freud a two-week notice (see Freud 1981, p. 101), her tacit identification of Freud and Herr K., and so on. Thus the transference is the cause of the premature termination of the analysis insofar as this involves hostile feelings *in* the analysis and insofar as these feelings in some degree derive from hostile feelings *outside of* and *earlier than* the analysis, specifically from events and fantasies appertaining to the neurotic conflict.

The crucial question, then, is—how exactly does this derviation function? Is it, for example, merely a shifting of feelings or affects? In other words, is it just that Dora has certain feelings about Herr

K. which, in the course of the analysis, simply come to be directed at Freud? Certainly there is such a redirecting of feeling, but to say this is merely to restate the problem, not to propose a solution. Surely, a transference of affects cannot occur spontaneously or independently of any other attitude and still be considered a *transference*. If Dora is angry with Herr K. and is then subsequently angry with Freud, but her conscious and unconscious relations to the two men are assimilable in no other way, then it seems that we merely have two distinct instances of anger and not the transferral, redirection, reincarnation, etc., of a single instance. Here we cannot distinguish transference from a choleric temperament.

Much the same is true of a transference of patterns of behavior. If Dora behaves similarly with Freud and Herr K., but her conscious and unconscious relations to the two men are once more entirely unlike, then it seems that we simply have two instances of one type of behavior—say, rejection—rather than the transferral, redirection, reincarnation, etc., of a single instance. Here we cannot distinguish transference from mere habit.

Now for Lacan, it is quite clear that there is indeed a transferral of affects. Thus there is a positive transference involving positive feelings and a negative transference involving negative feelings. He defines these, if somewhat facetiously, in *Les quatre concepts fondamentaux de la psychanalyse*, saying "the positive transference, that's when whomever it concerns, the analyst in this case, well! one has a soft spot for him[/her]—negative, one keeps an eye on him[/her]" (p. 114; my translation here and throughout). As this indicates, for Lacan the negative transference centrally involves an attitude of scepticism—and such an attitude is certainly one salient affective feature of Dora's negative transference.

As to patterns of behavior, Lacan just as clearly accepts these. Indeed, in the first volume of the *séminaire*, Lacan indicates the centrality to psychoanalytic method of the isolation of such patterns. As he puts it, "what Freud teaches us, the good analytic method, consists in recovering always the same rapport, the same relation, the same schema, that presents itself at once in actual forms, comportments, and, equally, in the interior of the analytic relation" (p. 53). For Lacan, as for most writers, the transference is a form of repetition. Indeed, it is an *acting out*, a sort of *behavior* in which the analysand, unbeknown to him/herself, expresses in action precisely those beliefs and desires which the analysand is unable to express in words. As Lacan puts it in *Les Quatre Concepts*, echoing Freud's claims in "Recollection, Repetition, and Working-Through," "the transference is the acting out [*la mise en acte*] of the reality of the unconscious" (p. 133).

But here the question is—upon what is this acting-out based? What does it mean for Dora to act out her unconscious conflicts in the analysis such that she behaves toward Freud as towards Herr K., etc.? Lacan gives a concise but very revealing answer to this question in the "Intervention sur le Transfert." The transference, Lacan tells us, is the apparition in the analysis "of the permanent modes according to which [the analysand] constitutes his[/her] objects" (p. 225). *Prima facie*, this seems to be a very simple assertion—and also one which is not very informative or helpful. However, there is a great deal concealed in this brief statement—in fact, an entire network of phenomenological claims and an implicit phenomenological analysis. It cannot be accidental that Lacan chose the phenomenological verb "constituer"—which translates Edmund Husserl's "konstituieren"—in this context. Lacan was not only familiar with phenomenological principles, but considered himself engaged in a sort of phenomenological enterprise from very early on. For example, in his 1933 essay "Le problème du style et la conception psychiatrique des formes paranoiaques de l'expérience," Lacan refers to his own 1932 dissertation, *De la psychose paranoiaque dans ses rapports avec la personnalité* as one of "the works of phenomenological inspiration" (p. 385). In his "Exposé général de nos travaux scientifiques" of the same year he emphasizes the indispensability of phenomenological analysis (p. 399). In another early essay, "Au-delà du 'Principe de réalité,'" Lacan begins his reconstruction of the "*Revolution of the Freudian Method*" with a "Phenomenological Description of the Psychoanalytic Experience." Lacan also makes explicit reference to phenomenology and phenomenological constitution in his discussions of the mirror stage, refers to the phenomenological notion of "bracketing" in "Variantes de la cure-type" of 1935 (p. 337), and so on. It seems clear then that this brief definition of the transference refers implicitly to both the original, 'pure' phenomenological principles of Edmund Husserl and the partially derivative, psychoanalytic-phenomenological principles of Lacan himself. Thus, to understand

Lacan's conception of the transference, we must step back for a moment and consider the notion, varieties, and function of constitution in Husserl and in Lacan.

In its broadest sense, 'constitution' refers to the synthesis of a unity. Specifically, it involves the relation and integration of various separately grasped aspects of a single object. Perceptual constitution, which we examined briefly in Chapter 2, is probably the easiest to illustrate. Imagine that you are looking at a statue. You approach, seeing one aspect of the statue. At the edges, this aspect, you might say, shades off into the outline, providing hints as to what might be found on the other side or sides. As you move around the statue, you perceive different aspects. Suppose the statue is of a man or woman. If you first see the front, you have hints of the sides. Moving clockwise, you now see the right side of the statue. The frontal aspect is now reduced to a mere hint—and a hint of the back, formerly completely occluded, is now available. Continuing clockwise, you view the back, with hints of the sides again, and so on. Now, your perceptions of the various aspects of this statue are not entirely discrete and unrelated phenomena. As you proceed about the statue, you, so to say, put the aspects together to form a unity. You relate the frontal aspect to the dorsal aspect, the dorsal aspect to the lateral aspects, and so on, in such a way as to form an understanding of the statue as *one* thing. This synthesis is the perceptual *constitution* of the statue.

Now, imagine the same thing for another subject. You see this person act in certain ways, hear the person say certain things; hear things about him or her, and so on. Again, you do not experience these as entirely discrete, unrelated phenomena. Rather you synthesize them in order to *constitute* another subjectivity, to come to an understanding of this subject as *one* subject. Finally, imagine this for yourself. For Lacan, the same process is involved in self-constitution as in the constitution of others. One forms a unified intentional object of oneself through the same sort of synthesis of experience, inference, and hearsay. (For a more extended discussion of this, see Hogan forthcoming b.)

In this context, it is extremely important to recognize that for Husserl and, as I understand him, for Lacan constitution is not and cannot be presuppositionless. Let us return to our example of the statue. When you view the frontal aspect, you recognize it as a man or woman and you project expectations beyond those given by the outline. More generally, you understand the statue in a constitutive manner before you begin to circumambulate, before you scrutinize its various aspects. You do this because you have seen both statues and people and you recognize the work in front of you as having certain features in common with these. As Husserl claims in section 38 of the Fourth Meditation, any constitution leads to a "history" of antecedent formations or constitutions of the same object or other objects of the same type. "Everything known points to an original becoming acquainted," Hussel tells us; "what we term unknown has yet a form of knownness, the object form, more exactly the spatial object form, cultural object form, tool form, and so on" (p. 82). This original acquaintance itself indicates a "primal instituting" (p. 82).

This primal instituting, then, derivative of an original becoming acquainted, determines our expectations. For example, our primal instituting of a *human form* might govern our expectations in viewing a certain statue. However, the expectations determined by our primal instituting may not always prove accurate. Our new experience may not cohere with the earlier form. Thus, as you move around the statue, you may encounter certain unexpected features which force you not only to specify but to *alter* your original judgment. You may find that the thing is not a human form at all, at least as you originally conceived of this—for example, it may turn out to have wings and thus be angelic, or a control box and thus be robotic, and so on. Jean Piaget refers to the entire process of recognizing and revising as the assimilation to and accommodation of a schema (see, e.g., Piaget 1971, p. 172; a recent, outstanding development and reformulation of these concerns may be found in Holland, et al. 1986; for an extension of this notion to literary analysis, see Hirsch 1976, pp. 32ff.; see also the related Gombrich 1972). Simply put, for Piaget, we have a schema or pattern or idea of a human form in our minds. Upon getting our first glimpse of the statue, we *assimilate* this glimpsed thing to our schema or pattern or idea. However, as we walk around the statue, we may encounter features which do not cohere with our schema. In that event, we *accommodate* the schema to the particularity of the object viewed. Thus while, as Husserl puts it, it is only "on the basis of already pre-given objects" that we may "originally constitute new objects"

(p. 80), it is still the case that the latter constitution is new, involving both specification and alteration or accommodation of the previously constituted form. In other words, we do not merely apply preconceived forms, we restructure them also.

Extending this notion to subjectivity, it should be clear that much the same holds. If we hear of someone's passionate interest in the music of Elliott Carter we begin to constitute that individual well beyond attributing to him or her a passionate interest in the music of Elliott Carter. As we become further acquainted with this individual we may come to recognize that the previously constituted form to which we assimilated the person is inadequate. For example, I take it that most of us would assume that someone passionate about Elliott Carter would not be passionate about Barry Manilow—except possibly in his or her revulsion. Thus if we met someone who was passionate about Carter, we would assimilate that person to a certain schema, constituting his or her subjectivity on the basis of prior constitutions, and thus assuming, among other things, that the person was not terribly enthusiastic about Barry Manilow's music or other music of Manilow's sort. However, we would have to *accommodate* this schema were it to turn out that he or she was, in fact, a Manilow enthusiast. In other words, we would have to *re-constitute* the person's subjectivity in light of this new datum.

It is easy enough to see how this hierarchical conception of constitution could enter into psychoanalytical considerations—specifically, in the young child's constitutions of him/herself and his or her parents. (This connection has been suggested by Paul Ricoeur, probably at least in part upon the basis of Lacan's teachings; see Ricoeur 1970, pp. 380ff.) These early constitutions, very similar to the self- and parental-imagos of classical psychoanalysis, are evidently the earliest fully articulated constitutions of subjectivity. This is not crucial in and of itself. After all, these could easily enough be accommodated to new individuals and for the most part they are. However, constitutions quite generally involve subjective attitudes and are integrated into our fantasies concerning the individuals in question. For this reason, certain constitutions imply repressed fantasies, and thus themselves come to be repressed along with those fantasies. In this way, for example, the unconscious oedipal complex may be understood as nothing more than a complex of oedipal constitutions of self and parents along with the oedipal fantasies in which these constitutions are embedded. Clearly, insofar as these or other ego- and parent-constitutions are unconscious—and this is what is crucial—they are not open to accommodation; they are not available for reconstitution. Repressed constitutions are necessarily ossified.

Here we arrive at the first point I should like to derive from Lacan's essay—that concerning the nature of the transference. For Lacan, I take it, in the transference there is an assimilation of the analyst and the analysand to certain infantile constitutions or schemata which are not open to reconstitution or accommodation. As these infantile constitutions involve both affects and patterns of behavior, they entail the sorts of phenomena observed above and thereby satisfy our 'identity of concept' criterion. Thus, we have an answer to our question concerning the nature of the transference— it is, so to speak, an 'arrested' constitution, an unaccommodatable, unconscious assimilation of the analysand and the analyst to unconscious, infantile (ultimately oedipal) constitutions, involving beliefs, aims, affects, patterns of behavior, and so on.

However, we have not yet touched the crucial question, the question to which most of Lacan's essay is devoted, the question concerning the *genesis* of the transference. I should now like to consider this second problem.

2.2 HOW DOES THE TRANSFERENCE ARISE?

If the transference involves the assimilation of the analyst and analysand to infantile constitutions, how does it happen that the analyst and analysand come to be so assimilated? Is it merely a spontaneous act on the part of the analysand, for example? This hardly seems possible, for then it would be difficult to explain why at least some of the analysand's non-analytic relationships are or may be non-transferential while his or her analytical relationships are necessarily and have necessarily been transferential; why even transferential relations differ one from another, and so on. Could it be then that the transference relations are generated by the repressed contents closest to the analysand's reflections and associations at a given time in the analysis? This is certainly more plausible, but still does not explain why certain contents come to be *recalled* and *expressed* while others come to be *acted out*.

According to Lacan, the problem with these and related accounts of the transference is that they make reference to the analysand alone. No doubt everyone recognizes that the analyst plays a part in what the analysand discovers about him/herself. Indeed, if the analyst did not, then he or she would be entirely superfluous to an analysis. But given that the analyst has a part in what the analysand does come to know, it would appear that he or she must have a part in what the analysand does not come to know, but rather transfers, as well. This, then, is Lacan's first point about the transference—the analyst has a part in it ("l'analyste y a sa part," p. 218).

If we return for a moment to Lacan's conception of constitution, we should be able to see why and how this might be the case. Clearly, constitution involves a *dialectic* of the usual sort parodied by Hegel with the terms "thesis, antithesis, synthesis." The initial schema—for example, that of a *human form*—functions thetically; the contravening datum—for example, the pair of wings—functions antithetically; and the resultant, accommodated schema— here, the angelic form—functions synthetically. Lacan is quite clear that in his view the subject-constitutions germane to psychoanalysis must be understood to be dialectical. Thus, in his essay on criminology, Lacan says of the mirror stage, the initial stage of self-constitution, that "man[/woman] constitutes him[/her]self *dialectically*" (p. 141, my emphasis).

Now it should be clear that the proceeding of *psychoanalysis itself* involves a sort of constitution also, a constitution of subjects, states of affairs, and so on. Thus when Dora speaks of her father's effectively exchanging her for Frau K., she constitutes a state of affairs which could hardly be directly present to her as a whole. Moreover, when Freud intervenes and asks Dora to explain her own complicity in this exchange, he in effect presents her with a negation of or antithesis to her constitutive thesis, as Lacan explains. Dora must then accommodate her constitution of the situation, reconstitute it incorporating the 'negative moment' introduced by Freud—and she does precisely that, Lacan tells us. In this analysis, constitution remains dialectical, but it is the analyst, and not the thing itself, that provides the negative moment and the impetus for reconstitution. For Lacan, such a dialectic of constitution by the analysand and re-constitution spurred by the analyst is absolutely crucial to any psychoanalytic practice. As Lacan argues early in his essay on transference, "In a psychoanalysis . . . the subject . . . *constitutes him/herself* through a discourse into which the mere presence of the psychoanalyst introduces *the dimension of dialogue*, even prior to any intervention" (p. 216, my emphasis). Moreover, this dialogical constitution, which makes up "the psychoanalytic experience" is precisely "*a dialectical experience*" (p. 216).

A dialectical conception of psychoanalysis was, of course, important to Lacan's thought throughout this period and after. The necessity of a dialectical conception of the subject is stressed in *Les complexes familiaux* of 1938 (p. 94), the "Discours de Rome" of 1953 (see pp. 292f., 385), *Les écrits techniques de Freud* of 1953–54 (see pp. 7, 306), even the "Subversion du sujet et dialectique de désir dans l'inconscient freudien" of 1960, and elsewhere. Here, however, its importance is precisely in explaining the genesis of the transference—more exactly, the negative transference. As Lacan puts it, "we are going to attempt to *define, in terms of pure dialectic, the transference* which is termed negative" (p. 218). Specifically, Lacan maintains that the "permanent modes according to which" the analysand "constitutes his/her objects" appear "in a moment of stagnation of the analytic dialectic" (p. 225). In other words, the transference sets in when the dialectic which defines the analysis fails to continue, stagnates, fails to provide the negative, contravening, reconstitutive moment.

Now Lacan's point should be perfectly clear. The transference, we have seen, is for Lacan the institution of a specific sort of 'arrested' constitution, a constitution in which present subjects, situations, etc., are unconsciously assimilated to specific unconscious prototypes, with no accommodation on the part of the prototypical constitutions. In ordinary life, accommodation is spontaneous. However, in analysis it is, as we have seen, the job of the analyst to trigger accommodation. The analyst, in other words, plays the antithetical role in the dialectic of constitution. The analysand proposes a constitution. The analyst in response provides the negation, antithesis, or contravening datum that forces a *re*constitution, which reconstitution must, in turn, be negated, and so on. This dialectic stagnates then only as the result of "an error of the analyst" (p. 226), an error in which he or she fails to produce the proper negation which will effect reconstitution.

Unfortunately, Lacan does not seem to recognize that the anti-thetical, contravening function must be fully reciprocal, that both analyst and analysand must be free to adopt the negative position, if true dialectic is going to occur. Similarly, Lacan appears to ignore the fact that the institutional authority of the analyst establishes a dissymmetry in the analytic relationship which inhibits dialectic right from the beginning and lends to the analyst's statements—whether negative or positive—a weight which any assertions of the analysand necessarily lack. These factors, I think, distort his inter-pretation of the Dora case and limit his understanding of the broader concerns of justice which attach to any dialectic, including that of psychoanalysis.

But Lacan is not entirely silent on the question of authority. Indeed, in later writing, Lacan comes to analyse the transference in terms of what he calls the "sujet supposé savoir" (the "subject supposed to know"). And it is here that Lacan provides us with an indication of some practical and political consequences of his anal-ysis of the transference.

2.3 AUTHORITY, IDEOLOGY, AND DIALECTIC

Already in *Les écrits techniques*, Lacan claims that readiness to transference is to be found whenever the analysand seeks his or her "truth" in the analyst (see p. 306). By the time of *Les quatre concepts*, he has gone so far as to conclude that "As soon as there is a sujet supposé savoir somewhere . . . there's transference" (p. 210). A sujet supposé savoir is a subject who is in an absolute position of authority. Lacan's claim, then, is that supposed doctrinal authority is the root of the transference as it is necessarily the antithesis of dialectic—though once again he evidently fails to recognize the institutional contexts of such supposition.

Dialectic, of course, began with the Socratic practice of interro-gation. This practice was designed in the first place precisely to undermine dogmatic certainty, as Plato has Socrates emphasize in the "Apology." In other words, the first task Socrates set for himself in his dialectical work was to undermine the position of the sujet supposé savoir, to demonstrate to everyone that "He, O men, is the wisest, who . . . knows that his wisdom is in truth worth nothing" (p. 65). Moreover, Socrates undertook this 'negative' dia-lectical project precisely in order to open the way for 'positive' dialectic on substantive moral, epistemological, and related topics. The point to be drawn from Lacan, then, is that if either analyst or analysand takes him/herself or his or her antagonist to be the sujet supposé savoir, then the dialectic must stagnate. One can listen to the sujet supposé savoir and repeat his or her dicta, but not address a response thereto, not engage in a dialectic.

In its general outlines, this view is not startling. In social terms, it is, for example, closely related to the claim that in what Karl Popper calls a "closed society" (see Popper 1962), rational, dialectical thought is stifled by dogma. What is important about Lacan's formulation, however, is the manner in which it points toward a way in which we might begin to address the question of the internal constraints which afflict us in our acceptance of the ruling, oppressive ideologies. Specifically, Lacan's work indicates that we establish a sujet supposé savoir, or many sujets supposés savoir, based upon our original, unconscious constitutions of such a sujet in our childhood in the authoritarian nuclear family. In this context Lacan's work on technique implies that a central task of any critique of ideology is the relentless criticism, in a negative dialectic, of the supposed certainty of sujets supposés savoir, even outside of clinical analysis. But this, however important, is not sufficient. We must add to Lacan's personal dialectic a practical response to the *institutions* which re-establish the notion and the structure of a dialectic-inhibiting sujet supposé savoir—the schools, the churches, childrens' organizations, and so on.

Thus to the degree that our acceptance of an other-serving ideology is a matter of transference in Lacan's sense, we must undertake a two-fold praxis. We must first criticize relentlessly others and ourselves; we must continually engage in negative and positive dialectic. This involves a rigorous adherence to the fundamental principles of logic and the principle of minimal interpretation, without which dialogue is impossible; it involves a commitment to truth along with an eschewal of dogma and dogmatic certainty; it involves intellectual sincerity and human decency; it involves observation, study, and reflection. Finally, it involves something which, as we have already remarked, Lacan does not appear to recognize in the psychoanalytic dialectic—absolute reciprocity.[2]

Second, we must seek to dismantle all those structures which establish or reenforce the constitution of a sujet supposé savoir.

This means that we must restructure, or abolish, the family in which children are conceived to be the property of the parents and in which reason has no place when confronted with authority; it means that we must restructure, or abolish, the schools in which dialectic is replaced by indoctrination or undisciplined, narcissistic effusion; it means we must restructure, or abolish, religion and the various associations which serve to accustom children to accepting thoughtlessly the dicta of authority. It means that we must do away with the state, and with private ownership—or ownership *tout court*—of capital goods. It also means that we must do away with ownership of knowledge. It means that we must struggle against the subtler forms of intellectual intimidation, from conformism to rhetorical manipulation. It means that we must never dismiss new ideas because they do not adhere to accepted principles or reject older views because they are no longer fashionable. The point of dialectic is to foster further study, refinement, reflection, rigor, circumspection, and invigorated investigation, not dogmatically to foreclose investigation. Thus, our second task is to work to create the social and political conditions in which dialectic will thrive and the tendency to constitute others as *sujets supposés savoir* will wither. It is such institutional concerns, specifically those of the university and the profession of literary study, to which we now turn in conclusion.

5

The Ideology of the Humanities and the Political Economy of Criticism: Notes Toward the Constitution of an Anarchist University

> The university should be a center for radical social inquiry. . . .
> It should loosen its 'institutional forms' even further, to permit
> a richer variety of work and study and experimentation, and
> should provide a home for the free intellectual, for the social
> critic, for the irreverent and radical thinking that is desperately
> needed if we are to escape from the dismal reality that threat-
> ens to overwhelm us. The primary barrier to such a develop-
> ment will not be the unwillingness of administrators or the
> stubbornness of trustees. It will be the unwillingness of stu-
> dents to do the difficult and serious work required, and the
> fear of the faculty that its security and authority, its guild
> structure, will be threatened.
>
> NOAM CHOMSKY, "The Function of the University
> in a Time of Crisis" (Chomsky 1973, p. 315)

A few years ago, in an article in *The Chronicle of Higher Education*, Michael D. Yates, Professor of Economics at the University of
Pittsburgh, argued that "Nowhere in the industrialized world is
anti-communism more the official, state-sponsored ideology than it

is in the United States, and nowhere are academics as subservient to state interests as they are here" (Yates 1986, p. 84). Yates went on to explain the imperialist function of this ideology and the complicity of American universities in the atrocities of U.S. imperialism. He also pointed to the racism of these institutions. To Yates' charges, I would add that the university is not only racist and imperialist, but sexist and internally exploitative also. Subservient to capitalist ideologies and the exploitative hierarchies they function to support, academicians go on to foster further *academic* ideologies which assure the continued existence of their own exploitative hierarchies. Moreover, academicians seek rigorously to maintain their ideological purity. As Yates pointed out, "let a curriculum vitae appear that gives the sender away as a leftist, never mind a communist, and the applicant will be rejected out of hand." Only when one's 'radicalism' is confined to 'decentring the subject' in Pope or 'overturning the hierarchies of signs' in Wordsworth is it fully acceptable in the academy. Then one's 'radicalism' is not political, and may even serve to substitute for political radicalism. Thus it is not only accepted, but encouraged.

The extensive ideological uniformity of the American university, its frequent operation as a sort of organ of state propaganda (in, e.g., the sense of 'state' proposed by Chomsky in Chomsky 1985, p. 230), has been widely discussed and analyzed (see, e.g., Chomsky 1969, pp. 23–158 and 309–67; and Chomsky 1982, pp. 60–86). The concrete economic reasons for this uniformity have been explored also (see, e.g., Ridgeway 1968 and, more recently, Noble 1989; there are also narrower studies which touch upon these issues for specific disciplines—on Medicine, see, for example, Moss 1980, pp. 253–301 and throughout). I will not undertake to cover this ground again. Rather, in the following pages, I should like to discuss some of the ideologies of the discipline of English and some of the political and economic factors which may be said to condition these ideologies.

Specifically, I will begin by looking at some of the ways in which English departments serve to disseminate official, government ideologies. Richard Ohmann has discussed in detail the way in which the teaching of composition tends to encourage, for example, ahistorical thinking (see Ohmann 1976, pp. 133–206) and thereby tends to support the ahistorical, capitalist ideology dominant in the

United States today. In stressing this theme, Ohmann expresses what is perhaps the main concern of literary critics who have in recent years examined the problem of ideology in the teaching of literature and composition. Since my own concerns in the following pages will be quite different from those of Ohmann and others, it is worth saying a few words about classroom instruction and historicism before continuing.

To begin with, I am unsure that the practices Ohmann describes actually foster ahistorical thinking or the like. Moreover, I am not sure that ahistorical thinking is all that crucial to capitalist ideology today, despite the claims of Marx and Engels that such thinking gives rise to the "misconception that induces [one] to transform into eternal laws of nature and of reason, the social forms springing from [the] present mode of production and form of property" (Marx and Engels 1975, p. 54). In other words, it seems to me that John and Jane Doe are just as likely to draw cynical as radical conclusions from a knowledge of the historical development and conditions of capitalism. Finally, and most important, the relevance of 'historicization' to a given issue is a matter for empirical study. Particular aspects of psychology, language, economy, social organization, gender, and so on, may or may not be 'historical products.' Issues of historicism cannot be decided *a priori.*

Unfortunately, there is a very strong tendency among Marxist and other politically oriented literary theorists to decide issues of historicism globally and without serious empirical study on specific issues. A particularly striking case is that of Fredric Jameson, who, at the outset of *The Political Unconscious*, asserts that the injunction "Always historicize!" is "the one absolute" (Jameson 1981, p. 9). I would agree with Jameson, Ohmann, and others that historical analysis is extremely valuable for gaining any adequate understanding of a broad range of issues. But in each case the historicist view must be treated as an hypothesis. While it may be of some political benefit to encourage students to consider historicist hypotheses, particularly in a few specific areas, the pedagogical insistence upon an historicist dogma which frequently verges upon religion can only be detrimental to the sort of critical thinking we should like to encourage in our students and in ourselves.

For these reasons, when I discuss the dissemination of official ideologies in our classrooms, I will not take up the common theme of ahistorical thought. Rather, I will be concerned with the more narrowly and obviously political function of directly teaching imperialist distortions of history, explicitly confining the range of possible debate within the problematic of capitalism, and so on. This, I will argue, is not at all unknown in our composition classes—or, for that matter, our literature classes.

Following a discussion of this issue, I should like to turn to the economy and political structure of the English department and its place in the university. English departments, like most university departments, are residually feudal, guild-structures impacted into the capitalist economy of the university and, thereby, that of the society as a whole. In this context, the English department has generated its own mythologies of quality in instruction and 'scholarship,' mythologies which I should like to examine.

From here, I will turn to the economics of criticism in the profession as a whole. Intellectual products are commodities and, like all commodities, the 'value' they are judged to have is primarily *market* value. Professional ideologies tell us that the value of a theory or a piece of criticism is its truth, its subversive force, its humanizing potential. Similarly, professional ideologies tell us that the value of a literary work is its aesthetical excellence, its moral perfection, and so on. In fact, I will maintain, these considerations are rarely important to actual judgments and practices.

Following this, I will conclude with some utopian conjectures on the way in which the university might be restructured, to its intellectual and moral benefit, along anarchist lines, lines which might foster the sort of dialectic which we discussed in the preceding chapter and which is to a great extent suppressed by the actual structures of the university today.

National Ideology and Literary Study

1. Imperialism and the Example of Composition

As I have remarked, the ideological uniformity of the university as a whole has been widely discussed, though it remains widely denied at the same time. The complicity of academicians in ideologization and oppression is most clear in the physical sciences, where the bulk of research is oriented directly toward military or industrial concerns—as Marx and Engels put it, "Big industry . . . made natural science subservient to capital" (Marx and Engels 1976, pp. 77–78). Sometimes it is thought that the humanities are non-ideological or even anti-ideological, at least as regards the crudest imperialist, sexist, and other ideologies. It is my contention, on the contrary, that the teaching of English, and most particularly the teaching of composition—which is, in effect, the prime task of and principle justification for an English department in most universities—is frequently a far more ideological undertaking than that of any discipline outside the social sciences. Specifically, in composition, students are taught the 'proper' modes of argument. While claiming to teach valid argumentation, composition classes in fact function, at least in part, to inculcate ideologically defined 'limits of rational discourse.' Those who adopt theses which fall outside the problematic of dominant ideology, cite ideologically impure sources, etc., are swiftly informed that their 'writing' is inadequate. It does not take students long to learn what 'good writing' really is and to seek to conform their essays thereto.

As a graduate student, I recall several friends complaining about advanced placement tests administered by their department to ascertain which incoming undergraduates should be allowed to skip the introductory writing courses. The incoming students were asked to write an essay on one of several topics. One of these topics concerned U.S./Soviet relations. It appears that uniformly the authors of those essays which, with relative clarity, asserted that the United States must be wary of the treacherous "Russian bear"—a recurrent expression in this context—were passed into the advanced courses or allowed to test out of composition entirely. On the other hand, with equal uniformity, authors of essays which placed comparable blame for Cold War tensions, the arms race, etc., on the United States and the Soviet Union, no matter what the clarity and rigor of the writing, were sent into the basic courses. (Evidently no one claimed that the Soviet Union should be wary of the treacherous United States.) The ideological equation of 'bad writing' with writing which does not conform to the imperialist/capitalist problematic dominant in the United States appeared overwhelmingly clear.

At the time, I thought this case might be exceptional or exaggerated. However, since then I have had direct experience, or heard from others with direct experience, of so many similar cases that I cannot help feeling that this sort of equation of 'good writing' with dominant ideology is far from exceptional. I should like to relate two such cases.

The first case concerns my younger brother. A few years ago, he was enrolled in the ordinary freshman composition sequence at a midwestern Catholic university. In the first course, his writing had improved drastically but was hardly perfect. For the most part he had received—though he did not always deserve—A's on essays which were not uniformly excellent, but which were uniformly apolitical. At the end of the semester, he wrote what was to my mind his finest essay by far—an attack on capital punishment. He advocated a preventive, rather than a retributive conception of justice and argued that capital punishment has no preventive force. Predictably, his grade was lowered.

The following semester, for another teacher, he was given an assignment on media coverage of the Vietnam war. First of all, this was, bizarrely, *not* a research project. Evidently, the students were all expected to know the nature of such media coverage by intuition alone or intuition guided by ideology. In any event, asked to submit a tentative opening paragraph, my brother submitted the following: "Many people claim that the mainstream U.S. media opposed the war in Vietnam. These people are right to the extent that the U.S. media did in fact oppose the war on practical grounds, especially after the Tet Offensive. However, the mainstream media supported the war on moral grounds from beginning to end." The instructor, asserting that the "language" was not "descriptive," took my brother aside and worked an entire period trying to construct a superior paragraph. Her result: "The attitude of the U.S. media towards the war in Vietnam, as evidenced by their reporting of the war, was ambiguous. This ambiguousness [sic] was manifest in three areas: the moral, the political, and the practical."

An outline had been assigned at the same time. They subsequently turned to this. My brother's outline indicated that he would discuss the military prognosis in the early years of the war, Johnson's "light at the end of the tunnel" promises, the shock of the Tet Offensive, and the reversal of press opinion about the prognosis following that offensive. These would constitute the section on 'practical opposition.' In the section on 'moral complicity,' he planned to address the systematic understatement or suppression of U.S. massacres and the insistence of the media on propagating the myths of the North Vietnamese Land Reform massacres and the Hue massacre. The instructor explained that in the early 1960's *Harper's* devised some sort of game with blue and, yes, red markers, representing the United States and North Vietnam. By playing this game, they "proved," she explained, that the United States could not win the war. She then went on to claim that the 'unwinability' of the war was the *only* thing my brother should discuss in the section on moral complicity. In this she was quite explicit: the *only* moral question of the war concerned the sacrifice of U.S. troops when we 'knew' we could not win.

When my brother submitted the first draft of the essay, he tried to insert a little moral sense, saying, "When someone argues that the war was immoral because of the number of United States soldiers killed, they also have to question the morality of these soldiers themselves and look at the number of Vietnamese civilians that were murdered." The instructor's revealing comment was a large red "Why?" at the end of the sentence.

After more disasters with other versions of the same paper, and a predictably low grade, Sean went to see the chairman of the English department about the situation. He was told, very nicely, that, because he had relied for a number of points on the writings of Noam Chomsky—who is not a "professional" in the field—the response of the instructor was justified. Clearly, Chomsky was beyond the bounds of rational debate—as was any discussion of the hundreds of thousands of civilians slaughtered by the United States in its ruthless invasion of Southeast Asia, and much else. (It is interesting to note that only a few months earlier, this chairman and I had appeared together on a panel concerning, of all things, the critique of ideology!)

A possibly more significant example may be found in an experience I had while supervising a Teaching Assistant at another university. This example is, I think, more significant because the composition program at that university—with which I had no association—was in my opinion very good from administration to instruction. Moreover, the TA I was supervising was one of the very finest teachers I have ever seen at any level. The day I was visiting this TA's class, she was examining two student papers. These were not papers from her own class, but sample papers given her by a more experienced TA during orientation. One paper argued that the United States was right to drop two atomic bombs on Japan, that dropping the bombs was, indeed, the only moral thing to do. The other paper argued that the compulsory draft, such as that operative during the Vietnam war, or compulsory registration, such as that operative now, are morally wrong.

The instructor made particularly insightful critical comments on the second paper. There were a number of sentences which were unclear, several connections missing, and so on. On the other hand, for the most part the missing links could be filled in and the basic points puzzled out. Moreover, there was a genuine attempt to address the opposition. This attempt was not entirely successful, as the instructor pointed out, but it was nonetheless intelligent and suggestive. Overall the argument was solid, though not fully compelling, and the opposition was nicely handled. The instructor did not mention, and probably did not see, these virtues.

The Hiroshima/Nagasaki paper, on the other hand, was more uniformly clear in presentation. The instructor remarked upon this and contrasted it with the preceding paper. However, this essay failed entirely to deal with the opposition. For the writer of this paper, there were two possible positions at the time the decision was made to drop the bombs: (1) drop the bombs and (2) launch a land invasion of Japan. Thus the only question is—would it have been better to invade? In this framework, then, to oppose the bombings is to support an invasion. For this writer, an option of neither bombing nor invading was beyond the bounds of rational discourse. Indeed, even as regards these alternatives, the author never considered the difference between civilian and military casualties, the possible biases of his one source (Henry Stimson, the Secretary of War), etc. Clearly the most significant issues were brushed aside. The instructor mentioned none of this.

What is most interesting here is that the instructor really had no sense she was being harder on the first paper than on the second. She simply found it easy to see the flaws in an argument against the draft, but not easy to see the flaws in an argument defending the bombing of Hiroshima and Nagasaki. I take it that this is because the flaws of the latter are, precisely, the flaws of the dominant ideology, in this case as articulated by Henry Stimson. The flaws of the former, as an explicitly *counter*-ideological statement, appear, so to speak, in relief against the background of our common, ideological beliefs. The flaws of the latter, however, blend into that background and thus tend to become invisible.

As soon as I pointed this out to the instructor, she agreed. We concurred that in terms of organization and clarity of exposition the Hiroshima/Nagasaki paper was better, but that in terms of argument the paper on the draft and registration was superior.

What makes this case particularly interesting is that the instructor did not say anything incorrect or explicitly adopt a political stance herself. In and of themselves, her criticisms were excellent. Moreover, her own political opinions were pacifist and thus she was inclined to oppose the draft and the bombing of Japan. However, because of her ideological training, she was in effect blinded to the ideological character of the one essay while being sensitized to the even minor errors of the other. I have no doubt that this is the most common form of ideologization to be found in the teaching of English and hence the form to which we should most carefully attend in our work to inhibit the ideological function of the English department.[1]

2. Political Judgment in the Classroom and in the Profession

Certainly many on the left would agree that imperialist and other ideologies absolutely should not be taught in classes. Moreover, many would extend the claim, insisting that professional bodies should at all cost avoid supporting such ideologies. But not everyone finds it so clear that politically 'correct' views should be rigorously excluded in this same way. This dilemma gives rise to two important general questions: (1) To what degree is it morally permissible (or obligatory) to teach ethics and (normative) politics in our classes? And (2) to what degree is it morally permissible (or obligatory) to constitute institutions in such a way as to allow majority political or ethical views to stand as the, in some sense, 'official' views of that institution? In other words, can/should we teach our *Beowulf* students about contra atrocities and can/should we allow/encourage the MLA to condemn such atrocities?

In both cases, the answer seems to me a clear *no*.

The first is less controversial. Most people would agree that in general the urgency of contemporary social issues does not justify the interruption of normal classroom teaching for the discussion of political events and ethical considerations : relevant to the topic of the course. In fact, this is true quite generally. Thus most would agree that we have no business teaching calculus, or ornithology, or sewing—or even *Bleak House*—in a course on *Beowulf*, just as we have no business teaching anti-imperialism. This appears to me the morally correct attitude for the following reason.

Let us suppose that, despite all its flaws, the university system is at present morally justifiable in some degree and that the teaching of English literature in that context is justifiable as well. Assuming this, then, it follows that the structure of the English curriculum— for example, its division into specific courses with specific guide- lines—is itself at least partially justifiable. Thus once we accept the justifiability of the university and of the teaching of English litera- ture within that university, we grant to the curricular structure of English what Alan Gewirth would call a *prima facie* obligatory character (see Gewirth 1982). In other words, if it is in some sense good to teach students English literature and if the general univer- sity format for teaching is justifiable, then we have a *prima facie* obligation to follow the official institutional principles laid down for that teaching, insofar as they are crucial to the operation of that department and university, insofar as they function to disseminate English literary knowledge.

Certainly a university may have many rules that do not bear on the dissemination of such teaching. These have no relevant moral force. However, rules governing, for example, what a student can reasonably expect to study in a given course—that is, the topic as generally described in the university catalogue—have *direct* bearing on this teaching and thus have considerable, if only prima facie force. In general, these rules exclude any extended, formal consid- eration of political or other questions irrelevant to the defined topic of the course. It follows that we have a prima facie obligation to refrain from addressing such questions in an extended, formal manner in the classroom.

But, as Gewirth emphasizes, prima facie obligations can be over- thrown. Under what conditions, then, might the 'relevance obliga- tion' be cast aside in relation to political and ethical concerns?

There would seem to be two possible justifications for abandoning the prima facie obligations of a university insofar as these affect the dissemination of knowledge: (1) the need to change the university in relevant ways, and (2) the presence of a certain sort of ethically critical situation which gives rise to ethical imperatives in conflict with the prima facie obligations and of greater moral force. Thus, as to the first, a certain sort of obligation to a university or other institution may, under certain circumstances, lose its force if the moral ideal of that institution demands the elimination of the obligated practice. Will the morally ideal university—the non-sexist, non-racist, non-imperialist university—eliminate the obligation in question, then? Will we be able to offer courses on *Beowulf* and teach Ho Chi Minh? No, of course not. An anarchist university, such as we will outline below, might eliminate explicit rules to this effect, but the obligation would in any event remain. One does not treat others as ends in themselves or further the justified principles of the university by luring students into one's class with a literary description only to subject them to unrelated political and moral tirades.

Thus it would appear that the first possible justification for abandoning the prima facie obligations of the university—their incoherence with the ideal of the university—never applies in the case of the irrelevant politicization of classroom teaching.

The second consideration, relating to the presence of an ethically critical situation, could apply in certain very unusual cases. For the most part even ethically critical situations can be addressed—and addressed most effectively—outside the classroom, though in certain revolutionary and related circumstances, the very *possibility* of a depoliticized classroom might be eliminated.

I should emphasize, however, that depoliticization should not be understood too narrowly. I have no doubt that in the examples cited above concerning teaching about Vietnam, Hiroshima, and the draft, the teachers in question thought that they were being politically neutral. But they were not. In seeking to avoid irrelevantly politicizing our classes (obviously the degree of relevance depends upon the class—less in *Beowulf*, more in 'Vietnam War Novels') we should be extremely careful not to mistake ideology for neutrality or non-politicality. Indeed, as should be clear from the preceding, *implicitly* ideological teaching which presents itself as neutral or non-political is often the most pernicious form of irrelevant politicization of teaching.

Turning to our second, and more controversial problem—that of political stances taken by professional bodies—the question we must consider is, once again, whether or not it is incumbent upon or even permissible for any department, professional society, or related body to denounce oppressive policies and struggle against oppressive ideologies. Richard Ohmann has discussed the furor surrounding an MLA resolution condemning the Vietnam war (see Ohmann 1976, pp. 31f.). In this context, Ohmann implicitly raised these questions and answered in the affirmative. Although I think that Ohmann and I would agree virtually across the board on what policies are to be considered oppressive, etc., and thus we would agree on what policies are to be condemned, we do not agree on who can and should do the condemning. It is my view that professional and related institutions have neither the obligation nor the right to take stands on political or moral questions except in the unusual circumstance that there is virtual unanimity among members with regard to the issue in question. There are two principal reasons why I maintain this position.

First, as to the *obligation* of institutions: we should begin by recalling that obligations are to a considerable degree related to functions or descriptions. Thus as someone teaching *King Lear*—that is, insofar as I am operating under the description 'teacher of *King Lear*'—I am obligated to seek in class to make *King Lear* comprehensible to my students, to meet with these students outside of class in order to help them understand *King Lear*, and so on. My obligations as a human being in general do not obligate me to make *King Lear* comprehensible. It is only my obligations as an instructor that do so. Conversely, my obligations as an instructor go no further. My obligations *as an instructor* do not encompass, for example, charity. If I am charitable, I am, in that regard, a *good person*, but I am not necessarily a *good teacher* in *any* regard. Similarly, if I am overall a good person, then I am probably charitable, though I may not be a lucid expositor. On the other hand, if I am overall a good teacher, then I may or may not be charitable, but I will certainly be a lucid expositor.

Quite generally, it is incumbent upon me to oppose oppression because I am a human being, not because I am an instructor, scholar, etc. There are, of course, some unusual cases in which oppression directly affects my teaching—for example, if I am teaching in El Salvador and the fascists have rolled in the U.S.-supplied tanks and closed down the university. In these cases, I am obligated both as a person and as a teacher to oppose the oppression. However, these cases are the exception. For the most part what we would normally consider *moral* obligations fall outside the purview of my *professional* obligations.

Now, a professional body such as the MLA is a gathering of individuals insofar as they share a certain function or description. The MLA does not gather individuals as persons quite generally, as general moral agents, but rather as scholars, teachers, and students of language and literature. Like any other organization, the obligations of the MLA mirror the obligations of the members *in the function or under the description germane to their constitution of the MLA membership.* Thus the obligations of the MLA as an institution are merely the obligations of its individual members *as scholars, instructors, and students of language and literature* (full stop). Thus while the MLA is obligated vigorously to oppose any censorship of teaching or publication, any prejudicial hiring, the closing of universities, and so on, it is not obligated to oppose U.S. imperialism, the general racism, sexism, homophobia, or tyrannization of children in a society, etc.

But does the MLA have any *right* to oppose—or support—these, even though it has no obligation? In other words, is the MLA in fact obligated neither to support nor to oppose U.S. imperialism, and so on? In this regard, I would argue that there is indeed one obligation that a democratic institution may be said to have over and above the obligations of its constituent members insofar as they are members—or rather I would argue that in being a member of a democratic institution, one acquires a new and specific obligation to the other members of that institution. This obligation concerns the relation between majorities and minorities. Each member of a democratic institution is obligated to live by the decision of the majority as long as he or she is a member of that institution. This obligation appertains most particularly to those who find themselves in the minority. Correlatively, just as those in the minority are obligated to abide by the will of the majority, so too are members of the majority obligated not to abuse their position, not to force the minority into the position of having to choose between leaving the institution or abiding by a decision they find repugnant, morally or otherwise. Part of this obligation of the majority is, then, refraining from taking stands *in the name of the institution* on matters which do not appertain to the members of the institution insofar as they are such members. For example, for the most part U.S. policy in Central America is not in any usual sense directly relevant to our obligations, interests, etc., as scholars, teachers, and students of literature and language. Thus if it happens that the majority of the MLA membership opposes the U.S. policy in Central America, but a minority supports it and would find repugnant any official MLA opposition thereto, the majority is obligated to defer to the minority and *not* to take an *institutional* stand on the issue.

I should emphasize, however, that 'rights of members to the apoliticality of their institution' should not be understood too narrowly. To take a somewhat outdated example, suppose that the majority of the membership of the MLA is indifferent as to whether or not the MLA convention city is in a state which has not passed the ERA. A significant minority of members, however, finds it morally repugnant to attend a convention in a state which has not passed the ERA. In other words, a significant minority finds repugnant one option (say, meeting in Chicago) and virtually no one finds repugnant the alternative (say, meeting in New York City). In such a case the majority is clearly obligated to seek a convention city in a state which has passed the ERA (though it remains obligated not to take an official stand on the amendment itself, unless, again, there is only insignificant opposition among the membership). Here and elsewhere, assuring the apoliticality of an institution and protecting members of the institution with minority political views does not mean pretending that political issues do not exist. Indeed, it not infrequently means taking such issues carefully into account in making institutional decisions.

Before going on, I should like to answer the common objection that the sort of apoliticality I have been urging is a myth. To be apolitical, the argument goes, is in effect to support whatever policies are actually in place. It seems clear that an institution can be said to support a policy if and only if the policy gains by the existence of that institution. It is ridiculous to claim that an institution supports a given policy if the existence of the institution makes no difference whatsoever to the success or failure of that policy. Thus the U.S. war in Central America is supported by the MLA only to the degree that U.S. imperial ideology and U.S. imperial policy would be weakened by the dissolution of that institution. Similarly, the U.S. war is successfully opposed by the MLA only to the degree that U.S. ideology and policy would be strengthened by the dissolution of that institution. It seems clear, then, that by not taking a stand on the U.S. campaign of mass terror, the MLA really is neither supporting nor opposing that campaign as the campaign is neither strengthened nor weakened by the existence of the institution.

The location of a convention city is a different matter, however. If the MLA did not exist, then the convention city would not receive the thousands of extra holiday tourists it does receive—there would, after all, be no convention and hence no convention city. Thus, if we accept the premise that monetary gain or loss to urban entrepreneurs—at least in the context of the breaching or honoring of boycotts—is a significant factor in state equal rights legislation, then choosing to convene in Chicago, when Illinois has not passed the ERA, does in effect support the opposition of Illinois to the ERA.

Thus institutions such as the MLA have neither the obligation nor the right to take stands on political and moral issues which do not bear directly upon the members of the institution *as* members of that institution. Indeed, the members of the majority in any institution are obligated to prevent this. However, in doing so they must carefully discriminate when a decision in fact constitutes taking such a stand and when it does not—a discrimination which is not as straightforward as it may at first appear.

Much as in the case of teaching, professional and institutional obligations are only *tentative*—prima facie if the institution itself is morally justifiable. Thus they are morally binding only to the degree that they are not overridden by larger, more critical ethical concerns. Once again, however, even in critical situations, these concerns are, I believe, best addressed by individuals or groups *from* the institution, and not by the institution as a whole. If 80% of the membership of the MLA opposes contra aid and 10% supports it (with 10% neutral), there is no reason why the 80% should not fill a lengthy petition or buy an advertisement in the New York *Times* or otherwise act as a group. But there are many reasons why they should not claim to speak for the entire 100% of the MLA. Moreover, there is little reason to believe that such a claim would make their protest any more effective.

Unlike many politically oriented writers, who have advocated the extension and development of political concerns in teaching and professional activities, I have urged their limitation. This is not because I conceive of politics narrowly, but because I conceive of ethics broadly and believe that all obligations should be taken seriously—even though, in cases of real conflict, some rights must supersede others.

Obligations to Authors, to Students, and to Colleagues

In the preceding section, we assumed that the university and its literature curricula are, in their general structure, morally justifiable. Evidently, there are two principal ways in which a university might, in principle, be justified morally: (1) by reference to the pursuit of knowledge, in other words, research, and (2) by reference to the dissemination of knowledge, in other words, teaching. Under the latter, I would distinguish justifications resting upon considerations of learning *per se* and those resting upon vocational considerations. In connection with these, our principal, relevant institutional obligations are to colleagues and to students, though we have some further relevant obligations to the authors whom we study, their families, etc., and to the public at large.

Concerning our obligations to authors, I should first of all state my disagreement with E. D. Hirsch's view that we have a moral obligation to authors to concern ourselves with authorial intent in literary interpretation (see Hirsch 1976, pp. 90ff.). Hirsch's claims here show a degree of sensitivity to questions of moral obligation rare in critical writing today. But as soon as one fully recognizes the stipulative nature of meaning and interpretation, Hirsch's claims lose their point and force, for we are evidently obligated to seek authorial intent when and only when we *claim* to be seeking authorial intent. Thus we are obligated to be honest, as well as careful in our researches, etc. We are obligated actually to seek intent when we claim that intent is what we are seeking. But there is no obvious reason why we might be obligated to claim we are seeking intent to begin with, or why we might be obligated to seek intent independent of our claims. (Oddly enough, Hirsch's widely misunderstood arguments in fact imply something very much like the 'stipulationism' defended above. But, possibly because he never explicitly formulates a strict 'stipulationism,' he fails to recognize that such a position is incoherent with a global ethical imperative to seek authorial intent, in whatever variety of authorial intent he might have in mind.)

More generally, our obligation regarding authors is simple—we should treat them as ends in themselves. This means that, in the relevant circumstances, we should seek to understand them, to criticize them justly to the degree that all men and women may be publicly criticized, and not to humiliate or degrade them. We have further obligations not to humiliate or otherwise cause suffering to the families of these authors, their friends, and so on. Clearly, these obligations apply most strongly when the authors, their relatives, or their friends are alive. They weaken, but do not necessarily disappear, subsequently. Such issues of obligation to an author arise most insistently in the writing of biography and in related activities, though they are not absent elsewhere. Unfortunately they appear to be all too rarely considered in any area.

As to colleagues, our first obligation here, beyond general human decency, is that of fostering dialectic to the greatest extent possible. More specifically, our obligations involve complete open-mindedness and a rigorously critical attitude toward all the research projects which our colleagues might wish to undertake. Of course, we must always keep in mind that our obligations are not only to the advancement and dissemination of knowledge, but to the far more practical concern of vocation as well. By definition, our colleagues are already employed. That is what makes them colleagues. However, they still have legitimate vocational concerns—specifically, those of retention and promotion. Thus we must always temper our support and criticism with a recognition of the vocational consequences of these acts. For example, we would not wish too strongly to encourage an untenured professor in his or her pursuit of an apparently unpromising project, for fear that the professor might not receive tenure. On the other hand, we would not wish too harshly to criticize the work of an untenured—and therefore inse-cure—professor, who might panic or lose confidence and therefore become paralyzed in his or her work. Finally, we have self-evident obligations to honesty and care in decisions concerning promotion, publication, etc.

In all cases, I should emphasize, the duties in question obtain independently of the personal relations of the individuals involved and even independently of the professional actions of those whom the obligations concern. Thus I am bound to encourage the col-league who votes to fire me, and I am bound to criticize the professor who votes to retain me. This is precisely because my obligations are *institutional*, not *personal* and thus their justifica-tion is an institutional and not a personal matter.

As to our own work, we should freely disseminate the results of our own researchers, seeking the comments and criticism of others, opening our work to the intellectual community. In this context, it should be evident that we have an actual moral obligation to strive for rigor, scholarship, and clarity in our work. Of course, I do not mean by 'clarity' what is most often meant—easy-seeming compre-hension of empty clichés. I call an essay, presentation, etc., clear to the degree that it presents theses that astute and informed readers can understand literally. The sort of lyrical metaphorics which literary critics often confuse with clarity is quite the contrary of what I here intend.

Our obligations regarding students are virtually identical with our obligations regarding colleagues—a fostering of dialectic through open-minded encouragement combined with rigorous, scholarly, and lucid criticism, in the context of honest and careful evaluation and sensitivity to vocational concerns. Whether we are teaching freshmen or directing a dissertation, the same holds. Of course, we must regulate our encouragement and our criticism by reference to the pomposity or insecurity of the individual student. Dialectic is not fostered by crushing the fragile self-esteem of one student or honoring the bloated self-confidence of another. On the other hand, dialectic is not encouraged by the facile generation of self-esteem through unwarranted praise or the deflation of pride through scorn. In both cases the only response is careful work to begin dialectic—often in private conferences in which honest effort and improvement are rewarded.

I find among many professors of English that a particular sort of seminar format—one in which everyone is allowed to opine uncritically about some text—is conceived to be the very best way to 'get students to open up' and 'bring them out of their shells,' and thus, one would assume, strengthen their self-esteem. In my experience, however, this is not the case. In a seminar based on unexamined and uncriticized opinion, the students who are already self-confident, or even self-important, are the ones who speak. Ultimately, the more timid students may be drawn into the discussion, but this is only because there is *no* risk whatsoever, because the seminar is little more than amiable chat. This is no way of building a student's self-esteem. Rather, a student's self-esteem can and should be built only by allowing and encouraging the student to think rigorously and individually and to risk proposing conjectures in an environment which is supportive but at the same time critical. This can only be achieved when the student has gained a certain degree of knowledge and achieved a certain level of competence.

Much of what I have just said about the duties of a critic and professor of literature may appear obvious, even banal. For example, who would disagree with the claim that our evaluation of student performance must be careful and honest? However, in the first place, the main underlying principle of our obligations, as just presented, is not obvious and banal. In its most general form, this principle asserts that the justification of an institution of higher education obligates us principally to foster dialectic. More specifically, as regards research, this means that we should be open to *all* research projects—including those which we find ridiculous or disagreeable—and at the same time critical of *all* analyses, including, indeed especially, those which conform to the standard theories or principles and thereby appear unexceptionable. As regards teaching, this means that we are obligated to strive equally to eliminate dogmatism and uninformed conjecture from our classroom, neither teaching a doctrine which the students may parrot nor allowing them aimlessly to opine on matters of which they are fundamentally ignorant. These do not seem to me necessarily banal or uncontroversial implications—though I certainly wish they were.

Moreover, beyond these, the uncontroversial implications are uncontroversial in the imaginary alone. For example, I find it quite impossible to believe that teachers are, in fact, entirely honest in grading. Some students expect A's, others B's, others C's, and most of us feel a strong inclination, conscious or unconscious, to follow the students' expectations—an inclination reenforced by an awareness of the concrete importance of student evaluations (see Cahn 1987, p. B3). More generally, some students present themselves as A students or have other characteristics, from dress to speaking style, which we associate with A students. I do not believe it can be denied that such students will be in general more likely to receive A's than comparable students who are less confident, wear different clothes, speak non-prestige dialects, or whatever. We have already mentioned confirmatory bias and seen how it functions to distort gender perceptions by, in effect, skewing our unreflective and unsystematic perceptions in the direction of gender stereotypes. In fact, as we have indicated, this bias is much more general. As Michael Mahoney explains, confirmatory bias is "the tendency for humans to seek out, attend to, and sometimes embellish experiences which support or 'confirm' their beliefs," no matter what the field. "Confirmatory experiences are selectively welcomed and granted easy credibility," he continues; "Disconfirmatory experiences, on the other hand, are often ignored, discredited, or treated with obvious defensiveness" (Mahoney 1977, pp. 161–62). Confirmatory bias is a nearly ubiquitous human tendency. As we will discuss below, it is particularly pronounced in a broad range of academic evaluations—including, for example, peer review. It is almost impossible to imagine that this bias would be absent from our evaluations of student work.

Thus our care and honesty in grading is often controversial in reality, if not in imagination. The frequently imaginary character of our commitment to vocational obligations, for example, placement, our commitment to clarity, which is more often a commitment to its inverse (i.e., fluent metaphorics), and so on, is even more obvious.

In general, we might say that our institutional obligations as critics and professors of literary studies today concern precisely the commitment to making research, teaching, and vocational work approximate as nearly as possible the research, teaching, and vocational work which would be fostered and to a degree systematized in an ideal university—the university as a kingdom of ends. Our *obligations* in a *real* system, then, are to protect as far as possible the *rights* guaranteed in an *ideal* system. But clearly the university in its present form does not approximate a kingdom of ends and this is true for structural reasons which go beyond the simple good will of individuals. All the obligations we have been discussing are correlated with rights. If we are obligated to be careful and impartial in tenure decisions, those being judged have a correlate right to be judged carefully and impartially. More generally, all students and faculty have the right to a university structure which fosters the advancement of knowledge through rational and informed dialectic and which provides a context in which all may be treated as ends in themselves. It is my contention that contemporary universities fail miserably on this score and that this situation can be altered only through a massive anarchist or libertarian socialist restructuring of the university. It is the burden of the final section to explore and defend this claim.

The Political Economy of Literary Study

1. The Guild Hierarchy of the Department

In many ways, the most salient fact about English and other departments in the contemporary university is that they are hierarchical guild-structures in competition for a decreasing amount of central funding in a capitalistic institution. Universities are rather like factories run at a loss. Within the university, the various levels of administration mirror the various levels of management in industry. The faculty as a whole—in the sense of all teaching personnel—constitutes a highly differentiated, rigidly hierarchized, and for the most part narrowly individualistic workforce. Within the department the oppressive structure of the guild hierarchy is clear, most particularly in the relations between tenured and untenured faculty. However, members of the department guild, Full, Associate, and Assistant professors, the 'workers' of the university, are not in general exploited. At many universities, teachers receive a relatively low hourly wage, given their level of education; however, for the most part professors manage to gain the means for quite comfortable lives with shockingly little work. Thus they cannot be said to be truly exploited by the capitalist system of the university. Teaching Assistants, Instructors, and Part Time Instructors form the class of capitalistically exploited laborers in the university in general and, most importantly for our concerns, in the English department in particular. Marginal to the profession and socially ostracized, the Part Time Instructors are the most exploited of the lot. They are often drastically overworked and always underpaid. Teaching Assistants have the advantage of being potential members of the professional guild, defined by Full, Associate, and, tentatively, Assistant professors. Part Time Instructors, however, are, for the most part, considered beyond hope; they have been held up to the ridiculous standards of the profession and found wanting. They are the outcastes of the English department.

Intermediate between the faculty 'laborers,' exploited or not, and the administrative managers, though often closer to the latter, is the chairperson. As Caplow and McGee put it in their 1958 *The Academic Marketplace*, "The chairman's role has some resemblance to that of the working foreman in industry. In order to function as a chairman, he must represent management to the boys in the shop, and the boys in the shop to management. . . . The chairman's ability to carry out his duties . . . may depend on his closeness to management" (p. 195). Indeed, the chairperson operates to manage the department and, in doing so, competes with other chairpersons for the limited resources of the university. Again this is much like any capitalist organization. The chairpersons compete for funds in large measure by proposing criteria for allocation which favor their particular departments. Publications, enrollments, and quality of teaching are the three general criteria which the debates concern. It is their nature and relative status that are at issue.

Of course, publication is always extremely important. The craze for publication in all departments is clearly a direct result of the departments' real, financial need to be filled with 'productive scholars'—that is, individuals who manage to churn out massive numbers of publications each year, whether these be admirable advances in learning or mere wasted paper. More important, the obsession of English departments with *books* is in many ways a direct result of this. In colleges of Arts and Sciences, English departments must compete with Physics, Chemistry, and other departments of experimental science. Professors in these departments publish many articles, but relatively few books. One way of undermining their authority is to establish criteria such that books count far more than articles, or, at best, such that articles do not count at all. (For example, I know of one English chairperson who, faced with competition from productive departments of physical and social science, proposed the intriguing equation: one book equals twenty articles.)

Enrollments are also important. We are all encouraged to lure more students into English classes, to undertake to convert more engineers to English-majorship, etc. In and of itself this is innocuous enough, though at the graduate level moral questions enter insofar as we are unable to place in suitable employment the men and women we seduce. However, even at the undergraduate level, I suspect that this understandable frenzy for increasing enrollment contributes to the profoundly anti-intellectual 'seminar' method of 'teaching' so common now in English departments. Rather than attending to intellectual backgrounds, sources, historical context, and so on, teachers often enough give their students, say, Book One of *The Faerie Queen*, enter class, have everyone sit around in a circle, and ask, 'So, what do you think this poem is really about?' Many students leave the class still unfamiliar with the basic literal plot, but often grateful for the opportunity to turn off their minds— and receive great praise in doing so—between real courses like calculus and biology.

One might think that the third criterion for funding—excellence in teaching—would discourage this slovenliness. In fact, the opposite is more nearly the case. Many departments rely almost entirely upon student evaluations to judge teaching. In his study of ethics in academia, Steven Cahn argues that this reliance constitutes a "subtle, yet . . . serious, threat" to good teaching quite generally (Cahn 1986, p. 34). He goes on to cite one study of teaching evaluations which indicates that "student satisfaction with learning may represent little more than the illusion of having learned" (p. 39; quoting the researchers—Naftulin, Ware, and Donnelly 1973). In a subsequent article further defending his thesis, Cahn quotes the conclusion of a literature survey in the *Annual Review of Psychology*: "Most research on student ratings of teachers does not indicate that the ratings measure the effectiveness of teaching, good teaching, intellectual achievement, nor understanding of basic concepts. The ratings appear to be measuring student satisfaction, the attitudes of students toward their teachers and classes, the psychosocial needs of the student, and the personality characteristics, popularity, and speaking quality of the teacher" (Cahn 1987, p. B2).[2]

But what gives rise to student satisfaction, etc.? Or, rather, how, if at all, do student satisfaction and other factors relevant to student evaluations relate to serious pedagogical issues? In my experience, aimless seminars with plenty of mutual back-patting, as well as dogmatic lecture courses, encourage very good evaluations. Courses which provide much information, but then challenge the students to think independently and rigorously—in other words, courses which are the most intellectually beneficial for the students, courses which encourage, precisely, *dialectic*—are much riskier business. Certainly many factors contribute to any given student's evaluation of a professor's performance, and rigorous, non-dogmatic instruction by no means ensures weak evaluations. My point is merely that, because dialectic—like physical exercise—is sometimes painful, it is far from a sure method for gleaning congratulatory evaluations. Thus, taking student evaluations—material objects which can be physically presented to a dean and even mathematically tabulated—as definitive of teaching quality seems less likely to foster than to discourage dialectical pedagogy.

All these criteria combine in a most pernicious fashion in tenure decisions. An assistant professor who learns nothing, but mechanically churns out and publishes a fashionable interpretation of some literary work or works—for example, a deconstruction of Milton's sonnets—will probably be given tenure while someone who publishes nothing, but spends six years gaining fluency in Greek and Latin better to read and understand the backgrounds of Renaissance literature, or learning programming languages and techniques for the manipulation and machine analysis of texts, will probably be fired. Similarly, someone who challenges his or her students and, with excellent results, encourages them painfully to think might well be considered a mediocre teacher while one or another dogmatist or sycophant may be held up as a model of excellence. Of course this is by no means true in all cases. Many assistant professors learn much *and* write brilliant books. Similarly many excellent teachers receive excellent teaching evaluations. The point is merely that the economy is not such as to reward scholarship and teaching *per se*, but rather publication and teaching evaluations, and that excellence in one is far from a guarantee of excellence in the other.

2. The Guild System of Specialization

"Intellectual authority and the authority of scholars and critics," writes Jim Merod, "are the first of all guild creations, products of the credentials conferred by schools that exercise their norms of judgment in order to reproduce themselves" (Merod 1987, p. 65). There are, in effect, two sorts of guild system in the profession of literary study. The first, historically more assimilable to early manufacture (see Marx 1967, pp. 336ff.) is to be found within the individual department as manifest in its hierarchy of authority, as we have been discussing. The second sort of guild system is to be found in the formal and informal professional societies—principally author societies in the case of English—which in effect function to monopolize or at least control work in their particular fields. The first sort of guild concerns faculty standing. The second concerns specialization. The first functions to maintain a hierarchy of authority in the department—the tenure and rank systems being often little more than systems of social control and stratification. The second has a similar controlling function, but one defined by object of study rather than institutional affiliation.

Specifically, the guilds defined by specialization are far from being guarantors of excellence, scholarship, and rigor, as is often claimed. Rather, in my view, Marx's discussion of the detail-labor in industry applies with equal force to the detail-labor in academia: "crippled by life-long repetition of one and the same trivial operation, and thus reduced to the mere fragment of a man[/woman]," the detail-worker must be replaced "by the fully developed individual, ready to face any change of production," for to him/her "the different social functions he[/she] performs . . . are but so many modes of giving free scope to his[/her] own natural and acquired powers" (Marx 1967, p. 488).

Far from functioning to improve intellectual life and assure excellence, specialization guilds function to regulate production and consumption, to the benefit of their members, in the fields in question. Principally they do this through the control exercised by their members in specialized journals, review committees for special topics in journals of broader scope, review committees for book manuscripts submitted to presses, as well as through conferences, awards, book reviews, citation practices within articles, and so on— clearly, when there is no official professional organization, a looser group of specialists fulfills the same function. Thus, for example, the American Shakespeare Association functions to regulate discussion of Shakespeare, thereby reserving at least the bulk of that subject for its members. It defines the 'bounds of rational discourse' concerning Shakespeare and seeks either to undermine or to incorporate and control the work which does not at least initially fall within these confines. (Needless to say, I am not claiming that anyone in the American Shakespeare Association or any other professional society has self-consciously decided to take on the task of market regulation—except, of course, insofar as this is ideologically conceived of as 'quality control.')

I should emphasize that there is a good deal of empirical research which indicates quite clearly that professional systems of 'expertise' function to confine professional discussion within quite narrow bounds—and thereby to control professional production and consumption. For example, Michael Mahoney has found that confirmatory bias—that is, again, bias toward arguments, data, etc., which tend to confirm or are presented as confirming dominant views—is enormously strong in peer review. Mahoney explains, "One study found that the vast majority of scientists drawn from a national sample showed a strong preference for 'confirmatory' experiments (Mahoney and Kimper, 1976). Over half of these scientists did not even recognize disconfirmation (*modus tollens*) as a valid reasoning form!" (Mahoney 1977, p. 162). In another study, Mahoney "manipulated the results and discussion sections of an experimental report and asked 75 journal referees to evaluate its worthiness for publication (Mahoney, 1976, 1977). Some reviewers read manuscripts reporting results consistent with their theoretical orientation. Others saw the same data but with the labels reversed so that they appeared to challenge their perspective. . . . The very same experimental procedures were applauded or strongly criticized depending on the direction of the data. Manuscripts reporting positive results were . . . much more likely to be recommended for publication than were those containing negative results" (Mahoney

1987, p. 168). In other words, "[w]ith identical experimental procedures, a positive results manuscript was rated as methodologically better than one reporting negative results" (Mahoney 1977, p. 169) and the positive results manuscript—that is, the manuscript which appeared to support disciplinary dogma—was *far* more likely to be accepted for publication (Mahoney 1977, p. 170). (It is worth mentioning here that much the same bias has been evident in hiring and promotion decisions [see, for example, Caplow and McGee 1958, pp. 19–22], though in these it is combined with an "anti-intellectual bias" and an overriding concern with the "prestige and compatibility" of the candidate [Caplan and McGee 1958, pp. 164, 160].)

Quite generally, then, to specialize in an area is to learn the 'limits of reasonable discourse' in that area, the truisms, the few great books, the proper clichés. Specialization is important not because it helps to preserve knowledge, but because it helps to preserve the most beneficial economic structure. A few exceptional critics can be allowed to write widely and in depth on various topics, but most critics must specialize if economic chaos is not to result. The entire predictable and banal structure of authority, which governs everything from who gets grants to what gets published, would crumble if the basis of guild specialization were removed. In my view, this would most certainly be a good thing.

3. The Literary Market

In capitalist society, all value tends to be reduced to market value. If this truism is obvious in the case of ordinary commodities such as automobiles, it is no less salient in the case of intellectual and academic commodities such as articles, books, and seminars. It is frequently thought that professors of literature have managed to escape the corrupt world of capitalist economy. In fact, as I will argue, literary production is governed by market concerns not only at the level of exchange value, but at the level of *use* value also.

Ordinarily, capitalists, or manufacturers quite generally, have two principal economic concerns. The first is that the market be adequately regulated. This is to assure that the entire economic system not be undermined by free-market forces. The contemporary system of state capitalism developed, most especially after the

Great Depression, in response to precisely this concern (see Kolko 1984, pp. 100–56). The second concern is that individual corporations always increase profit through innovation. This involves marketing innovation, the opening of new markets for old products, as well as production innovation, the creation of new products for old markets, the reduction of labor or other costs, and so on. The first concern touches on the fear of loss, the second on the hope for gain. The first attends to the benefits of capitalists as a class and is the product of cooperation. The second attends to the benefits of capitalists as individuals and is the product of competition. The first aims at economic constancy, the second economic change. The immediate pre-capitalist solution to the first and far more crucial problem was the guild system. For various reasons, principally due to the nature of most capitalist production, the guild solution quickly became untenable for industry. In its two forms, however, it remained the regulatory principle of academia and most particularly of the humanities, the sciences being more closely related to industry and industrial concerns and problems. We have already spoken of these guild systems. The ways in which the humanities, and most particularly English, have dealt with the second problem, however, are more narrowly and obviously capitalist, with no remnants of the university's feudal origins entering the picture.

Academics, like industrialists, produce commodities; they produce objects to sell. In this case the buyers—more exactly, entrepreneurs, buying in order to sell—are journals and presses and chairs of conference sessions, and the like. Of course, the academician is for the most part remunerated not by the buyers, but by his or her own corporation, the university. (Why the university functions in this way, why it thus pays, is an intriguing question, but one into which I will not enter.) In any event, the advancement of an academic is a function of sales—selling one's articles to journals, one's books to presses, one's courses to students, and so on. In this context, a university faculty member, insofar as he or she functions *as* an academic, must write and teach *in order to sell.* Though the faculty member may have other motives also, the specifically academic motive of writing and teaching is a *market* motive because the specifically academic value of writing and teaching is a *market* value.

Now, ordinarily, a commodity has both a market value and some other value as well (cf. Marx 1967, pp. 35ff.; though ultimately based on Marx's notions of 'exchange value' and 'use value,' my notions of 'market value' and 'satisfaction value' are somewhat different, as should become clear). Thus, a capitalist manufactures a product because it will sell, because it has a certain market value. But it will sell because it satisfies some need or want of a buyer, because it has a 'use value' or more generally a 'satisfaction value.' Most often this satisfaction value is *not* itself a market value. For example, Kellogg manufactures Rice Krispies not because they are nutritious (ha ha), or even because they taste good, but because they sell. They sell, however, because people think they taste good; people think that they satisfy their desire for something tasty. Here the satisfaction value is tastiness and thus the satisfaction value is not itself a market value. (That satisfaction value should be understood as 'marginal' in the usual economic sense, and that the usual considerations appertaining to demand apply, should be clear, though none of this is really important in the present context.)

There is, however, one case in which satisfaction value *is* market value—capital investment. Buying machinery, or stock, or labor is satisfying for the capitalist insofar as it produces a profit, insofar as it has market value itself or contributes to the market value of his or her products. As Marx explained in terms of the "general formula for capital," in ordinary purchases the acquisition of a commodity is an end, but in capital investment, the acquisition of a commodity is a means only (see Marx 1967, pp. 146ff.). I would maintain that this is precisely the case with academic products, that academic purchases are in effect capital investments.

Thus, in capitalist academia, the satisfaction value of a piece of writing is *not*, at least primarily, its explanatory capacity, profundity, truth, beauty, humanizing potential, etc. The satisfaction value of literary criticism or theory—or of literature itself—is often claimed to be one or another of these, but this claim is for the most part ideological. The satisfaction value of all writing in literary study is primarily a form of market value. That literary theory which allows the greatest production of literary analyses with the least effort will be the most salable in academia, hence that which is ideologically claimed the most true, ethical, etc. Similarly, that novel or drama or film which provides the most abundant materials for relatively effortless analysis and reanalysis will be the most salable in academia, hence that which is ideologically claimed the most beautiful, profound, etc.

For the most part, manufacturers manufacture for non-manufacturers. Some capitalists produce for other capitalists, but then these second capitalists produce for non-capitalists. In the industrial world, all production leads eventually beyond production and industry to the populace at large. In the industrial world, all market values are ultimately linked to satisfaction values. But imagine a society composed only of industrialists. The livelihood of each depends only on the bulk of his or her sales. For simplicity, suppose that the market for any given product cannot be oversaturated. Now clearly, each industrialist will be interested in buying *only* those products which will increase productivity. Similarly, the industrialist will be able to sell only those products which increase productivity. In this situation, the only value of commodities would be *market* value. Non-market satisfaction value would enter only as a secondary consideration if at all.

This may seem a totally fantastical situation, but it is almost exactly the situation of the humanities. Who buys literary theory? Certainly not the 'average American'—proletarian or capitalist, professional or bureaucrat, white collar or blue collar. Clearly, literary critics buy literary theory, both literally and metaphorically. This is not some esoteric inference of Marxist analysis. It is a well-known fact, important to the marketing decisions (and thus the publication decisions) of academic publishers. As Walter Powell points out in *Getting into Print: The Decision-Making Process in Scholarly Publishing*, scholarly publishers "operate with the knowledge that the readers of their books are, to a large extent, the same kind of people as those who write them" (Powell 1985, p. 19). "A great majority of the books published by scholarly houses," he explains, "are purchased either by members of the academic community or by university libraries . . . guided . . . by the advice of professors at their own universities. . . . In sum . . . the suppliers, the consumers, and the gatekeepers of scholarly publishing are all members of the academic community" (p. 195).

It is important to emphasize that the identity of producers and consumers here is not merely metaphorical. It is, rather, a literal and crucial fact of the capitalist economy in which academic publishing, like any other industry, is situated. Indeed, it has been widely attested that sales concerns have become much more serious in university publishing since the early 1970's (see Coser, Kadushin, and Powell 1982, p. 140; for a more detailed discussion of a single press, see Hall 1986 on changes at Harvard University Press at this time). This has made publishers very interested in the precise inclinations of their market constituents and has encouraged academic publishers to "'run with the crowd' and publish topics that other houses have found to be successful" (Powell 1985, p. 85).

The question that arises here, then, is: what makes the 'pack'— the academic producers/consumers—run in a certain way to begin with? What, for example, motivates literary critics to buy literary theory? Again, academic producers/consumers consume in order to produce. Literary critics buy literary theory in order to pick out a few things they can 'use' in reading Shakespeare or Sterne or Tichborne or whomever. Literary theorists buy literary theory in order to have something to develop or respond to. Who reads an article on the signifier in Pope? Popologists (members of the Pope guild), eighteenth-century specialists, experts in satire, a few theorists, and so on—in short, a number of people who, due to their job situation, have no choice but to search anywhere they can for something which they might 'use' in producing some precious lines of tenure-securing or salary-increasing print.

What is unusual about literary production in particular and what sets it apart from most other industries is that in the production and consumption of criticism and theory the *only* primary value is market value. Other values, such as explanatory capacity, enter only secondarily. Compare, for example, the physical sciences. For the most part the values of physicists' articles are market values. However, the claims of the physicists have real, practical consequences at some remove. Theoretical physics is linked to a technology. For this reason the market values of theoretical physics are ultimately linked to non-market satisfaction values. These, in turn, react back upon the market values of the theoretical physics such that explanatory capacity becomes a concern of at least some importance to market value. Thus theoretical physics really does in some degree concern explanatory capacity because explanatory capacity is a partial condition for market value, because market value is linked to complex non-market satisfaction values to which explanatory capacity is germane.

Unhappily, this is not the case with literary criticism and theory. For the most part, neither criticism nor theory is linked directly to a technology. Thus such criteria as explanatory capacity have no direct bearing upon market value in the humanities in general and in literary study in particular. As Caplow and McGee point out, whatever the problems with evaluation in other academic disciplines, "evaluation in English . . . is the most thoroughly subjective" (Caplow and McGee 1958, p. 88). In other words, among academic disciplines, evaluation in English is the least constrained by such factors as reasoning and evidence. Because of this, the principal consideration in determining the value of a literary, critical, or theoretical work is, again, the degree to which that work will or will not contribute to the production of other market-valuable works.

I should emphasize that this does not mean that the academic literary market is otherwise unconstrained. Due to the insertion of the professional economy into the university economy, there are in fact several crucial constraints. First, literary work must present at least the illusion of maintaining at least some degree of explanatory capacity. Principally, this is due to the fact that humanities departments must appear non-redundant. If the critical and theoretical works English professors produce seem to be nothing more than pointless verbiage, then other departments will be able to make a good case for a reallocation of university funds away from English and into physics, etc. Most often this problem is solved by the introduction of identifiably systematic procedures along with a technical vocabulary. In most cases, such systematic procedures and technical vocabulary adequately camouflage explanatory vacuity. In other cases, the reiteration of professional commonplaces and a veneer of scholarly research suffice.

Thus the most valuable writings in literary criticism and theory will generally be those which contribute to increasing production while at once decreasing labor and creating the illusion of explanatory capacity, etc. Moreover, for obvious reasons, the ideology of these criticisms, theories, etc., will be one which claims for them explanatory capacity, ethical power, and so on.

Post-structuralism in general—and deconstruction in particular—provides a clear illustration of this. During the period when deconstruction became the dominant ideology of English literary studies in the United States, the neat methods of New Critical text-production were proving less and less efficient. More and more people had less and less to say. They had learned the standard clichés and were now finding it difficult either to expand or reapply them. Moreover, the job situation was grim. There was a great deal of competition for very few places. As the competition would for the most part be won by publication, a method for drastically increasing publication was imperative. There was a brief interest in structuralism, but it clearly required too great labor. Deconstruction—as popularly understood—provided the perfect solution. Work was minimized as scholarship was discarded. The illusion of substance was maintained by the presence of an identifiably systematic—indeed mechanical—procedure and a highly technical vocabulary. Finally, and most significantly, a simple method for publication-generation was introduced. One need no longer find new ways of reiterating the old clichés, one could now either simply negate them or translate them into the new terminology.

As to the first, the deconstructive method of hierarchy-reversal may be and has been expanded so as to encompass the reversal of past critical judgments. Just as Rousseau's claims concerning origin may be 'demonstrated' to be undermined by the very language of his text, so too may Shakespeare's claims of providence be 'demonstrated' to be thus undermined. In this way, all the old articles asserting Shakespeare's providentialism may be paired with new articles asserting his *anti*-providentialism. Similarly, old articles on Shakespeare's misogyny may be paired with new articles on his anti-misogyny. And so on. Clearly this is a great boon for production—very little labor and no novelty are required thus mechanically to generate new publications. As R. Cairns Craig has pointed out, "deconstructionism is very much, now, a processing machine through which any work of literature can be fed" (Craig 1980, p. 527) and thus it fulfills a crucial function within the cycle of production and consumption in the academic economy.

Beyond the reversal of critical commonplaces, deconstructive argumentation also allows us easily to rewrite such commonplaces in a new, technical vocabulary. Both New Critical and Deconstructive methods are textualist and anti-intentional, but more important they supply parallel vocabularies. Thus where 'ambiguity' might have fit previously, now 'an unsynthesizable and irreducible free play' may be substituted. Where formerly 'irony' might have been found, 'a dehiscence which splits the *énoncé* and the *énonciation*' may be inserted. For example, I recently read an article which dealt with what would formerly have been called 'Greta Garbo's screen trademark.' A discussion of this topic is, of course, *passé*, unmarketable. But the topic was now the admirably innovative 'Greta Garbo's screen *signature*,' with a footnote to Derrida's influential "Signature Event Context" (in Derrida 1982) providing the aura of theoretical subtlety. This sort of substitution occurred throughout the essay with such predictability that one wondered if it had actually been written in a New Critical idiom and subsequently translated for salability. Of course, most often the relations of substitution and rewriting are not so clear.

I am not claiming, of course, that all slovenly argumentation and crude, mechanical criticism that calls itself deconstructive necessarily adheres to Derrida's principles. In fact, most does not. But precise theoretical accuracy and doctrinal purity are not important here. The present argument relies on more general connections, which I think are clear enough. While accuracy and purity are crucial in considerations of validity, only looser and more general connections are crucial to the market considerations we are examining. Similarly, I am not claiming that the New Critic's 'irony' is the post-structuralist's 'dehiscence,' etc. I am merely claiming that due to the parallels in the vocabulary, the one may be substituted for the other in the mechanical generation of publishable texts. It is irrelevant that educated use of the two terms is different. It only appears relevant due to the widespread illusion that the truth value or even precise claims of a piece of literary criticism are important to its acceptance or even of great interest to the author of that criticism.

It would seem, then, that—however they may be twisted, simplified, etc.—literary theories, such as that of Derrida, are accepted principally for reasons of market value. Whenever we buy a critical theory or interpretation, we make a capital investment. The function of political rhetoric such as that discussed at the outset of Chapter 2 is purely ideological. It provides an illusion which serves to mask the capitalistic interests which govern adjudication in literary study; it serves also to justify those adjudications, and the hierarchies based upon them.

I should emphasize that I speak of deconstruction only because it is, in my experience, the dominant theoretical ideology in the United States today—as John Ellis has pointed out, "there is a growing tendency to assume that an interest in theory of criticism automatically means an interest in the work of Derrida" (Ellis 1989, p. 18). But deconstruction is not unique in being commodified. All other critical ideologies also are accepted or rejected for assumed market value. Indeed, if this work is at all successful, it will be because some readers see potential for market exploitation therein. Though deconstructionists are, in my opinion, blameworthy for the extensive employment of an ideological rhetoric, they are hardly blameworthy for producing and distributing a theory widely perceived to be a good investment. It is capitalism, not deconstruction, that reduces all value to market value.

The Anarchist University and the Kingdom of Ends

I should like to conclude with some suggestions on how the university should be reconstituted in such a way as to approximate a kingdom of ends, to foster intellectual development, dialectic, and human decency, to substitute values of truth and justice for the now dominant market values. Of course, none of my suggestions is open to full implementation within a capitalist economy. As long as the society is capitalist, the university will itself be a capitalist institution, and thus an institution in which all teaching and research aspire to increased market value, *not* increased explanatory capacity, increased human decency, and so on. Ultimately, my suggestions could be followed through only in a socialist, anarchist society of relative prosperity and stability. A partially socialist democracy, such as Nicaragua, could probably allow for their limited implementation, were it not for the economic and social havoc wreaked by U.S. imperialism. A capitalist democracy, such as that in the United States, probably could not allow for their implementation at all. I discuss this reconstitution nonetheless because it is important for socialist libertarians to have a conception of how institutions might be restructured following a revolution (an unlikely event), or in the course of concerted non-revolutionary reform. Certainly, one of the major reasons for the profound failure of socialist revolutions—beyond their adherence to the Marxist-Leninist line of transitional statism and beyond the capitalist reaction in anticipation of which that statism was formulated—has been their inability to reconstitute institutions. On the other hand, it is probably unwise to specify this reconstitution in too great detail, in necessary ignorance of particular revolutionary or developmental conditions. Therefore, I will only indicate some of the major reforms I see as necessary to the reconstitution of a more just and more intellectually vigorous university, without filling in the details for any particular reform.

Beginning with course-work, first and most crucially, education should be entirely free at all levels. Like sustenance, education should be provided to all as fulfilling a basic need, though it should be required only until the child is able to make rational and responsible decisions regarding such study. As a protection to the rights of students—for example, those who are less self-assertive, more willing to accept lower grades, etc., as discussed above—there should be no grades, but only passes or failures, and there should be no permanent record of failures and no formal prerequisites for courses. A student should be allowed to enter any course he or she wishes, whatever the level. Requirements for passing courses should be strict, but, once again, only passes should be recorded permanently. In other words, any student should have the option of repeating a course as often as he or she likes and without penalty. Classes in which skills are taught—such as composition—should be *drastically* reduced in size. No teacher, whatever his or her subject, should have more than, say, forty students in a semester—fewer would be preferable. Correlatively, a significant tutorial component should be introduced into every course.

As to the faculty, they should have passed certain requirements—in most cases completion of a doctorate—in order to be accepted as paid instructors whose courses contribute to degrees. However, anyone should be allowed to present a non-credit course of lectures, without remuneration, if he or she so desires. There should be no ranks and no tenure.[3] A professor should be open to dismissal only under extraordinary circumstances. Quite generally, wages in the society should be identical for all occupations and at all levels of seniority, with a few qualifications such as those set forth in Russell's *Roads to Freedom* (Russell 1977, pp. 92–93). Course preferences should be awarded on a rotating basis. The balance between research and teaching should be decided individually and sabbaticals should be awarded at regular intervals to anyone with a project he or she is likely to pursue with diligence; in other words, any qualified person should be awarded a research sabbatical at the proper time if the person is likely to do the work, however ridiculous, unpromising, etc., his or her colleagues may think the project. *All* studies, theories, etc., should be pursued and encouraged in the manner advocated by Feyerabend (see Feyerabend 1975), though subsequent to their investigation all theories should be criticized rationally. I think Feyerabend is quite wrong in maintaining that rational disputation is not necessarily crucial to the development of theories. But I agree with Feyerabend that, with certain qualifications concerning availability of resources and the like, no research project should be foreclosed or terminated because it is generally agreed to be 'irrational.' The best theory is the most rational theory. However, we are often unable to recognize a theory as the most rational, or as rational at all, until it has been extensively revised and expanded through the pursuit of a vigorous project of research.

Given limited resources, I would support a lottery system for awarding research grants or a combination of lottery and peer review, with some awards granted by each. The advantage of peer review—review by a committee of 'experts' in the field—is that it guarantees a certain basic competence on the part of those receiving the grants. The disadvantage is that it encourages conformity. As David Horrobin has put it: "Peer review is the procedure that governs access to publication and money in modern science. Its function is to identify and reject poor work, to improve and accept good work, and to let the best through unimpeded. It performs the first two well but fails disastrously with the third" (Horrobin 1982, p. 217). 'Experts' in a given field are necessarily people who have a vested interest in the field as it is and thus have strong motivation to resist highly innovative proposals. Indeed, even when they are honest, this vested interest exacerbates the already strong confirmatory bias from which such researchers—and others—suffer. In work already cited, Michael Mahoney has shown the shocking degree to which this is in fact the case. A pure lottery system does not have the disadvantage of stifling innovation, but it also does not ensure competence—in principle, it could award a four year old money to build a time-machine. What is needed, I think, is a set of criteria determining competence—relevant degrees or experience, letters of reference from workers in the field, etc.—which would not bear on the value of the specific project, but on the relevant competence of those proposing the project. To enter the lottery, one would need to fulfill these criteria. But then the awards themselves would be given at random. (Oddly enough, according to the research of Cole, Cole, and Simon, National Science Foundation grants are in effect already given at random, after some basic eliminations. The difference, of course, is that under the present system the chance elements are denied and the elimination is to a great extent guided by bias, rather than being a straightforward matter of determining competence.) Also, after the awards have been granted, a committee of some sort could review and, if necessary, adjust, the proposed budgets. Finally, there would, of course, be certain sorts of projects—involving, for example, certain types of animal research—which would simply be illegal, and thus eliminated, by a legal panel, on those grounds.

As to the profession as a whole, professional societies should remain intact, but with considerably more fluid memberships. More important, the professional press should be *entirely free.* Now, "[t]he publication system is a type of control system," as Walter Powell has observed. Procedures for publication decisions, supposedly designed to guarantee that the very best work and only the very best work makes its way into print, in fact do something very different. As we have already noted, peer review functions at least in part to inhibit the publication of work which does not support prevailing views. Other research indicates that it functions to inhibit the publication of work by those from less prestigious institutions (see Peters and Ceci 1982) and to encourage a range of things from triviality in research focus to obscurity in prose style (Armstrong 1980, 1982; for a summary of peer-review research, see Mahoney 1985, p. 33). In order to put an end to this situation, and thereby to promote the sort of informed and full dialectic we are seeking, such evaluative constraints on publication should be eliminated. In other words, all books and all articles—and all reviews and all responses to reviews—which anyone might wish to publish should be published. Editorial suggestions for revision should be encouraged, but none should be binding. Similarly, all conferences should be entirely open and everyone wishing to speak should be allowed to do so. In both cases, the only possible qualifications should concern topic and length. Thus a journal of Shakespeare studies should be allowed to reject an analysis of quantum logic or ask that a study of Shakespeare be reduced in length. Similarly, a press should be allowed to limit the number of books published per person per year, though in general this should not be a problem. On the other hand, such a scheme as I am proposing would probably necessitate the transformation of publishing, such that there would be no journals or publishing houses, but only computer-stored texts, entered directly by their authors and available at terminals for reading or printing.

As to the *topics* of our teaching and research, it has been widely remarked that, with its almost exclusive emphasis on male writers and Europeans, mainstream literary study in the United States is hopelessly andro- and ethno-centric. To look only at the Indian tradition, when we teach literary theory, when do we mention Bharata-muni, *rasa* theory, or Abhinavagupta? When we speak of great world drama, how often do we include classical Sanskrit works such as *Shakuntala*? Our high culture is undoubtedly a culture based in part upon racial and sexual exclusion. Many writers have advocated revision of the canon for this reason, and I certainly agree. Indeed, I could see advantages to reversing the present curriculum for a time—say, a decade. Now-canonical authors (possibly excepting the few women, blacks, and third-world writers included in this category) could be confined to special topics courses, while the main curricular courses would concern Indian and African, possibly even Canadian or Irish literature, women's literature, especially that of the third world, black literature, and so on. Indeed, the entire curriculum could be restructured along such anti-Eurocentric, anti-imperialist, anti-sexist, anti-racist lines. Then we might study Sanskrit and Kinyarwanda and Cherokee to fulfill our requirements, with Latin and French and German available for those with special interests; ayurvedic and other alternative treatments could gain a prominent place in our medical schools (first in controlled tests, of course), and so on. Moreover, returning to literature, many scholars and critics might turn away from the canonical texts of European literature and devote themselves for some time to the excluded literatures of dominated groups.

A reform such as this—resulting, one would hope, in a more balanced curriculum at the end of the decade—could do no intellectual harm to students (e.g., we have no reason to believe that learning Kinyarwanda would be less intellectually stimulating than learning French, and in fact it might be more intellectually stimulating). Moreover, this could aid many students in beginning to overcome various sorts of ideology. Indeed, it would not even harm the scholarly disciplines as they now stand. Even our understanding of Virgil or of Shakespeare may be deepened and rendered more sensitive by our appreciation of other cultures, other works, other traditions. Breadth of study, if sincerely and rigorously undertaken, does not inhibit but expand our understanding of particular fields.[4]

Leaving aside considerations of vocation, all our institutional obligations as professors and critics reduce to a fostering of and engagement in a Socratic dialectic of literary study, a dialectic which is rational, empirical, and minimally interpretive; a dialectic which is at once generous toward all research and critical of all hypothesis; a dialectic which engages all as ends in themselves and strives toward the establishment of a kingdom of ends; a dialectic which continually seeks to understand the achievement of the fictional in the context of the real, and which continually seeks to judge the real in terms of the ideal; a dialectic, then, which seeks rigorously to understand both what is and what might be, and thereby ultimately to reconcile the actual to the possible. It is the aim of a libertarian and socialist university to allow precisely this dialectic. And it is the aim of political interpretation to practice this dialectic, with or without such a university.

NOTES

CHAPTER 2

1. Of course, there are many senses of 'ideology'—and of 'critique of ideology' also. I define the term as I will employ it hereafter. An excellent, lucid, and brief examination of the various senses of both terms, along with a helpful, introductory bibliography, may be found in Geuss 1981. To Geuss's list it is useful to add the original texts of Marx and Engels (e.g., *The German Ideology*) and those of the French school (e.g., Althusser 1981). I should emphasize that ideology in my sense is not the only thing which gives rise to or sustains, say, oppression. Unreflective mimetic behavior—e.g., 'spontaneous' ill-treatment of women—is an obvious case in point, as mentioned above.

2. Noam Chomsky offers other arguments against the notion of autonomous language—which he terms "E-language"—in several recent works. See, for example, Chomsky 1980, pp. 117ff. and Chomsky 1986, pp. 19ff.

3. Along the same lines, Rodolph Gasché claims that deconstruction operates at a level at which the Principle of Non-Contradiction does not apply (Gasché 1986, p. 104). Gasché refers here to the level of concepts at which contradictories are mutually definitive and thus, he claims, internally incoherent. Certainly, the Principle of Non-Contradiction does not apply to concepts, but for quite different reasons—specifically, it applies only to predicates with respect to fixed arguments. But in any event mutual definability in no way involves incoherence in the logical or any other ordinary sense. If salt is 'not pepper,' it does not mean that the concept of salt has 'pepperness,' hence its opposite, 'within it,' as Gasché indicates. If anything, it means that the concept of salt has 'not pepperness,' and thus *not* its opposite, 'within it' (though, as I argue below, this whole way of discussing meaning is inappropriate and misleading). In sum, the fact that one can define 'opposites' relative to one another simply has no consequences respecting logical contradiction or coherence.

214 Notes

4. Anyone who has heard a devotee of deconstruction speak of the "moving" experience of hearing Derrida lecture, or of the bitter suffering, repression, and academic rejection Derrida has suffered at the hands of the logophallocrats, cannot help recognizing the dᵣ ;ree to which he has been elevated to this status. I do not, by the way, blame Derrida for this.

5. This chapter was written before the discovery of de Man's Nazi past, or Heidegger's extensive involvement with German fascism. For an interesting discussion of the former, see Wiener 1988. I should emphasize that neither of these discoveries has any bearing on the validity of the linguistic or other intellectual work of de Man or Heidegger, not to mention that of related thinkers. However, it does add an obvious irony to deconstructive claims of political superiority.

6. It should be clear that my account here has definite points of contact with certain claims of Merleau-Ponty (see, for example, Merleau-Ponty 1962, pp. 364–65), as well Husserl's formulations concerning the *Lebenswelt* (see Husserl 1970, pp. 103–89, and Husserl 1973, pp. 41f.), Heidegger's exposition of the concept of the *zuhanden* (see, for example, Heidegger 1962, pp. 95–102), and various related notions. However, my metaphysical differences with these thinkers should be quite clear also. Further, in many ways closer connections with the preceding suggestions may be found in certain classical Marxist analyses, such as V. A. Lektorsky's treatment of the inseparability of "external practical activity, the process of cognition, and communication" (Lektorsky 1984, p. 259), and Vygotsky's earlier, related researches (see Vygotsky 1962 and Hogan 1980, pp. 51–53). M. H. Abrams has expressed a related view as well, in this case drawn in part from Anglo-American philosophy of language. As Abrams puts it, "language, whether spoken or written, is the use of a great variety of speech-acts to accomplish a great diversity of human purposes; only one of these many purposes is to assert something about a state of affairs; and such a linguistic assertion does not mirror, but serves to direct attention to selected aspects of that state of affairs" (Abrams 1988, p. 555).

7. Derrida recognizes that bi-polar oppositions may be multiple. For example, in his essay on the "Linguistic Circle of Geneva," Derrida lists the "series of oppositions nature/law, nature/convention, nature/art, nature/society, nature/freedom," and so on (Derrida 1982, p. 152). He does not explain why these form a series of bi-polar oppositions, rather than a part of the larger system of oppositions, etc. However, if they are mapped onto present/different, as I am suggesting, then their bi-polarity becomes clear.

8. I should point out that while Derrida does often adopt the generalized notion of writing (see, for example, Derrida 1976, pp. 44 and 60), he recurs to writing in the ordinary sense with equal frequency (see, for example, Derrida 1982, p. 95). Indeed, he even goes so far as to say that "I

would like to demonstrate that the recognizable traits of the classical and narrowly defined concept of writing are generalizable" (Derrida 1982, p. 316). The point here is that Derrida's arguments do not hold however he specifies the notion of writing.

9. I am indebted to Mike Walsh for suggesting this example concerning vernaculars. For this entire discussion, I am indebted to the work of Walter J. Ong. See, for example, Ong 1967, pp. 17–110.

CHAPTER 3

1. I pass over one interestingly problematic case where linguistic sexism may have separate force even in a relatively non-sexist society—compulsory gender-marking in the use of personal pronouns. Quite generally, when we speak we give only information germane to the topic under consideration. Thus, if we are discussing how to get somewhere and I say, 'There won't be much traffic on Main St.,' you will take me to be indicating that we might reach our destination by taking Main St., and not merely making some random, irrelevant comment. This is part of what Paul Grice calls the "rules of conversational implicature" (see Grice 1975). Now ordinarily we only give the height, weight, hair color, etc., of a person when it is relevant in the given context. However, we *always* give sex, at least whenever we use a third person singular pronoun. As Elizabeth Beardsley has argued, this grammatical fact might encourage children to consider gender as *essential*, as relevant in all contexts (see Beardsley 1973). On the other hand, as James McCawley has pointed out, "Hungarians and Turks don't appear to be less sexist than Americans despite the fact that their languages don't distinguish between *he* and *she*" (McCawley 1979a, p. 177).

2. These conclusions are also supported, in their general outline, by the inferences of Sandra Gilbert and Susan Gubar—see Gilbert 1985, pp. 114ff. As should be clear, I do not share Gilbert's and Gubar's high opinion of what they themselves refer to as the (counterfactual) "fantasies" of feminists of difference—see, for example, Gilbert and Gubar 1985, pp. 522–23, and 538–39.

3. This view may bear some relation to that of Hilary Putnam, who has recently advocated what he terms "internal realism" (see Putnam 1981, pp. 49ff.). However, I find Putnam's analysis somewhat difficult to follow in detail and suspect that he has not entirely rejected an essentialist conception of truth, that he has simply tried to 'steer a middle path' in the absolutist/ relativist debate, rather than rejecting the terms that debate. It is not clear that such a 'middle path' is possible. Perhaps this is why Putnam sometimes appears a relativist and sometimes an absolutist, at least in my reading.

4. In fact, beyond that, at a personal level, I myself feel that while superficial differences between cultures may be quite extensive and disorienting, profound differences between cultures are few and really no more difficult to comprehend than many—also profound—differences between individuals who share a culture. In other words, leaving aside very important but superficial differences—as well as problems of racism, closed-mindedness, and so on—the variations of degree between intra- and intercultural understanding do not seem to me that great. For example, in my experiences with in-laws in Kashmiri villages I have not felt any deeper conceptual or moral or other alienation than I feel when visiting my own relatives in the American midwest or in Europe. Admittedly, however, personal experiences cannot provide a solid basis for wide-ranging inferences about cultural difference.

CHAPTER 4

1. There is a particularly striking example of the failure to question a problematic in Irigaray's "Psychoanalytic Theory: Another Look." Having summarized the history of the debate on the castration complex, Irigaray undertakes to criticize its presuppositions by way of a series of seven questions. The first six questions (Irigaray 1985b, pp. 63–65) are very incisive and manage clearly to expose dubious premises common to all positions in the debate. For example, the first question is "*Why has the alternative between clitoral and vaginal pleasure played such a significant role?*" In the final question, Irigaray turns to what is in many ways the most critical issue—sublimation. The question we might expect is, 'Why has it been assumed that women fail to sublimate?' However, Irigaray does not ask this. Neither does she ask, 'Why have women failed to sublimate?,' which would at least imply a capacity for sublimation. Rather, Irigaray asks, "*Why is woman so little suited for sublimation?*" (p. 66). Thus Irigaray simply assumes, against all evidence, first of all that women have not sublimated and secondly that, indeed, women *cannot* sublimate. Thus, even in the context of a questioning of ideological presuppositions, Irigaray finds it impossible even to imagine doubting this most extreme and most obviously false form of patriarchal ideology. Elsewhere, of course, Irigaray 'celebrates' this 'understanding' precisely as would be expected from the preceding analysis, for in her treatment of the topic she has merely shifted [{male, sublimating, superior}, {female, non-sublimating, inferior}] to [{male, sublimating, inferior}, {female, non-sublimating, superior}].

2. Indeed, in this connection, Kant's views on moral pedagogy seem more to the point. In Part II of the *Critique of Practical Reason* (the

"Methodology of Pure Practical Reason") and even more in Part II of *The Metaphysical Principles of Virtue* ("The Methodology of Ethics"), Kant urges a dialogical approach to ethical instruction, at least for more advanced students. Specifically, Kant distinguishes an "acroamatic" method of inculcating virtue, "where all but the teacher are mere auditors," from an "erotematic" method, "in which the teacher asks of his[/her] students what he[/she] wants to teach them" (Kant 1964b, p. 146). Moreover, within the latter, Kant further distinguishes the catechetic from the dialogistic, "where both teacher and pupil question one another" (p. 147). The latter, a clear form of Socratic dialectic, is, for Kant, the highest form of ethical pedagogy, "For if anyone wants to ask something of another's reason, he[/she] can only do it through dialogue, i.e., teacher and student mutually questioning and answering one another. The teacher's questions direct his[/her] pupil's train of thought merely by developing the pupil's predisposition to grasp certain concepts through proposed cases (he[/she] is the midwife for his[/her] pupil's thoughts). The pupil, who thus becomes aware that he[/she] too is able to think, by his[/her] counterquestions (about obscurities or about his[/her] doubts that stand in the way of the propositions advanced) teaches his[/her] teacher" (p. 146).

CHAPTER 5

1. There are, of course, other, more explicit or self-conscious forms, which may be less common, but are no less important. Indeed, they may be far more important. A striking example may be found in the recent introduction into some influential composition texts of the gender ideologies of Cixous and Irigaray. Through these texts, ideologies become part of the very *content* of the composition courses in which the texts are used, rather than being confined merely to the occasional paper dealing with an explicitly political topic, as in the cases cited above.

2. Having cited Cahn on these issues, I should note that I disagree with Cahn's contention that peer supervision is the best method for teaching evaluation. The data which Cahn cites (in Cahn 1986) disputing the validity of student evaluations apply also, if in lesser degree, to peer evaluations resulting from classroom visitation and the like. Moreover, all the problems of peer review—which we will discuss below—recur in peer evaluation, sometimes with a vengeance.

Though it by no means entirely avoids the problems of peer review, it seems clear that the best method for evaluation, if evaluation must be done, is the perusal of student papers and exams—with the instructor's name concealed, if possible. A teacher who can give a challenging exam and receive excellent, considered answers, indicative of understanding and not rote memorization, is, in my view, an excellent teacher, no matter what students may write and no matter what a colleague may ascertain from a single class attendance. Oddly, as far as I am aware, student performance is simply irrelevant to teaching evaluation at virtually all institutions—and not, I am sure, due to a recognition of the degree to which various reviewer-biases limit the value of even this sort of evaluation.

3. In *American Professors: A National Resource Imperiled*, Howard Bowen and Jack Schuster present some cogent arguments for the retention of tenure (see Bowen and Schuster 1986, pp. 235–38 and following). Certainly anyone wishing to institute an anarchist university would have to take into account the arguments of Bowen and Schuster and seek to preserve the advantages of the tenure system in another manner. Bowen and Schuster cite four important benefits of a tenure system: (1) the encouragement of freedom of speech, (2) the granting of security, which is helpful in encouraging sustained research, (3) the fostering of collegiality, and (4) (again) the granting of security, which is in this case helpful in drawing talent into the profession. In my view, collegiality can be fostered otherwise than through a tenure system which often brutalizes younger faculty and security can be promoted otherwise than through a tenure system which renders many junior faculty insecure almost to the point of pathology. There is something in these suggestions of the old joke that it is good to beat your head against the wall because it feels so great when you stop.

As to academic freedom, I believe that Bowen and Schuster fail to seek the deeper causes of the limitations on academic freedom which do in fact exist. As Bowen and Schuster point out, Gerald Reagan "cites five contemporary constraints on academic freedom" (in Reagan 1982). These are "student consumerism, vocationalism, program planning, allocation of research funds, and the tenure-granting process" (Bowen and Schuster 1986, p. 127). This seems to me entirely correct and part of the point of the suggestions for the institution of a libertarian socialist university is to lift precisely these constraints—as well as comparable constraints on students. (I might emphasize that the staff members deserve similar considerations, but these are likely to fall under more general categories in libertarian socialist social transformation.)

Bowen and Schuster, however, more or less dismiss the final point, accepting only that "persons with weak market positions might feel inhibited," despite the fact that there could not be any "intention of actual wrong doing on the part of senior faculty, administrators, trustees, or legislators" (p. 127). Of course, none of these people thinks, 'I am going to engage in wrong doing.' The point is that, consciously or unconsciously, people will scrutinize for merits the records of tenure-candidates toward whom they are favorably inclined and scrutinize for flaws the records of tenure-candidates toward whom they are unfavorably inclined. Clearly, the vociferous expression of any but the most bland political views will color people's attitudes toward the one expressing these views. Thus it is extremely unlikely that a tenure-candidate's political activism, or non-activism, will not affect the degree to which the person is lauded or execrated in the process of a tenure judgment and thus his or her chances for achieving tenure (or for that matter being hired in the first place, passing third-year review, etc.).

Tenure may indeed secure freedom of speech for senior faculty, but it may render such freedom innocuous also. If most of the dissidents are eliminated, the few who remain may be treated as harmless cranks in a world of free consensus.

4. Indeed, there are cogent *practical* reasons for urging inter-cultural education. In his recent study of education, *Cultural Literacy: What Every American Needs to Know*, E. D. Hirsch, Jr., makes a convincing case for the establishment of an educational curriculum which would sustain and disseminate a common cultural knowledge. Common cultural knowledge, Hirsch argues, would ease communication, cooperation, understanding, etc., and thus benefit all concerned. This is almost certainly true. What is odd about Hirsch's book, though, is that he claims this cultural knowledge must be *national*. But surely every argument supporting the establishment of a common cultural knowledge based upon, say, American history, literature, etc., applies with greater force to support the establishment of common cultural knowledge which is *internationally* based. Of course, some common knowledge is national or even confined to states or cities (e.g., it is more important to know the speed limits in one's own state than in a foreign country). But beyond a few practical cases, home culture has no greater claim to our attention than foreign culture—and in some cases it has less. Even for the crudest, practical concerns, outside of ethical considerations, it is far from clear that modern American poetry is more important, for our students or for ourselves, than, say, the contemporary poetry of Central America.

REFERENCES AND
SELECTED BIBLIOGRAPHY

Abel, Elizabeth, ed. 1982. *Writing and Sexual Difference*. Chicago: University of Chicago.

Abrams, M. H. 1988. "The Deconstructive Angel." In Davis and Schleifer 1988.

Althusser, Louis. 1965. "Contradiction et Surdétermination (Notes pour une recherche)." *Pour Marx*. Paris: François Maspero.

————. 1981. "Ideology and Ideological State Apparatuses." *Lenin and Philosophy*. Trans. Ben Brewster. New York: Monthly Review Press.

————. 1981a. "Freud and Lacan." In *Lenin and Philosophy*. Trans. Ben Brewster. New York: Monthly Review Press.

————, and Balibar, Étienne. 1979. *Reading Capital*. Trans. Ben Brewster. London: Verso Editions.

Aristotle. 1965. περὶ ψυχῆσ. In *Aristotle De Anima With Translation, Introduction and Notes*. Ed. R. D. Hicks. Amsterdam: Adolf M. Hakkert.

————. 1984. "On the Soul." Trans. J. A. Smith. In *The Complete Works of Aristotle*. Vol. 1. Ed. Jonathan Barnes. Princeton: Princeton University Press.

————. 1984a. "Rhetoric." Trans. W. Rhys Roberts. In *The Complete Works of Aristotle*. Vol. 2. Ed. Jonathan Barnes. Princeton: Princeton University Press.

Armstrong, J. S. 1980. "Unintelligible Management Research and Academic Prestige." *Interfaces*. Vol. 10, pp. 80–86.

————. 1982. "Research on Scientific Journals: Implications for Editors and Authors." *Journal of Forecasting*. Vol. 1, pp. 83–104.

Bakunin, Michael. 1980. *Bakunin on Anarchism*. Ed. and trans. Sam Dolgoff. Montreal: Black Rose Books.

Baron, Dennis. 1986. *Grammar and Gender*. New Haven: Yale University Press.

Beardsley, Elizabeth. 1973. "Referential Genderization." *The Philosophical Forum.* Vol. 5.

Benderly, Beryl Lieff. 1987. *The Myth of Two Minds: What Gender Means and Doesn't Mean.* New York: Doubleday.

Bloom, Harold, et al., eds. 1979. *Deconstruction and Criticism.* New York: Continuum.

Booth, Wayne. 1983. "Freedom of Interpretation: Bakhtin and the Challenge of Feminist Criticism." In Mitchell 1983.

Borthwick, Meredith. 1984. *The Changing Role of Women in Bengal 1849–1905.* Princeton: Princeton University Press.

Bowen, Howard R. and Schuster, Jack H. 1986. *American Professors: A National Resource Imperiled.* New York: Oxford University Press.

Butler, Christopher. 1984. *Interpretation, Deconstruction, and Ideology.* Oxford: Clarendon Press.

Cahn, Steven M. 1986. *Saints and Scamps: Ethics in Academia.* Totowa, N.J.: Rowman and Littlefield.

————. 1987. "Faculty Members Should Be Evaluated by Their Peers, Not by Their Students." *The Chronicle of Higher Education.* Vol. XXXIV, no. 7.

Cameron, Deborah. 1985. *Feminism and Linguistic Theory.* London: Macmillan.

Caplow, Theodore and McGee, Reece. 1958. *The Academic Marketplace.* New York: Basic Books.

Chodorow, Nancy. 1978. *The Reproduction of Mothering.* Berkeley: University of California Press.

Chomsky, Noam. 1969. *American Power and the New Mandarins: Historical and Political Essays.* New York: Pantheon Books.

————. 1970. "Government in the Future." Audio-Forum cassette recording. Guilford, Ct.: Jeffrey Norton Publishers.

————. 1973. "Notes on Anarchism." *For Reasons of State.* New York: Vintage Books.

————. 1979. *Language and Responsibility.* Trans. John Viertel. New York: Pantheon.

————. 1980. *Rules and Representations.* New York: Columbia University Press.

————. 1982. *Towards a New Cold War: Essays on the Current Crisis and How We Got There.* New York: Pantheon Books.

————. 1982a. *Noam Chomsky on The Generative Enterprise: A Discussion with Riny Huybregts and Henk von Riemsdijk.* Dordrecht: Foris Publications.

————. 1983. *The Fateful Triangle.* Boston: South End Press.

_____. 1985. *Turning the Tide: U.S. Intervention in Central America and the Struggle for Peace.* Boston: South End Press.

_____. 1986. *Knowledge of Language: Its Nature, Origin, and Use.* New York: Praeger Publishers.

_____. 1987. "Equality: Language Development, Human Intelligence, and Social Organization." *The Chomsky Reader.* Ed. James Peck. New York: Pantheon.

_____. 1988. *The Culture of Terrorism.* Boston: South End Press.

_____, and Herman, Edward. 1979. *The Political Economy of Human Rights. Volume I: The Washington Connection and Third World Fascism, Volume II: After the Cataclysm: Postwar Indochina and the Reconstruction of Imperial Ideology.* Boston: South End Press.

Christensen, Peter Moller and Delman, Jorgen. 1981. "A Theory of Transitional Society: Mao Zedong and the Shanghai School." *Bulletin of Concerned Asian Scholars.* Vol. 13, no. 2.

Cixous, Helène. 1980. "The Laugh of the Medusa." In Marks and de Courtivron 1980.

_____. 1986. "Sorties." In Cixous and Clément 1986.

_____, and Clément, Catherine. 1986. *The Newly Born Woman.* Trans. Betsy Wing. Minneapolis: University of Minnesota Press.

Cole, Stephen, Cole, Jonathan, and Simon, Gary. 1981. "Chance and Consensus in Peer Review." *Science.* Vol. 214, pp. 881–86.

Coser, Lewis, Kadushin, Charles, and Powell, Walter. 1982. *Books: The Culture and Commerce of Publishing.* New York: Basic Books.

Craig, R. Cairns. 1980. "Criticism and the Truths of Literature." *Dalhousie Review.* Vol. 60, no. 3, pp. 517–35.

Culler, Jonathan. 1981. *The Pursuit of Signs: Semiotics, Literature, Deconstruction.* Ithaca: Cornell University Press.

_____. 1982. *On Deconstruction: Theory and Criticism after Structuralism.* Ithaca: Cornell University Press.

Davis, Robert Con and Schleifer, Ronald, eds. 1988. *Contemporary Literary Criticism.* New York: Longman.

de Beauvoir, Simone. 1974. *The Second Sex.* Trans. H. M. Parshley. New York: Vintage.

de Man, Paul. 1979. "Shelley Disfigured." In Bloom, et al., 1979.

_____. 1983. *Blindness and Insight: Essays in the Rhetoric of Contemporary Criticism.* Minneapolis: University of Minnesota Press.

Derrida, Jacques. 1972. "Structure, Sign, and Play in the Discourse of the Human Sciences." In Macksey and Donato 1972.

_____. 1973. *Speech and Phenomena.* Trans. David B. Allison. Evanston: Northwestern University Press.

———. 1976. *Of Grammatology.* Trans. Gayatri Chakravorty Spivak. Baltimore: Johns Hopkins University Press.

———. 1977. "Limited Inc abc." *Glyph.* 2.

———. 1978. "Freud and the Scene of Writing." *Writing and Difference.* Trans. Alan Bass. Chicago: University of Chicago Press.

———. 1979. *Spurs: Nietzsche's Styles/Éperons: Les Styles de Nietzsche.* Trans. Barbara Harlow. Chicago: University of Chicago Press.

———. 1980. *La Carte Postale: De Socrate à Freud et au-delà.* Paris: Flammarion.

———. 1981. *Dissemination.* Trans. Barbara Johnson. Chicago: University of Chicago Press.

———. 1981a. *Positions.* Trans. Alan Bass. Chicago: University of Chicago Press.

———. 1982. *Margins of Philosophy.* Trans. Alan Bass. Chicago: University of Chicago Press.

Dews, Peter. 1987. *Logics of Disintegration: Post-Structuralist Thought and the Claims of Critical Theory.* New York: Verso.

Dworkin, Ronald. 1983. "My Reply to Stanley Fish (and Walter Benn Michaels): Please Don't Talk about Objectivity Any More." In Mitchell 1983.

Eagleton, Terry. 1983. "Ineluctable Options." In Mitchell 1983.

Ecker, Gisela, ed. 1985. *Feminist Aesthetics.* Boston: Beacon Press.

Ellis, John. 1989. *Against Deconstruction.* Princeton: Princeton University Press.

Epstein, Cynthia Fuchs. 1988. *Deceptive Distinctions: Sex, Gender, and the Social Order.* New Haven: Yale University Press and New York: Russell Sage Foundation.

Fausto-Sterling, Anne. 1985. *Myths of Gender: Biological Theories about Women and Men.* New York: Basic Books.

Feyerabend, Paul. 1975. *Against Method: Outline of an Anarchistic Theory of Knowledge.* London: New Left Books.

Fichte, J. G. 1982. *The Science of Knowledge.* Ed. and Trans. Peter Heath and John Lachs. New York: Cambridge University Press.

Fish, Stanley E. 1980. *Is There a Text in this Class?* Cambridge: Harvard University Press.

———. 1985. "Anti-Professionalism." *New Literary History.* Vol. XVII, no. 1.

Flynn, Elizabeth. 1986. "Gender and Reading." In Flynn and Schweikert 1986.

———, and Schweikert, Patricinio, eds. 1986. *Gender and Reading: Essays on Readers, Texts, and Contexts.* Baltimore: The Johns Hopkins University Press.

Foucault, Michel. 1979. "My Body, This Paper, This Fire." Trans. Geoff Bennington. *Oxford Literary Review*. 4.

———. 1980. *The History of Sexuality. Volume I: An Introduction*. Trans. Robert Hurley. New York: Vintage.

Frege, Gottlob. 1980. *Translations from the Philosophical Writings of Gottlob Frege*. Ed. Peter Geach and Max Black. Third ed. Totowa: Rowman and Littlefield.

Freire, Paulo. 1986. *Pedagogy of the Oppressed*. Trans. Myra Ramos. New York: Continuum.

Freud, Sigmund. 1940. *Der Witz und seine Beziehung zum Unbewussten. Gesammelte Werke*, VI. London: Imago Publishing.

———. 1942. *Bruchstück einer Hysterie-Analyse. Gesammelte Werke* V. London: Imago Publishing.

———. 1954. *The Origins of Psychoanalysis: Letters to Wilhelm Fliess*. Ed. Eric Mosbacher and James Strachey. New York: Basic Books.

———. 1959. *Group Psychology and the Analysis of the Ego*. Trans. James Strachey. New York: W. W. Norton.

———. 1963. "A Note Upon the 'Mystic Writing Pad.'" Trans. Joan Riviere. In *General Psychological Theory*. Ed. Philip Rieff. New York: Collier Books.

———. 1963a. *Dora: An Analysis of a Case of Hysteria*. New York: Macmillan Publishing.

———. 1963b. *Sexuality and the Psychology of Love*. New York: Macmillan Publishing.

———. 1963c. *Jokes and Their Relation to the Unconscious*. Trans. James Strachey. New York: W. W. Norton.

———. 1965. *The Interpretation of Dreams*. Trans. James Strachey. New York: Avon Books.

———. 1965b. *New Introductory Lectures on Psychoanalysis*. New York: W. W. Norton.

Fromkin, Victoria and Rodman, Robert. 1983. *An Introduction to Language*. New York: CBS College Publishing.

Gardiner, Judith Kegan. 1982. "On Female Identity and Writing by Women." In Abel 1982.

Gasché, Rodolphe. 1986. *The Tain of the Mirror: Derrida and the Philosophy of Reflection*. Cambridge: Harvard University Press.

Geach, P. T. 1980. *Logic Matters*. Berkeley: University of California Press.

Geuss, Raymond. 1981. *The Idea of a Critical Theory: Habermas and the Frankfurt School*. New York: Cambridge University Press.

Gewirth, Alan. 1982. *Human Rights: Essays on Justification and Applications*. Chicago: University of Chicago Press.

Gilbert, Sandra. 1985. "Feminist Criticism in the University: An Interview with Sandra M. Gilbert." In Graff and Gibbons, 1985.

———, and Gubar, Susan. 1985. "Sexual Linguistics: Gender, Language, Sexuality." *New Literary History.* Vol. XVI, no. 3.

Gleason, Jean Berko. 1987. "Sex Differences in Parent-Child Interaction." In Philips, Steele, and Tanz 1987.

Gombrich, E. H. 1972. *Art and Illusion: A Study in the Psychology of Pictorial Representation.* Princeton: Princeton University Press.

Goodwin, Marjorie Harness, and Goodwin, Charles. 1987. "Children's Arguing." In Philips, Steele, and Tanz 1987.

Graff, Gerald. 1983. "The Pseudo-Politics of Interpretation." In Mitchell 1983.

——— and Gibbons, Reginald, eds. 1985. *Criticism in the University.* Evanston: Northwestern University Press.

Grassroots: The Newsletter of Grassroots International. 1986. Vol. 2, no. 1. (Spring.)

Grice, H. Paul. 1975. "Logic and Conversation." Excerpted in *Syntax and Semantics,* vol. III.

Grunbaum, Adolf. 1984. *The Foundations of Psychoanalysis: A Philosophical Critique.* Berkeley: The University of California Press.

Hall, Max. 1986. *Harvard University Press. A History.* Cambridge: Harvard University Press.

Hartman, Geoffrey. 1979. "Words, Wish, Worth: Wordsworth." In Bloom, et al., 1979.

Harvey, Irene E. 1986. *Derrida and the Economy of Difference.* Bloomington: University of Indiana Press.

Havelock, Eric. 1963. *Preface to Plato.* Cambridge: Belknap Press of Harvard University Press.

Hegel, G. W. F. 1969. *Wissenschaft der Logik.* 2 vols. Frankfurt: Suhrkamp Verlag.

———. 1970. *Phänomenologie des Geistes.* Frankfurt: Ullstein.

———. 1977. *Phenomenology of Spirit.* Trans. A. V. Miller. Oxford: Clarendon Press.

Heidegger, Martin. 1962. *Being and Time.* Trans. John Macquarrie and Edward Robinson. New York: Harper & Row.

Hiatt, Mary. 1977. *The Way Women Write.* New York: Teachers College Press.

Hintikka, Jaako and Hintikka, Merill B. 1983. "How Can Language be Sexist?" In Harding and Hintikka 1983.

Hirsch, E. D., Jr. 1976. *The Aims of Interpretation.* Chicago: University of Chicago Press.

———. 1983. "The Politics of Theories of Interpretation." In Mitchell 1983.

_____. 1987. *Cultural Literacy: What Every American Should Know.* Boston: Houghton Mifflin Co.

Hogan, Patrick Colm. 1980. "Meaning and Hegel." *The Southern Journal of Philosophy.* Vol. XVIII, no. 1.

_____. 1982. "Meaning, Intention, and Mind." *The Modern Schoolman.* Vol. LIX, no. 4.

_____. 1983. "Pomen, intenca in duh." Trans. Valter Motaln. *Problemi Razprave.* 1–2.

_____. Forthcoming a. "Preface: The Repression of Lacan." In Hogan and Pandit forthcoming.

_____. Forthcoming b. "The Symbolic—Structure and Ambiguity: Some Prolegomena to the Understanding and Criticism of Lacan." In Hogan and Pandit forthcoming.

_____ and Pandit, Lalita, eds. Forthcoming. *Criticism and Lacan: Essays and Dialogue on Language, Structure, and the Unconscious.* Athens: University of Georgia Press.

Holland, J., Holyoak, K., Nisbett, R., and Thagard, P. 1986. *Induction: Processes of Inference, Learning, and Discovery.* Cambridge: The MIT Press.

Holland, Norman N. 1982. *Laughing: A Psychology of Humor.* Ithaca: Cornell University Press.

hooks, bell. 1984. *Feminist Theory: From Margin to Center.* Boston: South End Press.

Horkheimer, Max and Adorno, Theodor. 1972. *Dialectic of Enlightenment.* Trans. J. Cumming. New York: Herder and Herder.

Horney, Karen. 1967. *Feminine Psychology.* New York: W. W. Norton.

Horrobin, David. 1982. "Peer review: A philosophically faulty concept which is proving disastrous for science." *The Behavioral and Brain Sciences.* Vol. 5, no. 2, pp. 217–18.

Husserl, Edmund. 1950. "Pariser Vortraege." In *Gesammelte Werke*, I. The Hague: Martinus Nijhoff.

_____. 1970. *The Crisis of European Sciences and Transcendental Phenomenology: An Introduction to Phenomenological Philosophy.* Trans. David Carr. Evanston: Northwestern University Press.

_____. 1973. *Experience and Judgment: Investigations in a Genealogy of Logic.* Ed. Ludwig Landgrebe. Trans. James E. Churchill and Karl Ameriks. Evanston: Northwestern University Press.

_____. 1977. *Cartesianische Meditationen.* Hamburg: Felix Meiner Verlag.

Irigaray, Luce. 1974. *Speculum de l'autre femme.* Paris: Éditions de Minuit.

_____. 1977. *Ce sexe qui n'en est pas un.* Paris: Éditions de Minuit.

————. 1985a. *Speculum of the Other Woman.* Trans. Gillian C. Gill. Ithaca: Cornell University Press.

————. 1985b. *This Sex Which Is Not One.* Trans. Catherine Porter. Ithaca: Cornell University Press.

Jack, J. C. 1916. *The Economic Life of a Bengal District: A Study.* Oxford: Clarendon Press.

Jameson, Fredric. 1981. *The Political Unconscious: Narrative as a Socially Symbolic Act.* Ithaca: Cornell University Press.

Johnson, Barbara. 1982. "Translator's Introduction." In Derrida 1981.

Kant, Immanuel. 1923. "Über ein vermeintes Recht aus Menschenliebe zu lügen." *Kant's gesammelte Schriften.* Band VIII. Herausgegeben von der Königlich Preussischen Akademie der Wissenschaften. Berlin und Leipzig: Walter de Gruyter.

————. 1951. *Critique of Judgement.* Trans. J. H. Bernard. New York: Hafner Press.

————. 1956. *Critique of Practical Reason.* Trans. Lewis White Beck. Indianapolis: Bobbs-Merrill.

————. 1964. *Groundwork of the Metaphysic of Morals.* Trans H. J. Paton. New York: Harper.

————. 1964b. *The Metaphysical Principles of Virtue.* Trans. James Ellington. New York: The Bobbs-Merrill Company.

————. 1965. *The Metaphysical Elements of Justice.* Trans. John Ladd. New York: The Bobbs-Merrill Company.

Katz, Jerrold. 1981. *Language and Other Abstract Objects.* Totowa: Rowman and Littlefield.

Klemenz-Belgardt, Edith. 1981. "American Research on Response to Literature: The Empirical Studies." *Poetics.* Vol. 10, pp. 357–80.

Kohut, Heinz. 1971. *The Analysis of the Self: A Systematic Approach to the Psychoanalytic Treatment of Narcissistic Personality Disorders.* New York: International Universities Press.

Kolko, Gabriel. 1984. *Main Currents in Modern American History.* New York: Pantheon Books.

————. 1985. *Anatomy of a War: Vietnam, the United States, and the Modern Historical Experience.* New York: Pantheon Books.

Kripke, Saul A. 1980. *Naming and Necessity.* Cambridge: Harvard University Press.

Kristeva, Julia. 1980. *Desire in Language.* Ed. Leon Roudiez. Trans. Thomas Gora, Alice Jardine, and Leon Roudiez.

————. 1982. *Powers of Horror: An Essay on Abjection.* Trans. Leon Roudiez. New York: Columbia University Press.

Kuhn, Thomas S. 1970. *The Structure of Scientific Revolutions.* Second ed. Chicago: University of Chicago Press.

Lacan, Jacques. 1966. *Écrits.* Paris: Éditions du Seuil.

_____ . 1973. *Le Séminaire, livre XI: Les quatre concepts fondamentaux de la psychanalyse.* Paris: Éditions du Seuil.

_____ . 1975a. *De la psychose paranoiaque dans ses rapports avec la personalité; suivi de Primiers écrits sur la paranoia.* Paris: Éditions du Seuil.

_____ . 1975b. *Le Séminaire, Livre I: Les Écrits Techniques de Freud.* Paris: Éditions du Seuil.

_____ . 1975c. *Le Séminaire, livre XX: Encore.* Paris: Éditions du Seuil.

_____ . 1978. *Le Séminaire, livre II: Le moi dans la theorie de Freud et dans la technique de la psychanalyse.* Paris: Éditions du Seuil.

Luria, Aleksander Romanovich. 1976. *Cognitive Development: Its Cultural and Social Foundations.* Ed. Michael Cole. Trans. M. Lopez-Morillas and Lynn Solotaroff. Cambridge: Harvard University Press.

Macksey, Richard and Donato, Eugenio. 1972. *The Structuralist Controversy.* Baltimore: Johns Hopkins University Press.

Mahoney, Michael. 1976. *Scientist as Subject: The Psychological Imperative.* Santa Barbara: Personal Empowerment Programs.

_____ . 1977. "Publication Prejudices: An Experimental Study of Confirmatory Bias in the Peer Review System." *Cognitive Therapy and Research.* Vol. 1, pp. 161–75.

_____ . 1985. "Open Exchange and Epistemic Progress." *American Psychologist.* Vol. 40, pp. 29–39.

_____ . 1987. "Scientific Publication and Knowledge Politics." *Journal of Social Behavior and Personality.* Vol. 2, no. 2 (pt. 1), pp. 165–76.

_____ and Kimper, T. P. 1976. "From Ethics to Logic: A Survey of Scientists." In Michael Mahoney, ed. *Scientist as Subject.* Cambridge: Ballinger, pp. 187–93.

Mao Tse-Tung. 1974. "Excerpts from *A Talk by Chairman Mao with a Foreign [Albanian] Military Delegation.*" In Milton, Milton, and Schurmann, 1974.

Marks, Elaine and de Courtivron, Isabelle, eds. 1980. *New French Feminisms.* New York: Schocken.

Marr, David. 1982. *Vision.* San Francisco: Freeman.

Marx, Karl. 1964. *The Economic and Philosophic Manuscripts of 1844.* Ed. Dirk J. Struik. Trans. Martin Milligan. New York: International Publishers.

_____ . 1967. *Capital, vol. 1: A Critical Analysis of Capitalist Production.* Ed. Frederick Engels. Trans. Samuel Moore and Edward Aveling. New York: International Publishers.

_____ and Engels, Frederick. 1975. *Manifesto of the Communist Party.* Peking: Foreign Languages Press.

———. 1976. *The German Ideology: Part One with Selections from Parts Two and Three and Supplementary Texts.* Ed. C. J. Arthur. New York: International Publishers.

Masters, William and Johnson, Virginia. 1966. *Human Sexual Response.* Boston: Little, Brown and Company.

McCawley, James D. 1979. "On Interpreting the Theme of this Conference." In *Adverbs, Vowels, and Other Objects of Wonder.* Chicago: University of Chicago Press.

———. 1979a. "Review of R. Lakoff, *Language and Woman's Place.*" In *Adverbs, Vowels, and Other Objects of Wonder.* Chicago: University of Chicago Press.

Merleau-Ponty, Maurice. 1962. *Phenomenology of Perception.* Trans. Colin Smith. London: Routledge and Kegan Paul.

———. 1974. "On the Phenomenology of Language." In *Phenomenology, Language, and Sociology.* Ed. John O'Neill. London: Heinemann Educational Books.

Merod, Jim. 1987. *The Political Responsibility of the Critic.* Ithaca: Cornell University Press.

Michaels, Walter Benn. 1983. "Is There a Politics of Interpretation?" In Mitchell 1983.

Miller, J. Hillis. 1979. "The Critic as Host." In Bloom, et al., 1979.

Millett, Kate. 1970. *Sexual Politics.* New York: Doubleday and Company.

Milton, David and Milton, Nancy. 1976. *The Wind Will Not Subside: Years in Revolutionary China—1964–1969.* New York: Pantheon Books.

Milton, David, Milton, Nancy, and Schurmann, David. 1974. *People's China: Social Experimentation, Politics, Entry Onto the World Scene, 1966 through 1972.* New York: Vintage Books.

Mitchell, Juliet. 1979. *Psychoanalysis and Feminism: Freud, Reich, Laing, and Women.* New York: Vintage Books.

———, and Rose, Jacqueline. 1982. *Feminine Sexuality: Jacques Lacan and the école freudienne.* New York: W. W. Norton.

Mitchell, W. J. T., ed. 1983. *The Politics of Interpretation.* Chicago: University of Chicago Press.

Moss, Ralph W. 1980. *The Cancer Syndrome.* New York: Grove Press.

Naftulin, Donald H., Ware, John E., and Donnelly, Frank A. 1973. "The Doctor Fox Lecture: A Paradigm of Educational Seduction." *The Journal of Medical Education.* Vol. 48.

Nagel, Thomas. 1986. *The View from Nowhere.* New York: Oxford University Press.

Nisbett, Richard and Ross, Lee. 1980. *Human Inference: Strategies and Shortcomings of Social Judgment.* Englewood Cliffs, N.J.: Prentice-Hall.

Noble, David. 1989. "The Multinational Multiversity." *Zeta Magazine.* Vol. 2, no. 4, pp. 17–23.

Norris, Christopher. 1982. *Deconstruction: Theory and Practice.* New York: Methuen.

Nussbaum, Martha. 1985. "'Finely Aware and Richly Responsible': Moral Attention and the Moral Task of Literature." *The Journal of Philosophy.* Vol. LXXXII, no. 10.

Ohmann, Richard. 1976. *English in America: A Radical View of the Profession.* New York: Oxford University Press.

Olson, Gary. 1988. "Execution Class." *Zeta Magazine.* July/August, pp. 111–13.

Ong, Walter J. 1967. *The Presence of the Word: Some Prolegomena for Cultural and Religious History.* New York: Clarion Books.

––––––. 1971. *Rhetoric, Romance, and Technology: Studies in the Interaction of Expression and Culture.* Ithaca: Cornell University Press.

––––––. 1982. *Orality and Literacy: The Technologizing of the Word.* London: Methuen.

Pannekoek, Anton. 1975. *Lenin as Philosopher.* New York: Breakout Press.

Peters, Douglas and Ceci, Stephen. 1982. "Peer-review practices of psychological journals: The fate of published articles, submitted again." *The Behavioral and Brain Sciences.* Vol. 5, no. 2, pp. 187–95.

Philips, Susan U. 1987. "Introduction: The Interaction of Social and Biological Processes in Women's and Men's Speech." In Philips, Steele, and Tanz 1987.

––––––, Steele, Susan, and Tanz, Christine. 1987. *Language, Gender and Sex in Comparative Perspective.* New York: Cambridge University Press.

Piaget, Jean. 1971. *Biology and Knowledge: An Essay on the Relations between Organic Regulations and Cognitive Processes.* Chicago: University of Chicago Press.

Plato. 1970. "The Apology." *The Dialogues of Plato, Vol. I: The Apology and Other Dialogues.* Trans. Benjamin Jowett. London: Sphere Books.

Popper, Karl. 1961. *The Poverty of Historicism.* New York: Harper and Row.

––––––. 1972. *Objective Knowledge: An Evolutionary Approach.* Oxford: Clarendon Press.

Powell, Walter. 1985. *Getting into Print: The Decision-Making Process in Scholarly Publishing.* Chicago: University of Chicago Press.

Putnam, Hilary. 1975. "The Meaning of 'Meaning.'" *Mind, Language and Reality.* New York: Cambridge University Press.

——— . 1981. *Reason, Truth and History.* New York: Cambridge University Press.

——— . 1983. "Models and Reality." In *Philosophy of Mathematics: Selected Readings.* Ed. Paul Benacerraf and Hilary Putnam. New York: Cambridge University Press.

Questions Féministes. 1980. "Variations on Common Themes." In Marks and de Courtivron 1980.

Quine, W. V. 1976. *The Ways of Paradox and Other Essays.* Revised ed. Cambridge: Harvard University Press.

Reagan, Gerald M. 1982. "Contemporary Constraints on Academic Freedom." *Educational Forum.* Summer.

Ricoeur, Paul. 1970. *Freud and Philosophy: An Essay on Interpretation.* New Haven: Yale University Press.

Ridgeway, James. 1968. *The Closed Corporation: American Universities in Crisis.* New York: Random House.

Rocker, Rudolf. 1989. *Anarcho-Syndicalism.* London: Pluto Press.

Rosenthal, R. and Rubin, D. B. 1978. "Interpersonal expectancy effects: the first 345 studies." *Behavioral and Brain Sciences.* Vol. 3, pp. 377–86.

Russell, Bertrand. 1938. *Principles of Mathematics.* New York: W. W. Norton.

——— . 1956. *An Inquiry Into Meaning and Truth.* London: George Allen and Unwin.

——— . 1977. *Roads to Freedom.* London: Unwin.

Ryan, Michael. 1982. *Marxism and Deconstruction.* Baltimore: The Johns Hopkins University Press.

Sachs, Jacqueline. 1987. "Preschool Boys' and Girls' Language Use in Pretend Play." In Philips, Steele, and Tanz 1987.

Said, Edward. 1978. *Orientalism.* New York: Pantheon.

Schneiderman, Stuart, ed. 1980. *Returning to Freud: Clinical Psychoanalysis in the School of Lacan.* New Haven: Yale University Press.

Searle, John. 1983. "The Word Turned Upside Down." *The New York Review of Books.* 27 October.

Showalter, Elaine. 1982. "Feminist Criticism in the Wilderness." In Abel 1982.

Siebers, Tobin. 1988. *The Ethics of Criticism.* Ithaca: Cornell University Press.

Singer, Peter. 1975. *Animal Liberation: A New Ethics for our Treatment of Animals.* New York: Avon Books.

Sorrels, Bobbye. 1983. *The Nonsexist Communicator: Solving the Problems of Gender and Awkwardness in Modern English.* Englewood Cliffs, N.J.: Prentice-Hall.

Stewart, Lea and Ting-Toomey, Stella, eds. 1987. *Communication, Gender, and Sex Roles in Diverse Interaction Contexts.* Norwood, N.J.: Ablex Publishing Co.

Taylor, Debbie. 1985. "Women: An Analysis." *Women: A World Report.* New York: Oxford University Press.

Tompkins, Jane. 1980. "An Introduction to Reader-Response Criticism." In *Reader-Response Criticism.* Ed. Jane Tompkins. Baltimore: The Johns Hopkins University Press.

Tucker, Robert, ed. 1978. *The Marx-Engels Reader.* Second ed. New York: W. W. Norton.

Vygotsky, Lev Semenovich. 1962. *Thought and Language.* Trans. Eugenia Hanfmann and Gertrude Vakar. Cambridge: MIT Press.

Wiener, Jon. 1988. "Deconstructing de Man." *The Nation.* (9 January).

Wittgenstein, Ludwig. 1958. *Philosophical Investigations.* Third ed. Trans. G. E. M. Anscombe.

Yates, Michael D. "South Africa, Anti-Communism, and Value-Free Science." *The Chronicle of Higher Education.* 14 May 1986.

Index

235